Remote Learning and Distance Education

Recent Titles in the
CONTEMPORARY WORLD ISSUES
Series

Foster Care in America
Christina G. Villegas

Women in Media
Amy M. Damico

Elections in America
Michael C. LeMay

Income Inequality in America
Stacey M. Jones and Robert S. Rycroft

Rape and Sexual Assault
Alison E. Hatch

Campus Free Speech
Lori Cox Han and Jerry Price

Global Terrorism
Steven J. Childs

Food Insecurity
William D. Schanbacher and Whitney Fung Uy

Conspiracy Theories
Jeffrey B. Webb

Advertising in America
Danielle Sarver Coombs

Cyber Warfare
Paul J. Springer

Extremism in the Police
Carla Lewandowski and Jeff Bumgarner

The US Criminal Justice System
Sarah Koon-Magnin and Ryan J. Williams

Women and Girls in STEM Fields
Heather Burns Page

Remote Learning and Distance Education

A Reference Handbook

William H. Pruden III

BLOOMSBURY ACADEMIC
NEW YORK • LONDON • OXFORD • NEW DELHI • SYDNEY

BLOOMSBURY ACADEMIC
Bloomsbury Publishing Inc
1385 Broadway, New York, NY 10018, USA
50 Bedford Square, London, WC1B 3DP, UK
29 Earlsfort Terrace, Dublin 2, Ireland

BLOOMSBURY, BLOOMSBURY ACADEMIC and the Diana logo are trademarks of
Bloomsbury Publishing Plc

First published in the United States of America 2025

Copyright © Bloomsbury Publishing Inc, 2025

Cover image: insta_photos/Alamy Stock Photo

All rights reserved. No part of this publication may be reproduced or transmitted in any form or by any means, electronic or mechanical, including photocopying, recording, or any information storage or retrieval system, without prior permission in writing from the publishers.

Bloomsbury Publishing Inc does not have any control over, or responsibility for, any third-party websites referred to or in this book. All internet addresses given in this book were correct at the time of going to press. The author and publisher regret any inconvenience caused if addresses have changed or sites have ceased to exist, but can accept no responsibility for any such changes.

Library of Congress Cataloging-in-Publication Data
Names: Pruden, William H., III, author.
Title: Remote learning and distance education : a reference handbook / William H Pruden III.
Description: New York : Bloomsbury Academic, 2025. | Series: Contemporary world issues (CWI) series | Includes bibliographical references and index.
Identifiers: LCCN 2024029004 (print) | LCCN 2024029005 (ebook) | ISBN 9781440879487 (hardback) | ISBN 9798765131107 (paperback) | ISBN 9798216172291 (epub) | ISBN 9781440879494 (pdf)
Subjects: LCSH: Distance education–Law and legislation. | Internet in education–Law and legislation. | Educational law and legislation. | COVID-19 (Disease)–Law and legislation. | COVID-19 Pandemic, 2020- | Web-based instruction.
Classification: LCC K3740 .P78 2025 (print) | LCC K3740 (ebook) | DDC 371.35–dc23/eng/20240625
LC record available at https://lccn.loc.gov/2024029004
LC ebook record available at https://lccn.loc.gov/2024029005

ISBN: HB: 978-1-4408-7948-7
ePDF: 978-1-4408-7949-4
eBook: 979-8-2161-7229-1

Series: Contemporary World Issues

Typeset by Integra Software Services Pvt. Ltd.
Printed and bound in the United States of America

To find out more about our authors and books visit www.bloomsbury.com and sign up for our newsletters.

Contents

Preface ix

1 Background and History 1
   The First Distance Learning 3
   Trends and Landmarks in Correspondence Education 5
   Radio Days 6
   The Television Age: A Revolutionary Tool or Wires in a Box 8
   Concerns Raised about Television's Dark Side 9
   Computers Enter the Game 11
   The Internet Starts to Make Things Interesting 13
   The Pandemic Changes Everything 20
   Confronting the Pandemic 22
   Emerging from the Pandemic: Navigating a Changed Landscape 26
   Here We Go Again?! 31
   Beyond the Pandemic: Looking Ahead to the Future of Distance Education in the New Normal 34
   References 40

2 Problems, Controversies, and Solutions 49
   Basic Elements of Distance Education 50
   Access and Equity 52
   Educational Quality 59
   Changing the Way We Teach and Learn? 64
   Protecting and Maintaining Academic Integrity 71
   Financial Costs 75
   Impact on Health: Physical, Mental, and Emotional 76
   Distance Education and the Corporatization of Higher Education 78
   The Conundrum of OPMs 81
   Remote Learning, Distance Education, and the Dangers of First Impressions 83
   Conclusion 86
   References 87

3	Perspectives	95
	Lindsey Barrett (*student*)	95
	Eleanor Campbell (*student*)	98
	Aidan Carroll (*instructor*)	100
	Laura Kovalaske (*instructor*)	103
	Guy Lancaster (*instructor*)	107
	Sarah Swain (*administrator*)	109
4	Profiles	113
	People	113
	Joan Ganz Cooney (1929–)	113
	Michael Grahame Moore (1938–)	115
	Muriel Oaks (1943–) and Janet Ross Kendall (1945–)	118
	Sir Isaac Pitman (1813–97)	121
	Charles A. Wedemeyer (1911–99)	122
	Organizations/Institutions/Corporations	125
	ASU Online	125
	Coursera	126
	Khan Academy	128
	Online Learning Consortium	130
	Southern New Hampshire University	132
	Telelearning Systems and the Electronic University Network	135
	2U, Inc.	137
	University of Phoenix	139
	Western Governors University	141
	References	144
5	Data and Documents	151
	Data	151
	Changes in Higher Education Online Learning Enrollment	151
	Table 5.1. Pre-pandemic Growth of Online Learning, 2013–18	151
	Table 5.2. Percentage of Students in Online Learning, 2019–21	153
	K-12 Parent Views on the Impact of the Pandemic on Their Children	153

Table 5.3. Parent Opinions of the Impact of the First Year of
Pandemic on Their K-12 Children's Education and
Well-being   153

Table 5.4. Differences by Race, Ethnicity, and Income in
Percentage of Parents Who Said the Impact of the First
Year of the Pandemic Was Negative   154

Table 5.5. Parents Who Said the First Year of the Pandemic
Had a Negative Emotional Impact, by Race, and Their
Views on Whether It Improved   154

Teen and Parent Views on Virtual Learning   155

Table 5.6. Teen Opinions on Post-Pandemic Schooling   155

Table 5.7. Teen and Parent Satisfaction Level with How Their
School Has Handled Virtual Learning   155

Table 5.8. Worry Level of Teens and Parents That They May
Have Fallen Behind in School Due to the Pandemic   156

Table 5.9. Access Issues for Teens, Encountered Often or
Sometimes   156

Documents   157

Press Release from Office of Senator Elizabeth Warren
Concerning Letters Sent to CEOs of Online Project
Management Companies (2020)   157

Letter Sent by Senators Elizabeth Warren and Sherrod Brown
to the CEOs of Five OPMs Concerning Business Practices
(2020)   159

National Council on Disability Statement to House
Subcommittee Regarding Educational Equity Post-Covid-19
(2021)   162

GAO Report, "Indian Education—Schools Need More
Assistance to Provide Distance Learning" (2021)   164

Press Release from the Office of Senator Edward J. Markey
Announcing the Introduction of Legislation Addressing the
Online Educational Needs Caused by the Covid Pandemic
(2021)   166

National Science Foundation, "Education Researchers Assess
Impacts of Long-term Remote Learning on Students" (2021)   168

Excerpt from "Distance Learning in the Pandemic Age: Lessons
from a (No Longer) Emergency" (2022)   172

6	Resources	177
	Books and Articles	178
	History, Overviews, and Compilations	178
	Theory, Philosophy, and Developing Practices	181
	Teaching Strategies and Tips	182
	Pedagogy, Curriculum, and Course Design	186
	The Business of Distance Education	188
	Administering and Developing Distance Education Programs	192
	Distance Education versus Remote Learning	196
	Pros, Cons, and Assessments	198
	Higher Education and Distance Education	201
	Hybrid and Blended Learning	202
	Issues and Impacts	203
	Opportunities for the Online Learner	207
	Websites	208
7	Chronology	213
Glossary		223
Index		226
About the Author		229

Preface

Courtesy of the Covid-19 pandemic, the idea of remote learning and the concept of distance education have moved to the forefront of global consciousness in the last few years, becoming a part of the educational landscape in a way no one would have anticipated just four short years ago. And yet they represent far more than the fix for an inability to provide safe in-person instruction, whether at the elementary, secondary, or collegiate level. In fact, the pandemic simply accelerated a process of educational exploration that was already under way. Indeed, not only does distance education have roots that go back to the early days of the American Republic, but the movement towards increased online learning is but the latest stage in the historic procession of distance education that was already advancing at a rapid pace.

That being said, it is important to distinguish between remote learning and distance education. Indeed, discussion of remote learning must begin with a definition, for while the recent pandemic-induced rush to virtual or distance learning has left most people with a definite sense of what it is—at least based on their own experience—in fact, it is very much more. Consequently, the very first thing we must do is define the term and then distinguish it as one of the approaches existing under the large umbrella of distance education. Indeed, that label can include a large number of educational approaches ranging from correspondence courses to virtual learning with countless others in between. But central to any and all of those examples and differing approaches is the fact that the teacher and the student are not in the same room, unable to directly connect and interact in person. While degrees of the distance and the remoteness can vary wildly, that fundamental distance, the human disconnect, if you will, is a defining aspect of anything that can be termed remote or distance learning.

Such a definition forces us to look at the history and development of the broader concept of distance education. This is critically important, for while the Covid-19 pandemic that began in early 2020 pushed the idea of remote learning to the forefront of global consciousness as an educational alternative, it also tended to impose a significantly narrower view of the concept and process, one that all but sweeps away its long history. For in fact, the idea and practice of distance education, a process we can define broadly as teaching and learning outside a traditional classroom, can trace its origins back well before Covid-19 penetrated our consciousness. And in tracing its evolution we can see the evolution of numerous aspects of education itself. This work will seek to trace that evolution while also offering insight into the advantages and the disadvantages, the promises and the pitfalls of its modern iteration and how it may impact the educational landscape.

Given where we are right now, it is hard to believe that it was only four years ago that the pandemic forced an almost instantaneous transition to virtual learning. Beyond the concerns about learning loss that have hovered over that period, perhaps the most important result of that transition was the way it forced (or perhaps more diplomatically, led) educators to speed up their ongoing conversations about the very nature of modern education, twenty-first-century education—at all levels—and more specifically, how remote learning and teaching and distance education fits into the modern educational landscape.

As we will see, the history of distance education stretches back centuries and has evolved and developed over the years. Beginning with correspondence courses, it has moved to radio to television and then, with the development of computer technology, we have seen the advent of webinars, online and virtual courses, and MOOCs. But from the start, all such efforts have raised questions about the very nature of teaching and learning. Questions about the role of the teacher in the process or about the value of the interaction among peers have always been a part of that debate.

Certainly, discussion among students was limited or in need of a redefinition in a correspondence course, although the dissemination of knowledge could certainly be achieved in that way. Similarly, technological advances like radio and television clearly facilitated the sharing of information in lecture-like formats, but they did not offer the opportunity for even cursory questioning of the speaker. And then the advent of public television for children, as seen in programs like *Sesame Street* or *Mister Rogers' Neighborhood*, did not just represent the new use of the latest technology but also served to broaden the definitions of both education and distance education, while also adding a new eager-to-learn audience to the mix.

There is certainly a case to be made that everything done outside the traditional classroom setting is not the same and that a more nuanced definition, one that distinguishes between online education and remote learning, and among the many distinctions that can be made there—should be developed. How exactly to do so is the question.

For the purposes of this book, while we will sometimes make very definite distinctions, the reader will come away with a well-defined understanding of the differences of the variety of types of teaching and learning all of which come under the umbrella of distance education. We will visit and distinguish the distinctive differences and the nuances of the approaches, but anything that is not a traditional, teacher-led, students in physical attendance in a brick-and-mortar classroom educational offering falls under the heading of "distance education."

Interestingly, one of the things that is most intriguing as both society at large and the educational world in particular wrestle with the idea of distance education or remote learning (the two most commonly used terms), is the variety of different labels and/or terms that are used to describe or identify the phenomenon. The online website "Powerthesaurus.org" offers sixty-three different terms for online learning (another favored term), be they words or phrases with similar meaning. And yet a quick review of the sixty-three options makes clear that many are less synonyms than examples of what online learning is and how it can be offered, as well as defined approaches to online learning. The plethora of options makes clear the wide application of the concept and the many ways, however specifically defined, it is being utilized.

In the end, one thing that today's distance and remote educational efforts make clear is the fact that it is an ever-evolving and advancing field. Starting with the correspondence course of long ago up to modern MOOCs and the increasing number of college and university sponsored course and degree offerings, remote learning and distance education have been transformed over time into a world unfamiliar, if not unrecognizable, to those from another time. Indeed, one of the things that education scholars agree on is how fast thing are changing and how quickly things once considered cutting edge can seem outdated. And then there is a question of whether these changes might not lead to a revolution in the world of higher education, a division into two industries, the brick-and-mortar post-secondary education and the online option. It is an intriguing possibility, one that all in the education world will watch with interest.

This book hopes to offer a starting place from which to better observe and understand that inevitable, yet powerful change.

Chapter 1 begins the effort by looking at the background and history of distance education. While the Covid-19 pandemic thrust it to the forefront of the international consciousness, in fact, distance education, in a variety of forms has been around for a long time.

Chapter 2 will offer a look at the role of distance education today. What it means, what its role is and can be, and the attendant issues that stem from all of that. We will look at the strengths and weaknesses as well as the new issues that the pandemic brought to the fore, and the new frontiers still to be addressed.

Chapter 3 offers a set of essays that share the personal experiences of a range of different individuals—educators and students—who detail and reflect on their experiences from both sides of the desk as well as in the trenches. They offer poignant reminders of the fact that at its core, distance education is still about people and how the process resonates on a personal level.

Chapter 4 offers a set of profiles of people and organizations which have had and are having an impact on the development of distance education in some form over the centuries. While it is impossible to offer a full and comprehensive treatment in this way, the profiles included are a representative sampling both topically and chronologically, while also offering ideas for further consideration.

Chapter 5 includes data and documents that help readers identify and understand how things have changed, where the world of distance education is going, and what issues and challenges will be central to discussions about its future.

Chapter 6 offers a resource guide that can help those seeking to pursue further research related to this changing field. It is by no means exhaustive, and with things moving and changing as fast as they are in the world of remote learning and distance education, new information appears regularly, but this does offer lots of valuable information on a wide range of relevant topics related to this vast field.

Chapter 7 offers a concise but informative timeline that traces the development of distance education over the last three centuries in which it has been a part of the commercial and educational worlds.

The book concludes with a **Glossary** of terms pertinent to the subject and a subject index to help the reader find specific information throughout the text.

INTERNATIONAL CORRESPONDENCE Schools

ANOTHER I.C.S. STUDENT

1

Background and History

The Covid-19 pandemic that began to impact the world in early 2020 pushed the idea of remote learning to the forefront of education at all levels. But the idea and practice of remote learning, a process we can define broadly as teaching and learning outside a traditional classroom, can trace its origin to well before Covid-19 unleashed its fury on the planet.

In going back to the roots of remote learning and tracing its evolution, we can also see the development of numerous aspects of the educational process itself. Such an inquiry makes clear that while the chaos Covid-19 wrought had an immeasurable impact on the educational world, in some ways it speeded up a process that was already under way, forcing whole schools and districts to adopt many practices never before imagined or at most tried in pilot or experimental ways before Covid-19. Indeed, the question now is whether practices that in some cases were forced on the educational world will endure and be further developed and refined, creating a new normal. Or will we revert to traditional models of in-school learning while adapting in a more deliberate way to technological advances that in different forms have been central to the development of remote learning for centuries.

This chapter traces the history and development of remote learning in all its forms, exploring the way it evolved from a process primarily focused on providing vocational training for blue collar workers to one that offers academic degree programs for professionals—and the many steps and stages in between. As we begin this inquiry, we must note at the outset that the pandemic forced millions to learn from locations remote from their standard classrooms. This sudden and stress-filled introduction to remote learning is one that advocates of

---

Automobile belonging to an International Correspondence Schools (ICS) student, 1940. The ICS, headquartered in Scranton, Pennsylvania, enrolled over 2.5 million students by 1923. (Photo by John Vachon. Farm Security Administration/Office of War Information Collection, Library of Congress Prints & Photographs Division)

distance education have viewed with mixed emotions. On the one hand, it raised the profile and heightened the awareness of the capacities of distance education, but at the same time, it also blurred the line between remote learning and true distance education.

The very real distinction that advocates see has, they fear, been lost in the turmoil and frenzy of responding to the pandemic. They fear that without increased public understanding of the real distinctions and differences, discussed in this chapter, the fortunes for distance education will be damaged in the long run. Consequently, at the outset, as we prepare to look at the long history of distance education, it is important that we distinguish between remote learning and distance education. In simplest terms, remote learning is all about distance between the teacher and student, and while distance education has that same component, it transcends that simple aspect by its use of a distinctive type of pedagogy developed for the teaching style it utilizes.

In an effort to address this confusion, the National Council for Online Education (NCOE) has offered a thoughtful presentation on the different approaches. The Council notes that "Remote learning is an emergency measure used to assure continuity of learning. It involves taking a course that was designed for the face-to-face classroom and moving it quickly into a distance learning modality (usually synchronous and held via web-conferencing tools, such as Zoom)." They note that "typically the aim is an attempt to replicate the in-person classroom experience." Given these circumstances, a reality of remote learning is that "most faculty have too little training, support or time to effectively pivot their face-to-face course to one we would characterize as high-quality online learning" (NCOE 2022). The Council further noted, "Online learning is a planned experience over weeks or months where the course has purposefully been designed for the online environment. The accompanying technology and tools have been carefully selected for the educational objectives. Faculty receive professional development and support to succeed in this modality" (NCOE 2022). These distinctions are real, but distance education advocates and educators believe that given all that has taken place in the last few years, there are fundamental misunderstandings about the very nature of distance education and how it differs from what most people over the course of the pandemic were experiencing in their online experience.

We will also look at the way in which attitudes towards distance education have changed. For example, two long-held perspectives on the process—one that argues that distance education is a self-contained approach and the alternative, which maintains that it is simply a vehicle of instruction—have evolved into a middle ground. The more modern view is something of a blend, resulting in a perspective where distance education represents a quasi-permanent divide between the teacher and student, one where the instructional process, in reaching across the divide, is facilitated by numerous types of technologically based media, including print, audio, video, or computer.

Interestingly, the U.S. Department of Education defines distance education as "education that uses one or more types of technology to deliver instruction to students who are separated from the instructor and to support regular and substantive interaction between the students and the instructor synchronously or asynchronously. The following types of technology may be used for distance instruction: Internet; Satellite or wireless communication; and Audio and video conferencing" (Distance Ed—IPEDS n.d.). In contrast, the Department of Education refers to remote learning only in the context of the emergency response to the Covid-19 pandemic (Remote Learning, Dept. of Ed n.d.).

Given the chaos that surrounded the introduction of millions of people to this type of teaching and learning, it is no surprise that while the modern view of distance education may represent something of a consensus, the timeline that connects the correspondence courses of old to the modern explosion of technology and pandemic-fueled advances is a lengthy and uneven one. Bursts of genius and innovation are followed by efforts to adapt and apply such ideas to the world of teaching and learning. These are followed by the organizational, management, and corporate interests that take the now developed idea and put it in the marketplace of both ideas and dollars. And always there are the unforeseen problems and impacts, the changes imposed on the educational landscape and their effects on existing operations and planned ones.

Indeed, few areas of society are more open to the ebb and flow of societal change than the world of education. Its centrality to so much of what we do and how we live means that countless interest groups and entities are engaged in educational reforms, advances, and controversies.

The First Distance Learning

While modern concepts of distance learning differ markedly from its roots, most would agree that from the very beginning those who pursued and offered distance education, however it was termed, were seeking to make knowledge accessible to a broader audience than the elitist few who had long held a monopoly on formal education. Indeed, the earliest examples of what we can broadly call distance or remote education appear to be the efforts of Caleb Phillips, a colonial entrepreneur who, in 1728, ran an advertisement in the *Boston Gazette* offering to teach shorthand to students through a process that would involve the exchange of letters through the then fledgling postal service (Sleator 2010). Some skeptics argue that because there is no evidence of any two-way communication affirming that anyone actually took Phillips up on his offer, the example does not technically qualify as distance education (Kentnor 2015). In any case, Phillips' idea was utilized and replicated over the years, and not just in the United States.

In 1833 Swedish newspapers across that nation carried advertisements for correspondence composition courses, and the practice soon spread across Europe, arguably reaching its peak in the 1840s in England when Sir Isaac Pitman offered correspondence courses that taught his "Pitman shorthand" style, one still widely used today (Kentnor 2015). Seeing the commercial potential of Pitman's efforts, the Phonographic Correspondence Society was founded in 1843 to publicize the style. The society was a forerunner to Pitman's own Correspondence College (Sleator 2010).

Reaching the United States in the early 1850s, correspondence course work became very popular among self-taught secretaries who enrolled in the course and then mailed their work to the Phonographic Institute in Cincinnati, Ohio. In a foreshadowing of the modern career enhancing benefits of distance education programs, the secretaries would receive a certificate attesting to their expertise in stenographic shorthand (Sleator 2010).

In 1856, instructors Charles Toussaint and Gustav Langenscheidt began to offer language classes via the mail from Germany, although their effort suffered from a lack of support (Pant 2014). However, that support proved to be right around the corner when, in 1858, the first institutional embrace of the idea of remote learning came with Queen Victoria of Great Britain signing a charter allowing the University of London to provide distance learning education to people regardless of where in the world they studied (Long n.d.). With the door now open, the University of London established the External Programme, an effort that stamped it as the first university to offer a degree via distance learning (Visual Academy n.d.). By the middle of the nineteenth century, numerous countries played host to mail-order courses, with the "Society of Modern Languages" in Berlin being among the leaders, offering correspondence courses in French, German, and English.

The first institution-based effort in the United States launched in 1873 with the creation of the nation's first correspondence course. The Society to Encourage Studies at Home was an enterprise headed by Ana Eliot Ticknor, the daughter of a Harvard University professor (Visual Academy n.d.). She sponsored the innovative venture until her death just over two decades later.

Trends and Landmarks in Correspondence Education

Another factor in the growth and acceptance of correspondence education in the United States was the development of the Chautauqua Movement, launched in the 1870s. From its beginnings as a summer training program for Sunday school teachers, it expanded and developed into a program that featured general education and the arts and included supplemental lessons and readings that participants would complete at home. In 1878, John Heyl Vincent founded the Chautauqua Literary and Scientific Circle in Chautauqua, New York, the nation's inaugural adult education program and correspondence school. Seeking to build upon these early efforts, Chautauqua University was launched in 1883, but its program of extension and correspondence courses, supplemented by summer terms, was short-lived. The business closed shop in 1892 (Kentnor 2015).

The entrepreneurial spirit led to correspondence course offerings in areas that might not immediately come to mind. One of these was the 1890 offering by the Pennsylvania Colliery Engineer School of Mines of a mine safety course. It was one of the initial schools in what became the International Correspondence Schools (ICS). Headquartered in Scranton, Pennsylvania, by 1900 ICS boasted 250,000 students, and its continued growth would ultimately result in an enrollment of over 2.5 million by 1923 (Watkinson 1996).

In 1892, in a pamphlet first produced by the University of Wisconsin-Madison, the term "distance learning" was used for the first time (Pappas 2013). That same year, the University of Chicago's president William Rainey Harper, drawing upon the Chautauqua University model, began offering correspondence courses at the school. The University of Chicago thus became the first traditional, brick-and-mortar, residential college to do so. Harper's innovative addition to the standard program proved a big success, with the university soon enrolling 3,000 students in 350 courses taught by 125 instructors (Kentnor 2015). The idea quickly spread, and by 1910 the University of California was said to have the largest academic correspondence program in the United States (Lienhard n.d.).

But the idea of distance learning was not limited to existing higher education programs. In 1900, at a time when women were often denied educational opportunities, Cornell University teacher and suffragette Martha Van Rensselaer established a remote education program that sought to connect with women in the rural areas of New York state. After receiving 2,000 responses to a letter sent to rural women across the state seeking to learn what subjects they were interested in studying, Van Rensselaer designed a correspondence course, the Reading Course for Farmers' Wives. It offered homemakers information on subjects including time-saving steps, sewing, and gardening. The positive response led to the creation of three courses for credit on campus in 1903 and the establishment in 1907 of the Department of Home Economics in the College of Agriculture (Aloi 2020).

In 1906 The Calvert School in Baltimore became one of the first primary schools to offer correspondence courses ("History ..." WorldWideLearn n.d.). That same year, The University of Wisconsin began recording lectures which were then sent to students in the form of phonograph records (Pappas 2013). Reflective of the wide-ranging appeal of the distance education of the time, in 1911 the University of Queensland in Australia founded a Department of Correspondence Studies with materials exchanged through the country's postal system (Visual Academy n.d.).

Radio Days

The 1920s saw distance education add another dimension with the advent of radio. The boom in radio that was so emblematic of the Roaring Twenties was also one of the first technological advances that promised to revolutionize education, while also improving it. At peak interest in the 1920s, more than 175 educational institutions across the United States had broadcast licenses in hopes of using the new technology to further education (Kentnor 2015).

Radio stations were constructed directly on the campuses of some of the nation's major educational institutions as schools looked to the newly developed technology as a vehicle for enriching teaching. Classes often used radio as a complement to existing correspondence courses with the audio addition enabling students to actually hear their teacher. One of the earliest pioneers was Pennsylvania State University, which began broadcasting some courses over radio in 1923 ("History ..." WorldWideLearn n.d.). Reflective of higher education's infatuation with the new technology was the fact that by 1923 over 10 percent of all broadcast radio systems were owned and operated by educational institutions. In fact, Congress passed the Radio Act of 1927 in an effort to regulate the broadcasting industry, but neither schools nor the radio industry were waiting on the government (Kentnor 2015). In 1928, for example, the Ohio Department of Education developed the Ohio School of the Air program which offered daily programs in literature, history, science, and music (Kentnor 2015). However, the onset of the Great Depression took a heavy toll on these educational programming efforts. Indeed, with the economic turmoil the nation experienced beginning in late 1929, the number of radio stations at educational institutions dropped from about 175 at the start of 1929 to only thirty-five by the end of 1930 (Kentnor 2015).

As a result, it fell to corporate-based interests to keep the idea of radio as an educational vehicle alive. The National Broadcasting Company (NBC) started the Radio Corporation of America (RCA) Educational Hour in 1928, and two years later, the Columbia Broadcasting System (CBS) started American School of the Air (Kentnor 2015). Indeed, the early part of the 1930s witnessed a rush to take advantage of the increasingly recognized potential of radio as an educational tool. In 1930 alone, the Rockefeller Foundation and the Carnegie Foundation organized and funded the National Advisory Council for Radio in Education (NACRE), while the Institute for Education by Radio (IER), an organization which focused on techniques used in educational broadcasting, was founded in Columbus, Ohio (Kentnor 2015). That same year, the National Committee on Education by Radio (NCER) was founded "to secure to the [American] people ... the use of radio for educational purposes" (Kentnor 2015).

Franklin Roosevelt's ascension to the presidency in 1933, at the height of the Great Depression, brought to the office a man who clearly recognized the power and potential of radio as an educational tool in the broadest sense of that term. His celebrated "Fireside Chats" over the radio airwaves beginning early in 1933 revealed him to be a masterful teacher. Indeed, Roosevelt's chats utilized radio in a way that made the whole listening audience his students as he helped people understand the economic challenges posed by the Great Depression while explaining how his programs were intended to address them. He connected with his listeners on a personal level and in doing so made the airwaves more than just a vehicle for sharing information. While educators would work hard to develop ways to adapt radio to the educational setting, they were never really able to do so. In the end, the technological advances of the early part of the twentieth century that radio represented did not so much alter the approach of education as they simply expanded the classroom, allowing Roosevelt to offer civics lessons to the largest classroom America had ever seen, an effort that was increasingly repeated, although seldom so successfully, by his many political imitators (S. Smith 2014).

Although the Second World War slowed the development of new technology that might have further fostered distance education, one pioneer in the field, Charles A. Wedemeyer, who had already been involved in the University of Wisconsin's early radio-based teaching efforts, used his time as a naval instructor to build upon his Wisconsin efforts and create a number of effective teaching methods for "classes" that included sailors stationed around the world. These efforts left him ready to launch programs after the war that introduced a whole new approach to education, albeit one whose early usage was limited to a small part of the growing post-war university populace (Wedemeyer—HoF 1998).

The Television Age: A Revolutionary Tool or Wires in a Box

In the aftermath of the Second World War, the American educational landscape experienced tremendous change, and distance education was not immune to the changes. While radio had proven to be an effective, if limited, purveyor of distance education before the war, by the early 1950s, television had become the new technological media rage. People quickly recognized the wealth of possibilities of television as an educational tool. The arrival of television as a potential educational vehicle made real the basics of a 1913 prediction by Thomas Edison that, given the then recent invention of motion pictures, "Books will be obsolete in the public schools. Scholars will be instructed through the eye. It is possible to teach every branch of human knowledge with motion picture" (Kentnor 2015).

Many colleges and universities began to seek television licenses from the Federal Communications Commission (FCC). However, at a time when the FCC was being besieged with similar requests, the agency's response to the uncoordinated request from academia was slow (Kentnor 2015). Finally, in 1952, the FCC responded to the educational community, reserving just under 250 channels for educational purposes. That number, which grew to 632 in less than fifteen years, was equally divided between state and local education systems, colleges and universities, and community organizations (Kentnor 2015).

In 1953 the University of Houston offered the first televised college classes on KUHT, the first public television station in the United States. The station ran 13.5 hours of educational material a week, just under 40 percent of the station's weekly broadcasting content (Visual Academy n.d.).

Concerns Raised about Television's Dark Side

During the 1950s most people were tremendously excited about the potential of television as a vehicle for education, entertainment, and promoting businesses, products, and services. But from the outset there were concerns raised about the potentially toxic effects of television.

The legendary newsman Edward R. Murrow sounded an early cautionary note. When Murrow took the stage at the 1958 Radio-Television News Directors Association convention, he was one of the most revered and famous journalists in America. His harsh criticism of the still-fledgling industry—and his demand that they use the power of the new medium more responsibly—thus sent shockwaves across the nation: "This instrument [television] can teach, it can illuminate; yes, and it can even inspire. But it can do so only to the extent that humans are determined to use it to those ends. Otherwise it's nothing but wires and lights in a box. There is a great and perhaps decisive battle to be fought against ignorance, intolerance and indifference. The weapon of television could be useful" (Murrow 1958). But at the same time Murrow noted that Americans "are to a large extent an imitative society," a reality that has been made all too clear in the many ways that both television and the subsequent forms of electronic distance education over the years have, both directly and indirectly, built upon television's examples—both good and bad—while leaving it up to the teachers and students on the firing line to determine whether TV as an educational vehicle would prove to be something more than "wires and lights in a box" (Murrow 1958).

Murrow's warning notwithstanding, the government certainly saw television as a potential player in the education game. In 1967 the Corporation for Public Broadcasting (CPB) was created "to encourage the growth and development of public radio and television broadcasting, including the use of such media for instructional educational and cultural purposes" (Public Broadcasting Act of 1967). Suddenly, the very nature of education, as well as the ways of teaching and learning, were open to discussion and debate, with many seeing opportunities to expand the reach of teaching to places it had never gone before.

Efforts to find and develop ways to more effectively use television in the educational process for remote learning continued in an uneven manner for the rest of the 1950s and into the 1960s. One of the areas of exploration during this time was educational television for preschool children. Acting upon a study commissioned by the Carnegie Commission on Educational Television, in 1968, the Children's Television Workshop was founded. Soon, under the leadership of Joan Ganz Cooney, the CPB began to offer innovative television for preschoolers that broke the existing mold. Suddenly, *Sesame Street* and later the *Electric Company* became must-see children's television—but more than that, they were efforts that changed the way people thought about using television for teaching (Reichers 2003).

In their own way, Cooney's efforts were more influential and effective responses to Murrow's challenge to make television more than just wires in the box than any standard television programming with its news and documentaries. Not only did the programs resonate with a new audience that had never before been considered or provided with viewing options, they also filled a need. With more mothers working, it became necessary to occupy and stimulate children whose caregivers could not provide them with undivided attention. Suddenly there was a recognition that television could be used as an effective teaching tool for children. This recognition coincided with an increasing concern about children being ready for school, and it was well received by a parental generation that increasingly saw its children's accomplishments as a measure of their parenting and thus that it was never too early to prepare their children for the trip up the ladder (Adler 1972). Especially for those who couldn't afford individual tutors at the early stages of their child's education, quality educational television programming was suddenly an important, if still undervalued, commodity.

Television offered another version of a successful distance education approach with the 1972 debut of the program *Zoom*. While *Zoom* took some of its inspiration from *Sesame Street* and the *Electric Company*, it did not have the same focus and educationally based script. Instead, it was more freewheeling and, in fact, mostly unscripted. In some respects, it was a TV version and forerunner of the experiential education approach that would become so much a part of later twentieth and early twenty-first-century learning. Its design gave the on-screen child hosts a voice, while drawing upon them and the audience for new ideas. Produced by and aired initially on Boston's PBS channel WGBH-TV, *Zoom* encouraged children to "turn off the TV and do it!" Its original cast was seven children who presented a wide range of activities that included games, plays, poems, recipes, songs, science experiments, and informal chats on a range of subjects, such as hospitals and prejudice, all of which were suggested by viewer submissions ("Zoom" n.d.).

While it did not receive the same acclaim from educators as *Sesame Street* and the *Electric Company*, *Zoom* was nevertheless celebrated as an innovative offering that showed yet another way students could be educated from afar. The submissions from contributing audience members and ideas from a revolving cast helped keep the show vibrant. Its original episodes aired until 1978, and it remained a formative experience for countless viewers over its six-year run ("Zoom" n.d.).

As critical as education is to the development of children, any effort to make television an effective, innovative—and of concern to many, a profitable—venture required it be something that offered content to an audience whose upper age range exceeded seven.

Computers Enter the Game

It is worth noting that at the same time television was trying to find its place in the educational firmament, efforts to successfully utilize computers for educational purposes were under way. In 1960, Professor Donald L. Bitzer led a team at the University of Illinois at Urbana-Champaign (UIUC) that sought to address the problem of illiteracy. In the course of their work, they developed PLATO (Programmed Logic for Automatic Teaching Operations) a computer-based education system. PLATO served as a successful computer-based teaching tool in various iterations for four decades, but the cost and its cumbersome hardware prevented it from ever becoming a large-scale success. It was ultimately rendered obsolete by the technological developments of the late 1990s and the early twenty-first century. Indeed, while PLATO wasn't a form of eLearning, it was an important technology that did much to help in the ultimate development of eLearning. In fact, its spawning of the first successful online communities foreshadowed the ultimate development of the internet. Over the course of its lifetime, PLATO contributed to the development of Plasma Flat-Panel Displays, Interactive Touch Screens, and other software, making it an important factor in the development of much that was needed to make modern distance education a reality (Vo 2015).

But all that lay ahead. In the short term, while 1968 saw the University of Nebraska-Lincoln begin to offer an accredited high school diploma through distance education, through the end of the 1960s and into the 1970s the efforts to offer credible, engaging distance education programming got no real traction. Indeed, while the use of both television and radio in education grew, technology was not as much used as a form of distance education as it was something teachers used in their classes to better explain, illustrate, or demonstrate ideas, concepts, and lessons. At home educational broadcasts on outlets like Public Broadcasting and National Public Radio (NPR) saw an increase in viewers and listeners, but the use of technology in an actual direct, synchronous teaching and learning format was diminishing. In part this was attributable to the poor quality of the offerings, as well as the fact that all too often a class was little more than a professor reading his lecture notes in front of the screen, an approach that did little to keep a student's attention. Television had for the most part been unable to rise to Murrow's challenge.

The succeeding years did see some stabs at establishing distinctive distance learning programs. In 1976 Coastline Community College, a school based in southern California, became the first "virtual" college. Operating without a campus, it broadcast all its courses ("History ..." WorldWideLearn n.d.). In 1982, Western Behavioral Sciences Institute's School of Management and Strategic Studies, utilizing computer conferencing, began to offer a distance education program for business executives (Thompson 2021). Similarly, in 1983, former Atari president Ron Gordon launched the Electronic University Network, which made online courses available to anyone who had access to personal computers (Euchner 1983). While the effort marked a major psychological step forward, the venture was short-lived and unsuccessful, encountering numerous obstacles and ultimately being rendered obsolete by more refined and efficient uses of the new technology (Darling 1985).

These early programs and others were experimental efforts based in a belief, however vague and tenuous, that there were educational alternatives to the standard, expensive, and immobile brick-and-mortar model, especially at a time when it was clear that there was a nontraditional population that was hungry for an alternative better suited to their lives, in which full-time school was impossible but further education was a must. Television, while initially trumpeted as the next technological advance that promised to salvage the blackboard jungle, proved to be no more effective than radio. Despite efforts like *Sunrise Semester*, a joint production of CBS and New York University, a program that was launched in 1957 and for almost twenty-five years offered watch-at-home courses for credit, television never fulfilled the promise so many believed it held (Noer 2012). The advent of personal computers also failed to spur significant expansion of distance learning. Happily, a new form of technology, one based in computers and dependent on a new invention, the internet, whose "birth" is generally set at January 1, 1983, was about to make its debut. Its arrival quickly altered the educational landscape as it immediately became clear that it had the potential to change everything.

The Internet Starts to Make Things Interesting

But while the internet would eventually revolutionize distance education, not everyone immediately jumped on the bandwagon. The year 1984 saw the launching of the National Technological University (NTU). Based in Fort Collins, Colorado, NTU was founded as a nonprofit organization that offered graduate courses via satellite television (Crotty 2012). Yet another attempt to make television an effective educational medium, it was the product of a collaborative effort by a number of engineering and management schools. The program aimed to address the need for both graduate and continuing education opportunities for engineers, technological professionals, and managers engaged with advanced educational and telecommunication technology. Both graduate and non-credit courses were developed by a number of well-respected universities associated with the program, and the courses were offered at sites across the country and overseas. NTU was accredited by the North Central Association of Colleges and Schools and the Higher Learning Commission. In the beginning, NTU courses were delivered via videotape, but within two years the content was broadcast by satellite, and in that form, it could offer real-time courses which permitted an actual dialogue between the teacher and students who would call in during the broadcast and have their questions answered on air (Mays 1988).

The somewhat patchwork-like nature of distance education continued to grow over the course of the 1980s. In a preview of what was to come, in 1985 Nova Southeastern University in Fort Lauderdale, Florida, offered the first electronic classroom through an accredited online graduate program (Thompson 2021).

Yet while the internet was looking to be the force that could change the face of distance education and was shaping up as the go to technology, television still had its adherents, as evidenced in 1987 when entrepreneur Glen Jones launched the cable television network Mind Extension University (ME/U, later Knowledge TV), a venture which enabled 30,000 students to take courses from more than 30 colleges and universities via television (Walker 2021). However, in 1989, the University of Phoenix became the first fully online institution of higher education, offering courses leading to both bachelor's and master's degrees (Visual Academy n.d.). At its peak in 2010, the for-profit university had an enrollment of 470,000 students, a figure that quickly caught the attention of the nonprofit educational world.

Meanwhile, reflective of the growing interest in and potential of distance education in the educational world, 1987 saw the creation of the United States Distance Learning Association (USDLA). The first nonprofit distance learning organization in the United States, it was founded to provide support for distance learning research, development, and practice for the increasing number of parties utilizing the approach in education, business, health, and government. From the outset, the group provided an opportunity for those involved with distance education to network with others in the far-reaching field, while also serving as a representative voice for those same widespread constituencies as distance learning forces sought to become an ever more prominent player in the educational world ("About"—USDLA n.d.).

In the midst of an ever-changing educational landscape, the 1990s saw the launching of a number of well-supported and potentially far-reaching new initiatives. Some took advantage of existing technology while others sought to maximize the power of the developing internet. One early example of a more gradual approach was the Educational Technology Leadership Program offered through George Washington University's Graduate School of Education and Human Development. The master's program was first offered in 1992 and initially delivered its course content in association with Jones Intercable's Mind Extension University. The classes were broadcast via satellite television and students would communicate with each other through a Bulletin Board system (Clark 1992). The first class graduated in 1994, but by 1996 the ETL program had transitioned to the internet and the master's program was offered completely online. In addition to the full-scale transition to the internet, the program assembled a set of web-based tools and HTML pages that facilitated the teaching and learning process. It allowed for asynchronous communication among all parties as well as the delivery of lectures, drop boxes for assignments, and other features that have become common in the modern online classroom (GW Ed Tech n.d.).

In 1993, entrepreneur Glen Jones took another bite at the distance education apple, this time partnering with Bernard Luskin as they started Jones International University, the first accredited and fully web-based university (History—JIU n.d.). That same year saw the introduction of the first internet browser. Created at the University of Illinois, it helped online efforts flourish. In fact, in 1994 the United Kingdom's Open University became the first accredited school to offer a course over the internet when it offered an experimental Virtual Summer School (VSS) to some of its Cognitive Psychology students ("History …" WorldWideLearn n.d.). Later that year, CALCampus launched the first online-only curriculum featuring synchronous learning—real-time instruction and student participation ("History …" WorldWideLearn n.d.). The new effort offered a considerably lower priced college option, but it did not satisfy the often critical need for flexibility that was central to the desire of the growing legion of working adults who were a prime target of distance education providers.

While the landscape was littered with hits and misses, there is no denying the increased possibilities that technology represented in the world of education well before the pandemic opened even more eyes to the potential for online, remote, and distance education and learning. And for policymakers ever on the lookout for new, more accessible, and more appropriate educational opportunities, distance education offered a number of different ways to fill in some of the existing gaps in educational offerings while also becoming a way to expand access and, in turn, equity.

The year 1995 offered a prime example when, in a show of bipartisan problem solving, nineteen U.S. governors came together to propose the creation of Western Governors University (WGU) in an effort to maximize educational resources through distance learning (Thompson 2021). Officially incorporated in 1997, the start-up costs of the online distance education institution were covered by taxpayer dollars, but from the start the university was intended to be and did, in fact, become a self-supporting, private, nonprofit institution. The effort has been a resounding success. It has grown at an impressive rate with its flexible curriculum allowing students to earn either degrees or more specific credentials, whichever serves their needs and ambitions (Burt 2021).

The move to internet-based distance education led to the development of numerous auxiliary type programs all aimed at developing and disseminating better distance education programs. Typical was the arrival in 1997 of the

Interactive Learning Network (ILN) which was created and released to numerous schools as the first eLearning platform ("History ..." WorldWideLearn n.d.). Early users include Yale, Cornell, and the University of Pittsburgh. Another was Blackboard Inc., which was also founded in 1997. The content management system developed a standardized platform for course management and delivery. Helping to facilitate growth was central to many of these efforts, and Blackboard's model made it possible for many additional schools to come online ("History ..." WorldWideLearn n.d.).

Meanwhile, in the fall of 1997 California Virtual University opened its doors—or perhaps more properly its website (Thompson 2021). Supported by Governor Pete Wilson, who got over $15 million from the state legislature for online learning, the consortium of almost 100 of the state's colleges and universities, California Virtual offered almost 1,600 courses from its member schools when it opened in November of that year. But less than eighteen months later, by the spring of 1999, the "dream lay in ruins." Caught in the crossfire of competing political, academic, and business interests, the once grand plans for a virtual library, as well as counseling services, were abandoned and staff was laid off. All that remained was a listing of online courses offered by colleges and universities across the state (Downes 1999).

While these projects reflected an increased interest in distance education, the field certainly had its perils. In 1998, New York University (NYU) created NYU Online, an online, for-profit subsidiary of its existent continuing education program. At its launch many saw it as the only institution that could effectively compete with the developing behemoth, the for-profit University of Phoenix, but that hope was soon extinguished as NYU Online closed shop in 2001 as did the University of Maryland's for-profit distance education effort. But while their travails were not unique, during that same period the University of Phoenix almost doubled its enrollment (Kentnor 2015).

Analysts identified many reasons why online education efforts were failing, but first and foremost was a fundamental lack of understanding of online pedagogy and online learning styles. Equally important was the lack of buy-in from faculty. Given that online teaching and learning required a different pedagogy, faculty resistance was not surprising. No less a hurdle towards achieving faculty buy-in was overcoming the skepticism that faculty felt regarding the quality of online education. While these issues were central to the failure of some of the distance education start-ups, they were no less a problem in the more peripheral efforts at distance education being started at traditional institutions (Kentnor 2015).

In 2002 the Massachusetts Institute of Technology (MIT) announced its launch of the OpenCourseWare Project which offered free MIT courses to people across the globe (Abelson et al. 2021). In 2005, YouTube was launched, radically changing the way entertainment and information could be viewed, as well as how and what could be presented. By 2009, YouTube had created an auxiliary channel, YouTubeEDU, which offered thousands of free lectures online. But in some senses, Apple had beaten them to the punch when, in 2006, it had introduced iTunes U which offered lectures on a wide range of subjects to anyone willing to purchase them ("History ..." WorldWideLearn n.d.).

Continuing the ongoing evolution/revolution in 2008, Sal Khan, a one-time hedge fund financier, turned his family-based tutoring sessions into Khan Academy, an online educational bonanza with a wide-ranging menu of videos offering basic classes in math, science, and other areas. Khan Academy also partnered with the College Board to provide valuable, effective, and free standardized test preparation resources (Adams 2013).

In 2012, in an apparent acknowledgment of the growing audience hunger for online educational offerings—as well as a possible market test—Udacity, an American for-profit educational organization, and EdX, a venture developed jointly at Harvard and MIT, began to offer hundreds of university level MOOCs (massive open online courses) at no cost ("History ..." WorldWideLearn n.d.). The following year, the University of Florida announced that in 2014, as required by a newly enacted law, the state would be starting a top level online program specifically aimed at students who were either first time college students or transfers (Thompson 2023). The new program was a clear recognition of the potential value of distance education in a state whose student population was growing in leaps and bounds.

In 2017, in a move that reflected a blurring, if not a tearing down, of the longtime divide between the nonprofit and for-profit educational sectors, as well as the increasing corporatization of American higher education, Purdue University acquired the online for-profit, Kaplan University, and its 32,000 students. Purdue's bold and unprecedented move into the online education arena stunned the world of higher education, especially coming, as it did, at a time when the online efforts of many of the large for profits were slumping. Under the agreement Purdue acquired almost all the credential-issuing parts of Kaplan's higher education business, a group that includes the seven schools and colleges that made up Kaplan University. Also included were the approximately

32,000 Kaplan students, about 85 percent of whom were enrolled in fully online programs, with the other 15 percent in hybrid ones (Fain 2017).

The response to the Purdue initiative, rebranded as Purdue University Global (PUG), was generally positive. While the size of the effort was not small, given the way Purdue's president Mitch Daniels, a former Director of the Office of Management and Budget (OMB) and Governor of Indiana, had moved quickly to establish an Indiana affiliate with the Western Governors University, his interest in expanding Purdue's online presence did not surprise the higher education community (Fain 2017). And in fact, Daniels' vision and judgment were vindicated when, in December 2021, Purdue's Annual Financial Report indicated that the still comparatively new venture had broken even for fiscal year 2021 (Hill 2021).

There were others who also saw the potential of distance education before the pandemic put it front and center on the national landscape. One was California governor Jerry Brown. Going back to his first stint as governor in the 1970s, Brown had always had an eye on the future, and over four decades later in 2016, as the last of his four terms as Governor of California neared its end, Brown put forth an idea he thought could make the state a leader in virtual education.

Recognizing the distinctive needs of working adults, and seeing that too many of the existing options aimed at that group were based in for-profit institutions that too often made their profits off high debt student loans programs, Brown sought the development of an online community college program that would be a public option for adult and low-income workers, often caregivers, who were seeking to improve their skills so as to be able to get better paying jobs (A. Smith 2021a). The program, which Brown included in his 2018 budget and that was then approved by the state legislature, resulted in the launching of Calbright College in 2019. An online-only institution that awarded certificates, not degrees, it was intended to be "an attractive alternative for working people, not the fancy elites, but people struggling to improve their lot in life by upgrading their skills and doing so in a way that is affordable" (A. Smith 2021b).

The program was the poster child for many of the ideas that led distance education to be touted as a particularly appealing option for older working adults. First, as a state-supported public institution, it was low cost—in fact, it was free. Its program was also self-paced, thus providing a flexibility that is critically important for the working students. It was aimed at students in the 25–34 age range, and the program was rooted in a competency-based model, where demonstration of skill mastery, and not time spent in class, were the basis for advancement (A. Smith 2021b).

For Brown, Calbright was all about equity and the way it could provide new opportunities for potentially countless people who had been left out of the economic pathway that was ultimately so critical to success. Calbright was intended to use modern technology to widen that path. The program had a rocky start, and even Brown acknowledged that its initial leadership was not appropriate (A. Smith 2021b.) These early problems, coupled with disappointing completion rates made it a regular target of Sacramento legislators (Schwartz 2022b).

However, when critics sought to eliminate it and transfer the money to other programs, a retired Brown continued to fight for the school. In doing so he highlighted one of the continuing dilemmas of the distance education world, when, after asserting that "Calbright is all about equity," he added that if the school were to be eliminated, the only people hurt would "be the low-income Californians that will lose the opportunity that they can find in no other way unless they pay a handsome fee to a corporate vendor," a clear reference to the for-profit schools which Brown had long seen as a predatory force in the world of higher education (A. Smith 2021b). Despite these challenges, by the spring of 2023, Calbright seemed to have vindicated its supporters' faith, experiencing a consistent increase in enrollment at a time when many of the state's other colleges were working overtime to stem the enrollment drops that had begun with the pandemic (Zinshteyn 2023).

Beyond specific programs, one thing that has been central to the expansion of distance education programs in traditional colleges has been the rise and development of Online Program Management (OPM) companies. These companies partner with schools, providing the technological expertise necessary to enable colleges to offer school sponsored content to online students. And in performing that service they earn no small share of the revenue. Indeed, so lucrative has been the practice that in early 2020, before the onset of the Covid-19 pandemic, Senators Elizabeth Warren (Democrat from Massachusetts) and Sherrod Brown (Democrat from Ohio) expressed official interest in the operations of some of the largest companies in the business. In a letter addressed to the five largest OPMs in the country (2U, Academic Partnerships, Bisk Education, Pearson Learning, and Wiley Education Services), Warren and Brown sought copies of all the contracts the companies held with colleges, as well as samples of presentations they made to the schools and detailed reports of their expenditures and revenues.

They were concerned about the influence these companies were having on higher education, especially given the millions of dollars of federal aid that could be a part of their business (Schwartz 2020).

While this initial inquiry yielded nothing of great relevance and seemed to stall in the midst of the 2020 campaign, not to mention the onset of the pandemic, the issues did not die. While some of their success may have been fueled by the pandemic, the advances and growth experienced by the OPMs in subsequent years did nothing to assuage the senators' concern and in January 2022, Warren and Brown, now joined by Senator Tina Smith (Democrat from Minnesota), wrote to the CEOs of those same five companies, as well as three others (Kaplan, Inc., Grand Canyon Education, Inc., and Zovio), seeking "an update on [their] online degree programs for college and universities that accept federal financial aid" (Warren et al. 2022). Noting that since their previous January 2020 inquiry, "Online Program Management (OPM) companies appear to have significantly expanded, becoming a more integral part of American higher education," they sought updated data, with an eye to "inform[ing] effective policy towards this growing sector of higher education" (Warren et al. 2022). It remains a matter of ongoing concern.

The Pandemic Changes Everything

For all of these entrepreneurial and public policy initiatives, it took an international pandemic for the idea of remote learning and the concept of distance education to truly pierce the national consciousness. Suddenly, beginning in March 2020, with the advent of the Covid-19 pandemic fueled national shutdown, remote learning and the virtual classroom became commonplace, the new educational normal—at least for the short term. While the problems and challenges that attended that transition were many and real, the situation shined a spotlight on an idea that had been operating around the edges, thrusting a formerly peripheral activity to the front and center, albeit in an overly simplified way. In doing so it ushered in a new reality that forced millions—educators, parents, students, government officials, and corporate interests alike—to confront its reality and ponder its potential.

Initially, almost the whole educational world, at whatever level, was forced to go virtual or to close down. Schools and school systems across the nation scrambled to adapt to the technological needs that had to be addressed to make virtual online education a possibility. The issues that meticulously developing distance learning programs were working on suddenly could not wait. At the same time, those who had never intended to teach virtually, who had no facility with it and no real idea of how to do it other than to try to do what they always did but now on their computer's camera, were suddenly forced to do just that—and maybe more.

From tech needs to hardware demands to internet access, the challenges were many, and the stories of students and parents driving around their neighborhoods to find internet access become legion. To parents and psychologists, some of the longtime concerns about distance learning, including the isolation and questions of motivation and accountability, also became apparent. Questions involving the lines of development and the age at which lessons on a computer screen could be done effectively were brought to the forefront. Appreciation for all that had gone into making *Sesame Street* and the *Electric Company* such important parts of earlier generations' educational experiences skyrocketed. Educators found that certain approaches did not translate well into effective online teaching—at least not when change was happening on a dime. For the educational community on both sides of the desk, as well as in support areas, the transition to distance learning was a major challenge to making the best of the rest of the school year and brought into question what things should look like as the 2020–21 academic year began.

As the spring semester drew to a close and the specter of a continued distance learning experience loomed, countless students began to reassess their options. Suddenly, those programs that had lurked on the periphery of the educational world but that focused on and had a track record in distance education suddenly gained a new stature—and a new attraction. Filling a need caused by the continuing pandemic were programs like the University of the People, a nonprofit whose online program is free, charging only a small assessment fee for each course. In the aftermath of the onset of the pandemic, it experienced massive growth and has continued to thrive (D'Agostino 2023). Foreshadowing the trend and highlighting the turn to those experienced in the field was Modern States Education Alliance, a nonprofit that developed affiliations early in the pandemic with numerous states including New York, Indiana, and Ohio, allowing students in those states to use the organization's library of online courses, a resource that some students were able to use to complete their freshman year in college free of charge (Lubot 2020). Meanwhile, Straighterline, a for-profit operation that offers low-cost online general education courses, experienced a major increase in its use by students from non-partner institutions ("Straighterline Salutes ..." 2021).

All expectations were that distance learning enrollment would continue to grow as the line between the periphery and the mainstream became blurred and uncertainty about whether in-person classes would resume grew. People were reassessing their educational goals and options, and suddenly the not infrequent differences in quality, cost, and convenience became clearer to not only those who were only just becoming acquainted with distance learning but also to those for whom online learning was their focus and not just an emergency option.

Confronting the Pandemic

With the likelihood that remote teaching and learning would still be at least a part of their approach in the fall of 2020, educators at all levels, increasingly cognizant of the difference between effective distance education and their previous emergency efforts, worked hard that summer. They looked for ways to bridge that gap, to develop remote teaching skills and lessons appropriate to their new "classroom" in a determined and dedicated effort to offer a more effective and valuable educational experience to their students.

Those efforts proved necessary, for when the 2020–21 school year began the number of virtual learners remained high. Indeed, October saw the release of the annual report from the National Council for State Authorization Reciprocity Agreements (NC-SARA), an organization that oversees distance education in all states except California while also covering Washington, DC, Puerto Rico, and the US Virgin Islands. It disclosed that in the fall of 2020 approximately 5.8 million students were enrolled in exclusively distance-based courses in SARA participating institutions. That figure was almost double the number of students enrolled in entirely remote courses the previous fall (Schwartz 2021a).

But beyond the numbers, the report also revealed some pointed ways in which the pandemic had impacted some ongoing trends in online learning. One of these was the distribution between in-state and out-of-state enrollment. In 2019, the share of students enrolled in exclusively distance education (EDE) in their home state versus those in out-of-state institutions was 53.7 percent to 46.3 percent. In 2020, the percentage of those who were in home state EDEs increased to 67.6 percent. The report's authors surmised that "[t]he significant growth, both in sheer EDE enrollment reported and the proportion of reported enrollment, is likely attributable to the pivot to emergency remote learning" caused by the pandemic (Schwartz 2021a).

The report also noted that a majority of the surveyed institutions anticipated that they would continue offering some or all of the emergency remote learning options they had offered during the crisis. The 2020 EDE enrollment was overwhelming centered in public colleges, which boasted 85.3 percent of the remote enrollment, up from 78.7 percent in 2019. No less telling is the fact that according to federal government data, in 2020, 44.7 percent of students were enrolled entirely online as opposed to the 17 percent who were similarly enrolled in 2019 (Schwartz 2022c).

The increase in online and distance learning that occurred in the United States with the onset of the pandemic was phenomenal, and it raises numerous questions about modern education as well as society at large. At a time when higher education has increasingly been the subject of wide-ranging debate about its role and its sustainability, not to mention more specific questions about its cost and even in some quarters its fundamental value, distance education adds another element to the equation. The lean, no frills offerings that can characterize distance learning also raise questions relating to experiences that have long been hallmarks of a residential college, from the socialization that comes from living on campus to the role of athletics, fraternities, and societies in an educational experience. Yet as important as these matters are, in the fall of 2020 they were questions for another day, as remote learning remained a necessity for many students when the 2020–21 academic year began. Despite the circumstances, it did not take much to see distance education as a new and enticing, if not fully understood, option.

The reality of this change was apparent in the enrollment figures that emerged as the 2020–21 academic year unfolded. Educators across the globe have conceded that the pandemic had a profound impact on distance learning, both in real and perceptual terms. Whether because it forced both students and faculty to utilize it in a way that had never been intended, or because it proved to be a seemingly easy way to address the restraints imposed by the pandemic, distance learning was suddenly on everyone's radar. The way in which it suddenly became a fact of life, however awkward, in the homes of students around the world, many of whom had never contemplated it as part of their educational plans, forced them to confront its reality and its potential. Former naysayers, as well as those new to it all, had to admit to its practicality under the circumstances.

In the immediate aftermath of the onset of the pandemic, it became evident that the online educational landscape would be changing. With every faculty member delivering a remote form of education and every student receiving it in some fashion, it was inevitable that resistance to the practice would arise. But the bigger question was whether those who had simply done what needed to be done, offering video conferenced classes supplemented by emailed assessments, would truly embrace the possibilities of distance education and seek to develop new and creative technology-enhanced ways of teaching, especially if the following year would see a return to normal, in-person schooling.

Indeed, one thing that the spring 2020 turn-on-a-dime transition to virtual learning made clear was that teacher training is essential if schools and colleges want distance learning to be anything more than simply an in-class presentation offered on-screen. At the same time that such training was being contemplated, the nation's educational community was also forced to ask itself why. If virtual learning was only to be a short, stop-gap measure, then what kind of training was necessary? Did teachers and professors simply need instruction aimed at making them more facile with the existing technology, developing at least a comfort level that would allow them to do what they had been doing but in a virtual manner, or did faculty need training and encouragement that would lead to a veritable recreation of all they had been doing. In the midst of the oppressive conditions created by the pandemic, at a time when their resources were already being stretched and devoted to things never previously imagined or anticipated, schools had to make some immediate decisions with potentially critical long-term ramifications. Remote learning, if not true distance education, had arrived, however unexpectedly, but its sudden arrival was accompanied by a need to think—immediately—about its future.

One immediate concern was that of access, an issue whose importance, indeed centrality, to any real chance to maintain learning levels was evident. At the same time that educators and the government were struggling with ensuring that everyone could have the internet access needed to continue the virtual efforts still required in many places in the fall of 2020, the higher education community agonized over the enrollment drop-off that they experienced that same fall. But while overall enrollment decreased significantly, the nation's online schools' enrollment saw equally significant increases (Dist. ed Partic. 2019–20).

Two trends were emerging in the online world. First, as enrollment grew, so too did the divide between those online providers with established records and reputations and those still working to achieve that recognition and credibility.

The second trend was that as online education became a more accepted and available option, its mere availability was no longer enough in the eyes of its prospective students. In an increasingly competitive market, distance education providers were also having to pay more attention to the other aspects of their "product." Experienced programs understood this in the same way they understood the need for a distinctive pedagogy. The importance of support, not to mention the very nature of the course content, came to the forefront, as students and potential students began to focus on the whole online student experience (Westra 2018). This competition altered the way schools presented their online programs, with the student experience becoming an integral part of marketing efforts. The change in approach was a telling reflection of distance education's continuing move from the educational fringe to a position ever closer to the mainstream.

With the advent of new internet-based distance learning efforts, there emerged a definitive divide between asynchronous learning and synchronous learning. While exact definitions may vary depending in large part on how specific one wishes to be, at their core, these educational styles differ in the timing and nature of the interaction between instructor and students and amongst the students themselves. Asynchronous learning is best described as an online teaching experience where the instruction is presented in a way that does not require all students to be in attendance at the same time. In contrast, synchronous learning is more like a traditional, in-person class but is simply presented through an online platform. Like in a traditional classroom, all students are in attendance, with the teaching and learning process as well as the teacher–student and student–student interactions occurring in real time (Wintemute 2023).

The differences in the two approaches both reflect and highlight some of the issues at the heart of discussions about online education. Synchronous learning offers the obvious benefit of real-time instructor feedback as well as related interactions and true discussions as opposed to the types of idea-sharing methods that characterize the asynchronous learning experience. This allows for a more personally supportive experience. However, it also can replicate the problems that often crop up in an in-person classroom; for example, one student may dominate a discussion, or the quantity of contribution may trump quality. The human dynamic in the synchronous classroom may inhibit quieter students whose shyness or lack of confidence makes them reluctant to join the fray in a personal and public way. At the same time, real-time interaction allows for questions and confusion to be addressed immediately and directly, and thus students are less apt to suffer from the lack of clarity or nuance that may result from reading posts on comment boards or ideas shared via email, methods of communication that characterize asynchronous learning.

The most obvious, or at least the initial, advantage of the asynchronous learning experience is its flexibility. For a student to be able, albeit, within some predetermined constraints, to take their class and pursue their education on their own time is a huge benefit in the modern 24/7 world. Allowing the student to enjoy a more individualized experience, that experience can also be a more isolating exercise, one that reduces opportunity to draw upon the talents, experiences, and ideas of one's classmates in a real-time exchange. It can also result in a lack of personal instructor support. Communication can still occur through discussion board postings, online threads, and emails, but the nature of these interactions is clearly different. That said, there is also an element of anonymity that can lead to a type of equality that is often lacking in a class where one individual, however unintentionally or despite the instructor's best efforts, can dominate. The gift of time provides an opportunity to reflect on a lesson and to give more thought to the written ideas of classmates, another advantage of the asynchronous approach and one that may benefit all.

A major result of the boom in distance education has been the opportunities it has afforded teachers themselves to again become students, as online professional development programs and opportunities have skyrocketed. The reduced costs and the flexibility of such programs are making it easier than ever to provide teachers with additional training—often in technology or distance education related workshops—in ways that are less costly and less disruptive. Teachers can more easily pursue additional credentials and degrees that enhance their professional stature and advance their careers, while also getting training in the pedagogy appropriate to distance education teaching (Elliott 2017).

Emerging from the Pandemic: Navigating a Changed Landscape

As we look back at a country seeking to move on in the aftermath of the pandemic, its educational landscape now included a new, if still not fully understood, option. While higher education scholars Arthur Levine and Scott Van Pelt have noted the way that education technology mimics its predecessor, with the onset of the pandemic and the arrival on the national radar of remote learning, the situation was very different from the time when television took the baton from radio. The stakes were higher and the audience larger, but more importantly, events were out of the control of those who would have sought to achieve a smooth transition. The next step in the progression—formal, well-developed distance education—was still on the sidelines, preparing itself.

As we have seen, the late 1980s witnessed the first wholly online degree programs, but pretty much all comprehensive efforts at distance education were essentially niche offerings. They tended to serve their specific, mission-based audiences, usually aimed at working adults who sought further education, especially of the type that could further their careers or represented greater general access, like that at the heart of the Western Governors University's mission. Prior to the pandemic, online education was peripheral to the world of higher education, concentrated in a small number of institutions. Ten universities accounted for 10 percent of the enrollment, with established programs like Western Governors University whose enrollment was about 120,000, Southern New Hampshire University with 150,000 students, and the University of Phoenix with a little under 100,000, leading the way (Levine and Van Pelt 2021).

But in the aftermath of the pandemic, the number of programs increased and broadened. Each month has brought news of changes, but tellingly these changes are more often than not developments on the business side of distance learning. News of mergers and acquisitions, like that of 2U acquiring edX in the fall of 2021 or the public offerings of Coursera, 2DL, and Udemy in 2021, while not about curriculum or pedagogy, can offer insight into trends and expectations relating to alternative credentials and the still developing, ever-changing online education market (Schwartz 2021b).

Indeed, in its public offering prospectus, Udemy asserted that its efforts were helping to meet the rising demands for lifelong training that traditional providers were not adequately addressing. Its two-pronged approach by which it offers online courses both directly to consumers and through Udemy Business, which helps employers train their workers, is reflective of the different elements of the market. The company aims to serve a changing job market, one that has seen millions of workers leaving their jobs despite often needing new or additional training for their next jobs. Such training is often most accessible through a distance education option (Shah 2021a). This shift is a telling reflection of the multifaceted, changing educational landscape. Indeed, as one economic analyst observed, the first year of the pandemic was a banner year for the nation's MOOC providers, and as distance education moves from the periphery to the mainstream, becoming ever more closely tied to traditional educational institutions, its value will likely continue to grow. What exactly that means for education, especially in the long term, is an open question.

While OPMs were experiencing economic good news as a result of the pandemic-fueled growth of distance education, in 2021, Eastern Gateway Community College found itself serving as the poster child for questions that continue to surround the new distance education paradigm. As the Thanksgiving holiday approached, Eastern Gateway was the recipient of a ten-page letter from its accrediting agency, the Higher Learning Commission, announcing that the Steubenville, Ohio, institution had been placed on probation, with its accreditation to be further reviewed in two years. The letter criticized the college's unchecked growth while also noting the lack of a strong commitment to maintaining academic standards (Vasquez 2021).

Eastern Gateway's growth was exceptional to be sure. In 2015, the school enrolled 3,000 students, but by 2020, it boasted an enrollment of over 40,000 students, almost all of them online. Clearly its partnership with the online management company, Student Resource Center (which had profited handsomely from its partnership with Eastern Gateway), had achieved significant success, but at a no-less obvious price (Smalley 2021a). School officials noted that they had already responded to some of the Commission's criticisms, while admitting that being on probation would limit further growth. The school also noted the probationary period would provide an opportunity for it to review its procedures and policies while also preparing a response to the Commission's charges (Vasquez 2021). Central to the concerns about maintaining academic standards were charges of waiving fees as well as allowing many of its union-supported online students to forego the placement tests that were required of every one of the on-campus students. The uneven admissions standards were a specific point identified by the accreditors (D'Agostino 2022b). While Eastern Gateway officials were confident that they would again achieve full reaccreditation when next reviewed, the situation served as a cautionary tale for other schools that might have been contemplating hitching their wagon to the distance learning star (Vasquez 2021).

Another system that joined the fray was the University of North Carolina (UNC). In December 2021, the state announced that the University of North Carolina system would be launching a nonprofit ed-tech start-up whose efforts would be aimed at increasing adult online education, in response to the anticipated need for more skilled labor. Leveraging the $97 million that the state had received in pandemic recovery funds, Project Kitty Hawk, whose name was a nod to the state's having been the site of the Wright Brothers' first airplane flight, was a reaffirmation of North Carolina's commitment to technological innovation. UNC leaders hailed the program as one that would be transformative as it sought to connect with the estimated 1 million North Carolinians who claimed some college education, but no degree (Smalley 2021b).

The initial plan called for the launching of 120 new online programs over the first five years and was presented as a response to a clear state need. Indeed, with half of the state's workers eligible for employer educations benefits, the fact that as of fall 2019, Liberty and Strayer universities were the most popular online programs among the more than 60,000 state residents enrolled in what state officials called "high cost, out of state programs," caught the eye of state officials. Those same officials also realized that a new program, one that appropriately tailored its online services and infrastructure, had a fertile field from which to draw. A pre-launch white paper revealed that, as of 2021, only 9 percent of UNC system undergraduates and just 13 percent of students over the age of twenty-five were learning exclusively online. This offered UNC's leaders strong evidence that the state needed a more expansive adult online offering (Smalley 2021b).

At the same time, while the new program represented yet another traditional school entering the online world in a substantive way, UNC sought to avoid some of the now clear pitfalls, especially the expense of the popular OPM model that, while successful, often diminished much of the institutional earning potential. According to the white paper, Project Kitty Hawk planned to be self-sustaining by 2026, a result of a plan that will utilize a "private sector-like approach on behalf of a tremendous public good" (Smalley 2021b). The size of the venture was hailed by observers as unprecedented. At the same time, there were some who noted that given the decentralized culture of higher education, in choosing to centralize the program rather than creating sixteen separate online models, UNC needed to take particular care to avoid the pitfalls that had been experienced by other less successful efforts.

Comments from leaders from the various system campuses reflected their recognition of the value to their students, while also revealing a clear recognition of the potential for adult learners. Project Kitty Hawk was, said new UNC system president Peter Hans, an opportunity to provide the tens of thousands of North Carolinians for whom such education presented a chance to advance in their job and in their careers with an outlet, while also serving as one of the engines in the effort to achieve the state's goal of providing 2 million more North Carolinians with high-quality credentials by 2030 (Smalley, 2021b).

While the UNC initiative reflected an increase in established schools jumping more fully into the distance education pool, other news from 2021 offered reminders of why they were doing so. As noted earlier, as 2021 ended, Purdue University's distance education program, based in large part on its 2017 acquisition of Kaplan, reported that it was breaking even, a status it had reached with impressive speed (Hill 2021). This was reflective of the benefits that schools were getting as their distance education efforts, while often seeming to mimic corporate dealings, also furthered the corporatization of higher education.

In a move that had all the hallmarks of the mergers and acquisitions reports that frequently appear in the business news, in March 2021, Southern New Hampshire University (SNHU) acquired coding boot camp provider Kenzie Academy. This move not only added to an enrollment that was already consistently at or near the top of the pack but also enabled the university to expand its alternative credentials offerings. Under the agreement, SNHU got the for-profit Kenzie's programs and students, with Kenzie becoming a division of SNHU. The addition of the Indianapolis-based Kenzie, which was founded in 2017 and offers certificates in software engineering and user experience design, was to allow SNHU to expand its alternative credentials offerings which accounted for only a small part of the school's portfolio. With this new addition, they planned to focus on micro-credentials sought by people who are looking to retrain for newly in-demand jobs (McKenzie 2021). Ironically, the transaction would soon serve as a reminder of the way the distance education landscape could change remarkably fast. By the summer of 2023, citing both the rise of AI and increased competition, SNHU shut down Kenzie Academy (Coffey 2023).

Although it is impossible to read the national mind, the significant increase in online enrollment at the nation's top nonprofit online providers from 2019 to 2020—Southern New Hampshire University at 18 percent, Arizona State University with more than 20 percent, and Western Governor's by almost 7 percent—would seem to speak volumes about the increased willingness of the nation's students to pursue their education from distance learning providers, especially when the alternative was a distance learning experience at a place whose track record was far less established. Interesting, too, was the breakdown of those increases with Southern New Hampshire's upturn powered overwhelmingly by undergraduates while both Arizona State and WGU saw their greatest increase on the graduate school side of the ledger (Blumenstyk 2021).

Some observers see such numbers as a product of the pandemic, which appears to have impacted clientele differently. Many lower-income undergraduate students, victims of furloughs and layoffs, also abandoned their college dreams and did not return for the start of the 2020–21 academic year. In contrast, many younger, early-career professionals, having effectively transitioned to working at home, concluded that it was now a good time to take the plunge and do what they needed to do to advance in their professional journey. Online learning was the way for them to make that move (Blumenstyk 2021).

Here We Go Again?!

For all of this progress and change, as well as the developing optimism and the increasing focus on the future, as 2021 came to a close, the United States educational establishment discovered they were not yet out of the woods. Rather, the arrival of a new Covid-19 variant, Omicron, on campuses in the aftermath of Thanksgiving brought a new set of challenges. Recognized as spreading more quickly than earlier versions, the new variant brought a rash of cases to countless campuses just as the schools were heading into exams. The new threat led to pivots at some schools with a speed that rivaled that of the spring of 2020. But now with experience in hand and better developed capabilities, it was easier for places like Princeton, Georgetown, and NYU, among others, to move exams online while also limiting or canceling large group gatherings. They also urged students to vacate campuses as soon as possible (Jaschik 2021).

Not surprisingly, concerns about the status of second semester courses immediately surfaced, and both the nation and the higher education community that thought they had weathered the worst of the Covid-19 pandemic suddenly had to refer back to their hastily created, and constantly revised, pandemic playbook. All the while, they wondered whether they would be forced to relive their previous nightmare, and if so, whether they had truly learned from that earlier experience. With Christmas approaching, colleges and universities ranging from Harvard to the jewels of the University of California system, Berkeley and UCLA, and countless others in between, announced that the opening weeks of the second semester would feature online classes, a practice that generally carried through to the end of January 2022 (Arrojas 2021). For the most part, the decisions did not seem unreasonable, and they often were accompanied by regulations and guidelines—including the testing that now seemed to fall under that umbrella—that would allow for students to have the more normal aspects of residential college life, to at least some degree.

But of course, there was not only the question of what they had learned from the past but whether those lessons would be both appropriate to the current crisis and able to be adapted. Too, there was also the question of whether or not a nation of students, who had, for the most part, been willing to accept virtual educational offerings that had often been put together on a moment's notice, would be so willing to accept similar efforts on a second go around.

The first wave of the pandemic had caught everyone by surprise, and few would have argued that the quality of education that students received in the spring of 2020 was what they would have received in person. But as 2021 ended, the situation was different, for with so much of the 2020–21 academic year still having involved virtual instruction, even for in-residence students, faculty had ostensibly had the chance to adapt and improve their efforts, and so expectations were higher. Whether or not faculty had truly raised their game was open to debate. Indeed, whether they could meet the challenge if Omicron forced the nation to revert to an all or mostly virtual format remained to be seen. Would their efforts be good enough to satisfy an audience that had become increasingly critical of much that their college experience offered? There was no denying that, as the Omicron variant arrived in late 2021, the colleges utilizing remote learning found themselves preparing to address a new set of challenges, as well as an audience and consumer group whose attitudes and expectations were markedly different from that of March 2020.

With the experience gained from the previous shutdown, colleges were able to adjust comparatively quickly, and the spring semester 2022 proceeded in a manner far closer to normal than many had expected. But for other groups, it was not so easy. In the beginning days of 2022, as the Omicron variant surged, students, parents, teachers, and administrators across the country often felt as though they were thrust back in time. The holiday break had only fueled the surge of infections, and while previous experience had left most people determined to do in-person instruction, the impact of the virus on school personnel—a problem not limited to schools—was in some cases making virtual education, its logistical challenges notwithstanding, the only real option.

Indeed, with the surge coinciding with the post-holiday start of school in January 2022, distance education became something of a political football. For those like teachers' unions led by Chicago's powerful contingent, it represented a safe alternative, one that allowed teachers to teach all students in the same way, while reducing some of the health risks (M. Smith 2022). In fact, in a number of places, educational desires were overwhelmed by health concerns and vaccination rates. Cleveland, Detroit, and Milwaukee were among the major cities that started with online instruction after the holidays (Saul 2022). In contrast, schools in New York City, where vaccination rates ranked among the nation's highest, opened in person after the holiday break (Shapiro et al. 2022).

Even in places where people agreed with the decisions made, there was anger over the lack of notice, as last-minute announcements left families scrambling to juggle jobs and childcare. For all its advancement, the nation had yet to see a distance education menu that it could fully embrace by choice, one that reflected thoughtfully developed curricular options and not ones created with an eye to the clock and emergency usage, ready to be utilized at a moment's notice. While colleges had made the transition more smoothly, it was not without controversy. Indeed, Florida Governor Ron DeSantis declared that any college that shifted back to online instruction should offer students a full refund (Greenberg 2022).

Interestingly, there was one thing missing in almost all of these debates and discussions: any truly substantive consideration of the actual quality of the teaching and learning that was being offered. This often seemed little more than an afterthought. Certainly, broader concerns, not to mention the political pressures, were evident when Michigan Governor Gretchen Whitmer's January 2022 State of the State included the assertion, "I want to be crystal clear. Students belong in school. We know it's where they learn best … In-person learning is critical to social development and mental health. And that's why we will do everything we can to keep kids in the classroom" (Neher and Roth 2022). Indeed, those sentiments—or at least the bottom-line desire to get students in school—were evident in the many on one side of the divide, who, after the challenges of the previous year and a half wanted and needed children to be in school on an in-person basis. Whitmer's remarks highlighted many of their concerns, especially the belief that in-person instruction reduced many mental health and psychological issues and that it was the better learning experience while also being less disruptive of family and work life.

The health versus education debate was a real one, but where the core issue of distance education as a provider of quality instruction fit in was uncertain. This was no small concern and source of frustration for distance education advocates, who saw their distinct, effective, well developed, and responsible approach being undermined by factors not only beyond their control but also unrelated to the educational aspects central to their process. Remote learning, they emphasized, was not distance education, but they knew that the public perception was now skewed, affecting people's ability to effectively assess what distance education can truly offer and provide (Hodges et al. 2020).

Beyond the Pandemic: Looking Ahead to the Future of Distance Education in the New Normal

While the Omicron surge at the end of 2021 and into 2022 represented a setback, by the spring of 2022, things were back to a considerably more "normal" existence. With a massive drop in cases and an increase in vaccinations and boosters, mask mandates across the country were abandoned, and people on both sides of the school desk began to talk about remote learning in more fundamental educational terms and not simply as the response to a crisis. Discussions provided an opportunity for distance education advocates to take advantage of heightened awareness of their work and to show what well-designed distance education could do under appropriate educational circumstances.

While the educational world began to consider the potential of distance education as a transformative innovation at the end of the pandemic, the business sectors that had profited so handsomely from the pandemic-fueled remote learning boom wondered how they would fare when they were head-to-head with traditional higher education on a level playing field, no longer directly impacted by Covid-19. The financial success of the companies that had been at the center of the large corporate component of the distance education boom was mind boggling and evident in the public offerings and huge valuations associated with the companies. Indeed, by any estimation, 2020 and 2021 had been profitable in the extreme, with the massive boom in MOOC platforms clearly evident in the way Coursera's enrollment numbers increased from 44 million in 2019 to 71 million in 2020 to 92 million in September 2021, and they were not alone (Wood 2022). And yet while there were concerns about how these companies would compete, as well as doubts about their ability to continue to experience the growth trajectories they had recently enjoyed, there was also a recognition that in addition to the competitive aspect, there was also a parallel partnership, as the Course Management Systems (CMSs) and OPMs helped the colleges add to their existing options with things like immersion programs and boot camps as well as non-degree professional certifications and credentials programs. The potential was there for the distance education venture to be a win–win for all involved, at least financially.

During the pandemic, the remote classroom allowed for the continuation of the teaching and learning process but with no real concern about the quality of the experience. While the pandemic helped introduce distance education, or at least remote learning, to an audience that would likely have otherwise been uninterested or remained unexposed to its potential, the isolation central to pandemic-induced online learning certainly highlighted an aspect of distance education that must be addressed. Social needs and the desire for connection has proven to be a real concern, one that has manifested itself in mental health issues and higher dropout rates. While some argue that isolation is less of an issue when the distance learner has chosen that learning approach rather than being consigned to it, it nevertheless remains a concern, and at the very least raises the question of how to better motivate or engage online distance learners.

As the country looks to education on the far side of the pandemic, the question of where remote learning and distance education fit into the new educational landscape is a big one. As mentioned previously, scholar Arthur Levine observed that over the course of time, each communication technology has mimicked its predecessor. Radio programs brought live entertainment—theater, concerts, and sports—to the airwaves before they created their own distinctive programming. Television offered video versions of radio staples like *The Lone Ranger* and the *Jack Benny Show*, while on the education front, lectures were televised. Similarly, the earliest of online courses were for the most part simply lectures shared by computer, an approach that offered essentially one-way communication and was a source of frustration. But eventually, as Levine notes, outsiders, those on the periphery of change and more innovative than the mainstream, began to produce something more (Levine 2022).

Witness the way places like the University of Phoenix and others began to offer an online experience that was different. In the overall context of the world of higher education, they were an outlier, occupying the periphery while at the same time seeking to expand their presence and make inroads into the mainstream. The Covid-19 pandemic suddenly accelerated that process, with those on the periphery suddenly benefiting from new interest and awareness while the mainstream was forced to adopt some of the peripheral occupant's approaches. But once things calmed down, that initial exposure, as well as the still unsettled state of the mainstream, led many to reassess their options, and suddenly online options seemed a more inviting, if not viable, possibility. The result was an increase in online enrollment as well as a downturn for traditional providers. Whether it would last remained to be seen, but at least for the moment, as Levine noted, while the periphery remained the periphery, it was moving ever faster towards the mainstream.

The early days of 2022 shined a spotlight on remote learning but not in a way that distance education professionals appreciated. Rather, as the Omicron variant of the Covid-19 virus surged, schools at all levels were forced to assess the situation and determine whether the school year would continue in person, virtually, or in a hybrid mode, whether the start of colleges' second semester would be delayed and whether mask mandates would be affected. In the midst of this debate, the political football that was being tossed around amongst politicians, educational administrators, teachers, teachers' unions, not to mention students and their families, was the very concept of remote learning. The last two years had made clear it was a viable operational option. But as the politics of the situation became increasingly dominant, the way the term success was defined and how it related to actual teaching and learning became far less clear.

While these day-to-day pressures put remote learning back at the forefront of the debate, the world of distance education was looking to the future, after a pandemic era of remarkable expansion. As noted, the increase of MOOC platforms over the course of the pandemic was huge and could not be ignored, enabling companies like Coursera and Udemy to become publicly traded in 2021 (Mascarenhas 2021). The growth of the business side of the equation was illustrated no less clearly when powerhouse MOOC provider edX was acquired by the ed tech giant 2U for $800 million (Shah 2021b).

While some business analysts doubted the ability of these companies to continue their growth once the situation settled down, there was an increasing recognition that companies were competing both against each other as well as with traditional educational institutions, something that some of the schools were seeking to forestall by entering into partnerships that could be seen as a win–win proposition, allowing more traditional schools to benefit from the advances made by distance education proponents.

Another indication of the increasingly mainstream place that distance education was coming to occupy was the fact that in January 2022 *U.S. News & World Report* issued their 2022 rankings for the best online bachelor's and master's programs. Reflecting the divide between remote learning and distance education, the magazine's "Best Online Programs" rankings included only those programs that were specifically designed to be administered online and did not include any traditionally brick-and-mortar, in-person programs that were forced to go temporarily virtual due to the pandemic. In addition to the credibility and presence in the higher education landscape that the rankings represent, it is also worth noting that the 2022 edition included more than 1,700 programs, a substantive increase over the previous year's, at just over 1,600. Two areas of study that saw particular growth were business, which grew from 145 to 228 programs, and psychology, which more than doubled, jumping from 27 to 55 offerings. The numbers and the media reaction to the latest news were further evidence of the increasing impact of distance education on higher education ("US News Unveils ... Rankings" 2022).

Meanwhile, befitting its longtime standing as a distance education leader among more traditional schools, in January 2022, Arizona State University (ASU) announced the launching of a new initiative that sought to reach 100 million learners worldwide by 2030. The program would be centered in an online global management and entrepreneurial certificate program. Reflective of its global nature, the program will be translated into forty languages and will be offered through ASU's Thunderbird School of Global Management (Belkin 2022).

The initiative was spurred by a $25 million gift from businessman F. Francis Najafi and his wife Dionne Najafi, and ASU hopes to raise additional funds to build upon the Najafis' support. The intent is to make the certificate programs free. Those who pursue the certificate must complete five graduate-level courses. The fifteen credits earned in achieving the certificate can then be applied towards degrees at both ASU as well as other affiliated schools. Analysts note that ASU is not the first institution to try and reach a global audience through an online program, but the university's significant commitment of resources is certainly noteworthy (Schwartz 2022a). ASU plans to have small teams of faculty members curating the course content, which will feature interactive exercises while also allowing students to connect through peer groups. Students will receive feedback from associated faculty, and that process will eventually be further enhanced through artificial intelligence (Bleezer 2022). All of this led Thunderbird School dean Sanjeeev Kahgram to enthusiastically describe the initiative as a "MOOC 4.0" (Schwartz 2022a). At the very least, it makes clear that, in addition to recent successful corporate endeavors in distance education, there are also major academic players who see a bright future for their approach and offerings as well as a growing role in the world of American and global higher education.

As the world moved into the spring of 2022, with people seemingly ready for a return to some semblance of pre-pandemic normal, remote learning seemed to be taking a back seat to distance learning, with the many for whom the distinction had meant little now forced to think about what it held for the future. Had it been an emergency lifeline, or was it a preview and forerunner of what technology could offer education, especially at the high school level and beyond. Debate raged over whether it would lead to the demise of traditional higher education or serve as its savior, helping schools adapt to the demands and desires of twenty-first-century students. At the same time that companies like Coursera and U2 were taking their now publicly traded offerings to an ever wider set of potential customers, small schools like Simmons College saw in distance education a way to expand its online offerings as well as raise its public profile, all while enhancing and growing its business side (Swaak 2022a).

As the 2021–22 academic year drew to a close, educators could not ignore the upsurge in reported Covid-19 cases, but they were certainly optimistic that as in other sectors, life would go on. Signs that remote learning and distance education had worked their way ever more into the mainstream were evident, and the economic challenges that followed the pandemic triggered concerns for which remote learning could be a solution. For example, Southwest Tennessee Community College decided to conduct some of their classes online beginning in May of 2022. The reason for the school's decision to institute a "virtual Friday" was not an educational one—although they hoped it might help keep students in school—but rather an effort to help the school's many commuter students who were struggling with the massive increase in gas prices that descended on the nation as the summer approached (Moon 2022). Although not the path that distance education advocates would have wanted, it was yet another indication of the way that remote teaching and learning had altered the educational landscape.

As the 2022–23 academic year loomed, educators and the public were reminded of the fast-moving and ever-changing nature of remote learning and distance education. However, attitudes were beginning to change. A national survey released in the final weeks of July 2022 showed a major increase in the percentage of Americans who viewed online education positively. Specifically, it reported an almost 50 percent increase in those who believed that online education was roughly the same quality as in-person teaching and learning. However, those same respondents also made clear that they believed distance education should be cheaper (Seltzer 2022). Reminders of corporate involvement in much of the distance education world appeared when July also brought news that Byju's, a huge India-based ed-tech company, was seeking to buy the major OPM 2U (Swaak 2022b). At the same time, two years after the start of their promised "transformational" partnership, the University of Arizona and Zovio ended their operating agreement (Schwartz 2022c). The corporate aspects of the world of distance education were still developing.

As the 2022–23 academic year was getting under way, a sobering report was released, one that cannot help but impact the ongoing discussions surrounding the future of distance education and remote learning, while also reinforcing the concerns of educators, parents, and policymakers about the impact of the pandemic and the role of distance education in the educational landscape. The results from the spring 2022 administration (the first since the onset of the pandemic) of the National Assessment of Educational Progress, an assessment commonly known as the Nation's Report Card, revealed that the "pandemic has smacked American students back to the last century in math and reading achievement." The results "show the biggest drop in math performance in 4th and 8th grades since the testing program began in 1990. In reading, 4th and 8th graders likewise are performing on par with students in the 1990s, and about a third of students in both grades can't read at even the 'basic' achievement level— the lowest level on the test" (Sparks 2022).

Similar results were seen when officials in Washington, DC released the results of the 2022 PARCC exam. The test used by the nation's capital's schools as well as a number of states was given to students in grades three through eight and high school and the results were no less disappointing, with substantial declines extending across grades and racial and socio-economic divides (Lumpkin 2022). These results add a whole new dimension to the debate over the quality of the remote teaching and learning experience. While the results do not represent a final verdict, they do serve as a stark reminder of the many factors and questions central to the ongoing debates over the efficacy of this educational approach.

Although these results cast a cloud over the online experience of elementary school students during the pandemic, results of a survey done in 2022 made clear that online college among traditional age undergrads has become an increasingly attractive option. In fact, the results of a national survey released in October 2022 revealed a massive increase in the number of students in the 18–24-year-old range who were enrolled exclusively in online programs, with online giants Western Governors and Southern New Hampshire leading the way. WGU and SNHU both saw marked increases in traditional aged undergraduates pursuing their degrees through online programs that had previously mainly been the program of choice for working adults (D'Agostino 2022a).

While observers noted that both universities' numbers were on the rise prior to the pandemic, the shift in demographics seemed to represent yet another step forward for advocates of distance education. In conjunction with these findings were the results of another survey, this one of high school juniors and seniors concerning their college plans, conducted by Eduventures Prospective Student Research. The result was a doubling of those who planned to attend college fully online. While admittedly the overall number remained comparatively low, the result represented a significant change (D'Agostino 2022a).

Finally, the release in June 2023 of the latest report from the National Assessment of Educational Progress only reaffirmed what the October 2022 results had revealed. National test scores for thirteen-year-olds who took the test in the fall of 2022 showed massive drop-offs from the pre-pandemic 2019 results. Specifically, math scores dropped by nine points to their lowest level since 1990, while a reading drop of four points saw the average reading score at the same point as in 2004. Particularly disturbing was the fact that the lowest performing students saw a decline almost double that of their higher achieving peers (St. George 2023).

While remote learning certainly could not be blamed for all of the backsliding, the latest report could not fail to cast a cloud over the whole concept and fuel ongoing debates. Clearly, there was much to be learned, discussed, and studied. But in a fast-moving process that had seen each new answer met with many new questions, the next step in the evolution of remote learning and distance education remained very much a puzzle.

References

Abelson, Hal, Shigeru Miyagawa, and Dick K. P. Yue. 2021. "On the 20th Anniversary of OpenCourseWare: How It Began." MIT Faculty Newsletter, May/June. https://fnl.mit.edu/may-june-2021/on-the-20th-anniversary-of-opencourseware-how-it-began/

Adams, Richard. 2013. "Sal Khan: The Man Who Tutored His Cousin—and Started a Revolution." *The Guardian*, April 23. https://www.theguardian.com/education/2013/apr/23/sal-khan-academy-tutored-educational-website

Adler, Renata. 1972. "Cookie, Oscar, Grover, Herry, Ernie, and Company: The Invention of Sesame Street." *The New Yorker*, June 3.

Aloi, Daniel. 2020. "Snail Mail to Wi-Fi: Cornell's History of Remote Instruction." *The College of Arts & Sciences*, Cornell University, April 8. https://americanstudies.cornell.edu/news/snail-mail-wi-fi-cornells-history-remote-instruction

Arrojas, Matthew. 2021. "Colleges Plan to Go Remote to Start 2022 as Omicron Spreads." *Best Colleges*, December 21. Updated May 6, 2022. https://www.bestcolleges.com/news/2021/12/20/college-remote-2022-omicron-vaccine-booster/

Belkin, Douglas. 2022. "Arizona State University Looks to Enroll 100 Million More Students by 2030." *Wall Street Journal*, January 20. https://www.wsj.com/articles/arizona-state-university-looks-to-enroll-100-million-more-students-by-2030-11642674604

Bleezer, Kristy, 2022. "With $25M Gift, Thunderbird Launches Global Initiative to Educate 100 Million by 2030." *Poets and Quants*, January 20. https://poetsandquants.com/2022/01/20/with-25m-gift-thunderbird-launches-global-initiative-to-educate-100-million-by-2030/?pq-category=business-school-news

Blumenstyk, Goldie. 2021. "The Edge: Enrollment May Be Down, but Some Established Online Providers Are Seeing a Surge." *The Chronicle of Higher Education*, January 27. https://www.chronicle.com/newsletter/the-edge/2021-01-27

Burt, Chris. 2021. "Model for the Future? One Fully Online University's Stunning Success." *University Business*, December 6. https://universitybusiness.com/model-for-the-future-one-fully-online-universitys-stunning-success/

Clark, Kenneth R. 1992. "2 Cable Rivals Teach for Tomorrow." *Chicago Tribune*, March 23. https://www.chicagotribune.com/news/ct-xpm-1992-03-23-9201270093-story.html

Coffey, Lauren. 2023. "Southern New Hampshire Shuttering Kenzie Academy Boot Camp." *Inside Higher Ed*, August 24. https://www.insidehighered.com/news/tech-innovation/teaching-learning/2023/08/24/southern-new-hampshire-closing-coding-boot-camp

Crotty, James Marshall. 2012. "Distance Learning Has Been around since 1892, You Big MOOC." *Forbes*, November 14. https://www.forbes.com/sites/jamesmarshallcrotty/2012/11/14/distance-learning-has-been-around-since-1892-you-big-mooc/?sh=14219c572318

D'Agostino, Susan. 2022a. "A Surge in Young Undergrads, Fully Online." *Inside Higher Ed*, October 13. https://www.insidehighered.com/news/2022/10/14/more-traditional-age-students-enroll-fully-online-universities

D'Agostino, Susan. 2022b. "Education Department Shuts a 'Free' Program for Union Members." *Inside Higher Ed*, July 20. https://www.insidehighered.com/news/2022/07/21/us-shuts-community-colleges-free-program-union-members

D'Agostino, Susan. 2023. "Will University of the People Endure for the People?" *Inside Higher Ed*, March 14. https://www.insidehighered.com/news/2023/03/15/free-online-global-university-seeks-seal-approval

Darling, Sharon. 1985. "The Electronic University." *Compute*, September. https://www.atarimagazines.com/compute/issue64/electronic_university.php

"Distance Education in IPEDS." Accessed July 5, 2023. https://nces.ed.gov/ipeds/use-the-data/distance-education-in-ipeds

"Distance Education Participation." 2019–20. "Digest of Education Statistics." Department of Education. Accessed July 6, 2023. https://nces.ed.gov/programs/digest/d21/tables/dt21_311.15.asp

Downes, Stephen. 1999. "What Happened at California Virtual University." Stephen Downes: Knowledge, Learning, Community, April 14. https://www.downes.ca/post/270

Elliott, Joshua C. 2017. "The Evolution from Traditional to Online Professional Development: A Review." *Journal of Digital Learning in Teacher Education*. https://digitalcommons.fairfield.edu/cgi/viewcontent.cgi?article=1130&context=education-facultypubs

Euchner, Charlie. 1983. "Business Group Announces Creation of 'Electronic University'" *Education Week*, September 21. https://www.edweek.org/education/business-group-announces-creation-of-electronic-university/1983/09

Fain, Paul. 2017. "Purdue's Bold Move." *Inside Higher Ed*, April 17. https://www.insidehighered.com/news/2017/04/28/purdue-acquires-kaplan-university-create-new-public-online-university-under-purdue

George Washington University Educational Technology. n.d. Accessed July 5, 2023. https://gsehd.gwu.edu/ed-tech-leadership

Greenberg, Susan H. 2022. "DeSantis: Colleges That Move Online Should Refund Tuition." *Inside Higher Ed*, January 4. https://www.insidehighered.com/quicktakes/2022/01/05/desantis-colleges-move-online-should-refund-tuition

Hill, Phil. 2021. "Purdue University Global Breaks Even for The First Time in FY2021." On EdTech Blog, December 13. https://philhillaa.com/onedtech/purdue-university-global-breaks-even-for-the-first-time-in-fy2021/

"History of Distance Learning." n.d. WorldWideLearn. Accessed July 4, 2023. https://www.worldwidelearn.com/articles/history-of-distance-learning/

"History." Jones International University (JIU). Accessed July 5, 2023. https://jiue.org/history/#:~:text=Jones%20International%20University%20(JIU)%20is,to%20exist%20completely%20online%20globally

Hodges, Charles, Stephanie Moore, Barb Lockee, Torrey Trust, and Aaron Bond. 2020. "The Difference between Emergency Remote Teaching and Online Learning." *EDUCAUSE Review*, March 27. https://er.educause.edu/articles/2020/3/the-difference-between-emergency-remote-teaching-and-online-learning

Jaschik, Scott. 2021. "Georgetown, GW, NYU and Princeton Change Course." *Inside Higher Ed*, December 15. https://www.insidehighered.com/news/2021/12/16/georgetown-nyu-princeton-adopt-changes-because-covid-19

Kentnor, Hope. 2015. "Distance Education and the Evolution of Online Learning in the United States." *Curriculum and Teaching Dialogue* 17, nos. 1 and 2.

Levine, Arthur. 2022. "What Online Learning Reveals about Innovation in Higher Education." *EdSurge*, January 26. https://www.edsurge.com/news/2022-01-26-what-online-learning-reveals-about-innovation-in-higher-education

Levine, Arthur, and Scott Van Pelt. 2021. *The Great Upheaval: Higher Education's Past, Present and Uncertain Future*. Baltimore, MD: Johns Hopkins University Press.

Lienhard, John H. n.d. "Engines of Our Ingenuity, No. 1976: Correspondence School." University of Houston. Accessed July 4, 2023. https://www.uh.edu/engines/epi1976.htm

Long, Heather. n.d. "A History of Distance Education." Sutori. Accessed July 4, 2023. https://www.sutori.com/en/story/a-history-of-distance-education–JZwEKaM7VQagC8NypqMUU5fW

Lubot, Rebecca. 2020. "Modern States: A Timely Option for New Jersey." *Insider NJ*, August 19. https://www.insidernj.com/modern-states-timely-option-new-jersey/

Lumpkin, Lauren. 2022. "D.C. Math, Reading Test Scores Fall to Lowest Levels in More Than 5 Years." *Washington Post*, September 2. https://www.washingtonpost.com/education/2022/09/02/dc-schools-parcc-test/

Mascarenhas, Natasha. 2021. "Coursera Is Planning to File to Go Public Tomorrow." TechCrunch.com, March 4. https://techcrunch.com/2021/03/04/coursera-is-planning-to-file-to-go-public-tomorrow/

Mays, Marilyn Elaine. 1988. "The Historical Development and Future of the National Technological University." Dissertation, University of North Texas. August. https://digital.library.unt.edu/ark:/67531/metadc331714/m2/1/high_res_d/1002714762-Mays.pdf

McKenzie, Lindsay. 2021. "Southern New Hampshire Acquires Coding Boot Camp Kenzie Academy." *Inside Higher Ed*, March 9. https://www.insidehighered.com/quicktakes/2021/03/10/southern-new-hampshire-acquires-coding-boot-camp-kenzie-academy

Moon, Melissa. 2022. "Southwest Tennessee Community College Back to Virtual Learning to Help Students with Soaring Gas Prices." WREG.com, May 24. https://wreg.com/news/local/memphis-college-back-to-virtual-learning-to-help-students-with-soaring-gas-prices/

Murrow, Edward R. 1958. "Wires and Lights in a Box." RTDNA. https://www.rtdna.org/murrows-famous-wires-and-lights-in-a-box

National Council for Online Education (NCOE). 2022. "Emergency Remote Instruction Is Not Quality Online Learning." *Inside Higher Ed*, February 2. https://www.insidehighered.com/views/2022/02/03/remote-instruction-and-online-learning-arent-same-thing-opinion

Neher, Jake, and Cheyna Roth. 2022. "Why Whitmer's Call for In-person School Matters," WDET 101.9FM, January 31. https://wdet.org/2022/01/31/why-whitmers-call-for-in-person-school-matters/#:~:text=Remote%20learning%20is%20not%20as,the%20beginning%20of%20that%20quote

Noer, Michael. 2012. "One Man, One Computer, 10 Million Students: How Khan Academy Is Reinventing Education." *Forbes*, November 18. https://www.forbes.com/sites/michaelnoer/2012/11/02/one-man-one-computer-10-million-students-how-khan-academy-is-reinventing-education/?sh=17000d3244e0

Pant, Ashish. 2014. "Distance Learning: History, Problems and Solutions." *Advances in Computer Science and Information Technology* (ACSIT), 1, no. 2 (November). https://www.krishisanskriti.org/vol_image/02Jul201510072615%20%20%20ashish%20pant%20%20%20%2065-70.pdf

Pappas, Christopher. 2013. "The History of Distance Learning— Infographic." eLearning Industry, February 5. https://elearningindustry.com/the-history-of-distance-learning-infographic

"Public Broadcasting Act of 1967." https://cpb.org/aboutpb/act

Riechers, Maggie. 2003. "Joan Ganz Cooney." National Humanities Medal, National Endowment for the Humanities. https://www.neh.gov/about/awards/national-humanities-medals/joan-ganz-cooney

"Remote Learning: Resources for Educators, Administrators and Related Service Providers." U.S. Department of Education. Accessed July 5, 2023. https://www.ed.gov/coronavirus/remote-learning

Saul, Stephanie. 2022. "More Major U.S. School Districts Delay Reopening in Person Because of the Virus Surge." *New York Times*, January 3. https://www.nytimes.com/live/2022/01/03/us/school-closings-covid

Schwartz, Natalie. 2020. "Democratic Congressional Inquiry Targets OPMs." *Higher Ed Dive*, January 28. https://www.highereddive.com/news/congressional-inquiry-targets-online-program-managers/571275/

Schwartz, Natalie. 2021a. "Pandemic Fueled Huge Online-only Enrollment Growth, Report Finds." *Higher Ed Dive*, October 20. https://www.highereddive.com/news/pandemic-fueled-huge-online-only-enrollment-growth-report-finds/608522/

Schwartz, Natalie. 2021b. "3 Takeaways from Udemy's Initial Public Offering." *Higher Ed Dive*, November 2. https://www.highereddive.com/news/3-takeaways-from-udemys-initial-public-offering/609349/

Schwartz, Natalie. 2022a. "Arizona State Wants to Reach 100M Learners by 2030. Can It Meet Its Goal?" *Higher Ed Dive*, January 20. https://www.highereddive.com/news/arizona-state-wants-to-reach-100m-learners-by-2030-can-it-meet-its-goal/617468/

Schwartz, Natalie. 2022b. "Calbright Faces Another Attempt from Lawmakers to Close the College." *Higher Ed Dive*, February 25. https://www.highereddive.com/news/calbright-faces-another-attempt-from-lawmakers-to-close-the-college/619469/#:~:text=A%20new%20bill%20in%20California's,community%20colleges%20and%20their%20students

Schwartz, Natalie. 2022c. "University of Arizona Global Campus Terminates Contract with Zovio." *Higher Ed Dive*, August 1. https://www.highereddive.com/news/university-of-arizona-global-campus-terminates-contract-with-zovio/628603/

Seltzer, Rick. 2022. "Online Education's Reputation Jumps, Survey Says." *Higher Ed Dive*, July 26. https://www.highereddive.com/news/online-educations-reputation-jumps-survey-says/628064/

Shah, Dhawal. 2021a. "Analyzing Udemy's IPO Filing: $430M Revenue; $30M CorpU Acquisition; Consumer Segment Stalls, Enterprise Grows." *The Report*, October 13. https://www.classcentral.com/report/udemy-s1-analysis/

Shah, Dhawal. 2021b. "A Decade of MOOCs: A Review of Stats and Trends for Large-Scale Online Courses in 2021." *Ed Surge*, December 28. https://www.edsurge.com/news/2021-12-28-a-decade-of-moocs-a-review-of-stats-and-trends-for-large-scale-online-courses-in-2021

Shapiro, Eliza, Grace Ashford, and Jeffery C. Mays. 2022. "N.Y.C. Schools Are 'Staying Open,' Mayor Eric Adams Says." *New York Times*, January 3.

Sleator, Roy D. 2010. "The Evolution of eLearning: Background, Blends and Blackboard …" *Science Progress* 93, no. 3: 319–34. https://journals.sagepub.com/doi/pdf/10.3184/003685010X12710124862922

Smalley, Suzanne. 2021a. "An Enrollment Surge, a Decline in Quality—and a Sharp Rebuke." *Inside Higher Ed*, November 11. https://www.insidehighered.com/news/2021/11/12/eastern-gateway-community-college-put-probation

Smalley, Suzanne. 2021b. "UNC's $97 Million Plan to Reach Adult Online Learners." *Inside Higher Ed*, December 8. https://www.insidehighered.com/news/2021/12/09/unc-system-launch-ambitious-97-million-ed-tech-start#:~:text=The%20University%20of%20North%20Carolina,need%20for%20more%20skilled%20workers

Smith, Ashley A. 2021a. "Few Completions, More Dropouts as Calbright College Continues to Struggle." *EdSource*, October 21. https://edsource.org/2021/few-completions-more-dropouts-as-calbright-college-continues-to-struggle/662710

Smith, Ashley A. 2021b. "Former Gov. Jerry Brown Defends Calbright College." *EdSource*, May 27. https://edsource.org/2021/former-gov-jerry-brown-defends-calbright-embattled-online-college/655472

Smith, Mitch. 2022. "Chicago Says Classrooms Will Stay Open. Its Teachers Say Maybe Not." *New York Times*, January 3.

Smith, Stephen. 2014. "Radio: FDR's 'Natural Gift.'" APM Reports, November 10. https://www.apmreports.org/episode/2014/11/10/radio-fdrs-natural-gift

Sparks, Sarah D. 2022. "Two Decades of Progress, Nearly Gone: National Math, Reading Scores Hit Historic Lows." *Education Week*, October 24. https://www.edweek.org/leadership/two-decades-of-progress-nearly-gone-national-math-reading-scores-hit-historic-lows/2022/10

St. George, Donna. 2023. "National Test Scores Plunge, with Still No Sign of Pandemic Recovery." *Washington Post*, June 21. https://www.washingtonpost.com/education/2023/06/21/national-student-test-scores-drop-naep/

"StraighterLine Salutes Its 100,000+ Students on National Online Learning Day." 2021. Straighterline.com, September 15. https://www.straighterline.com/press/national-online-learning-day/

Swaak, Taylor. 2022a. "A Small, Private College Ups Its Bet on Online Programs. Will It Pay Off?" *The Chronicle of Higher Education*, March 17. https://www.chronicle.com/article/a-small-private-college-ups-its-bet-on-online-programs-will-it-pay-off?cid2=gen_login_refresh&cid=gen_sign_in

Swaak, Taylor. 2022b. "An Overseas Ed-Tech Firm Wants to Buy 2U. What Could That Mean for Colleges?" *The Chronicle of Higher Education*, July 21. https://www.chronicle.com/article/an-overseas-ed-tech-firm-wants-to-buy-2u-what-could-that-mean-for-colleges?sra=true&cid=gen_sign_in

Thompson, Ella. 2023. "UF Online Delivers High-quality Degrees Remotely." *The Independent Florida Alligator*, February 6. https://www.alligator.org/article/2023/02/uf-online-high-quality

Thompson, Evan. 2021. "History of Online Education." *The Best Schools*. https://thebestschools.org/magazine/online-education-history/

"U.S. News Unveils 2022 Best Online Programs Rankings." 2022. PR Newswire, January 25. https://www.prnewswire.com/news-releases/us-news-unveils-2022-best-online-programs-rankings-301467087.html

United States Distance Learning Association (USDLA). n.d. Accessed July 5, 2023. https://usdla.org/about/history/

Vasquez, Michael. 2021. "First, Meteoric Growth. Now, Probation." *Chronicle of Higher Education*, November 26.

Visual Academy. "The History of Online Schooling." n.d. onlineSchools.org. Accessed July 4, 2023. https://www.onlineschools.org/visual-academy/the-history-of-online-schooling/

Vo, Alix. 2015. "Before the iPad There Was Bitzer's PLATO." *Technician*, November 16. https://www.technicianonline.com/arts_entertainment/before-the-ipad-there-was-bitzer-s-plato/article_fa515510-8cdf-11e5-a2ac-07212ad7ad4a.html

Walker, Heather. 2021. "Important Events in the History of Digital Higher Education: Course Sharing Through Mind Extension University." *Digitex*, June 16. https://digitex.org/2021/06/16/important-events-in-the-history-of-digital-higher-education-course-sharing-through-mind-extension-university/

Warren, Elizabeth, Sherrod Brown, and Tina Smith. 2022. Letter to OPM CEOs, January 14. https://www.warren.senate.gov/imo/media/doc/2022.01.14%20Follow%20up%20letter%20to%20Online%20Program%20Managers%20(OPMs)_.pdf

Watkinson, James D. 1996. "'Education for Success': The International Correspondence Schools of Scranton, Pennsylvania." *The Pennsylvania Magazine of History and Biography*. CXX, no. 4 (October), 343–69.

"Wedemeyer, Charles A." Hall of Fame Class of 1998. International Adult and Continuing Education Hall of Fame. Accessed July 5, 2023. https://halloffame.outreach.ou.edu/Inductions/Inductee-Details/charles-a-wedemeyer

Westra, Kayla. 2018. "Online Student Services: What, Where, Who, When, How, and Most Importantly, Why." *EDUCAUSE Review*, October 29. https://er.educause.edu/articles/2018/10/online-student-services-what-where-who-when-how-and-most-importantly-why

Wintemute, Doug. 2023. "Synchronous vs. Asynchronous Classes: What's the Difference?" TheBestSchools, April 18. https://thebestschools.org/resources/synchronous-vs-asynchronous-programs-courses/

Wood, Johnny. 2022. "These 3 Charts Show the Global Growth in Online Learning." *World Economic Forum*, January 27. https://www.weforum.org/agenda/2022/01/online-learning-courses-reskill-skills-gap/

Zinshteyn, Mikhail. 2023. "Calbright's Star Is Rising: California's Online Community College Is Adding, Keeping More Students." *LAist*, April 12. https://laist.com/news/education/calbrights-star-is-rising-californias-online-community-college-is-adding-keeping-more-students

"ZOOM (1972–8): Children's Community and Public Television in the 1970s." American Archive of Public Broadcasting. Accessed July 6, 2023. https://americanarchive.org/exhibits/zoom

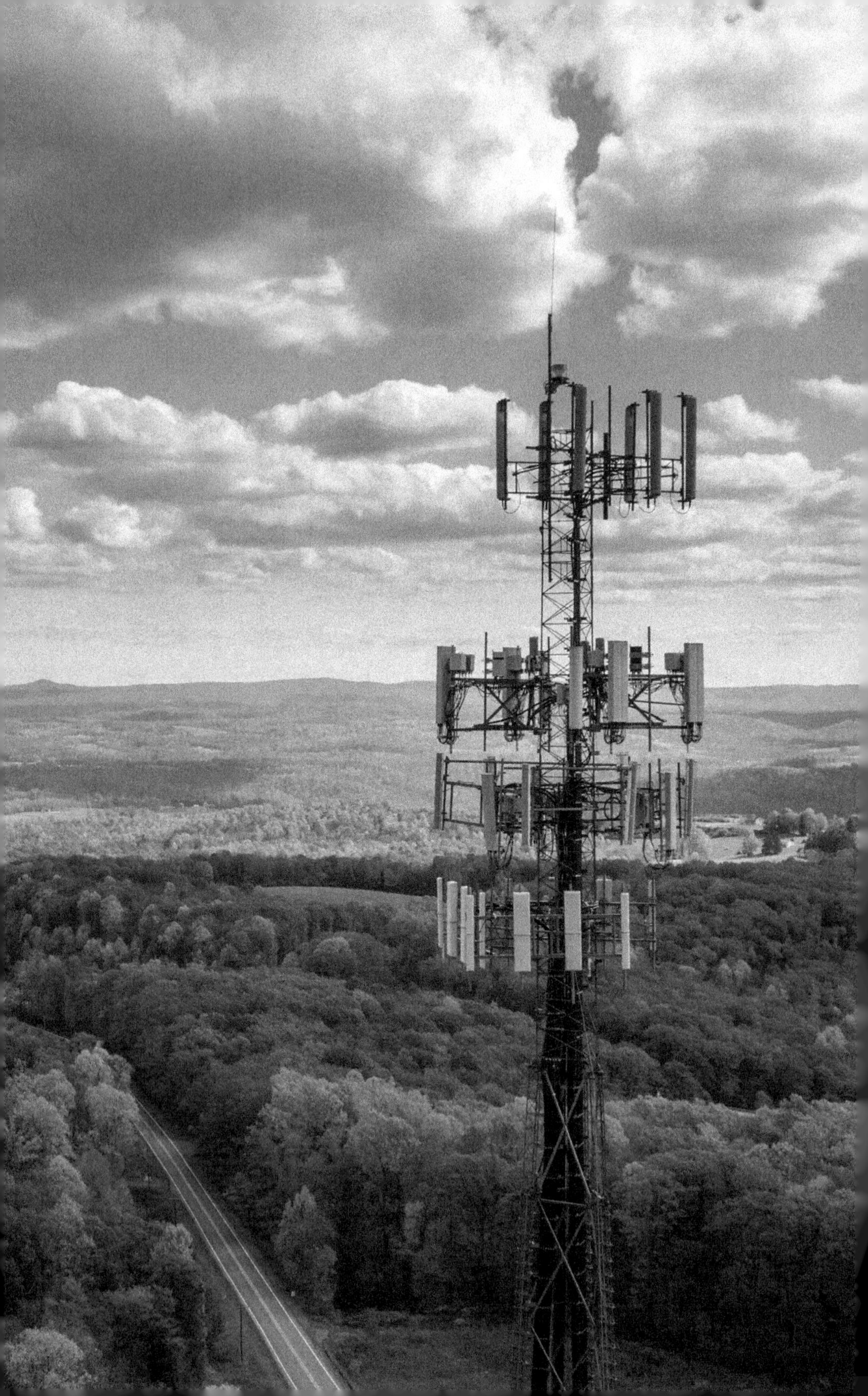

2

Problems, Controversies, and Solutions

Notwithstanding the long history of distance education detailed in Chapter 1, the modern tech-based version is developing and evolving at veritable warp speed. And, it has done so under an international microscope as the pandemic's forced shift to remote teaching and learning raised its profile higher and faster than could ever have been imagined, while also subjecting it to scrutiny that it neither sought nor was prepared for.

Even advocates of distance education, those who have been methodically shepherding its growth and development, have recognized the double-edged sword that the pandemic-induced exposure represented. Indeed, while they welcome the new-found awareness, they have had to work overtime to make clear to a suddenly aware populace that distance education and remote learning are not the same, and that the differences matter in countless ways (Roe 2020).

All of this serves as an important backdrop to any discussions about the issues, and especially the challenges, central to modern distance education—where it is now, what it offers, and what questions need to be addressed as it becomes an ever-larger facet of the modern educational world at all levels. While a historical review of the evolution of remote learning provides context, the modern version is so far removed from its roots that any reasonable discussion, especially one that seeks to assess its current role in education as well as its efficacy, must focus on the present and the future.

First, the distinction between remote learning and distance education must be recognized; it is not simply a matter of semantics (Stauffer 2020). As distance learning advocates forcefully assert, they are two very different things and the differences between them can make determinations about their comparative

---

The Covid-19 pandemic shutdown brought the issue of internet inaccessibility to the foreground as schools struggled to shift to distance learning. Many states used emergency Covid funding on broadband expansion projects to better reach their rural populations. (© Steveheap/Dreamstime.com)

strengths and weaknesses difficult to identify (Craig 2020b). Other questions that are central to an understanding and assessment of distance learning include consideration of whether or not it is an appropriate vehicle for serving the needs of individual students or educational institutions and in what areas. Distinguishing between the changes in modern education brought by technology and those that are, in fact, a product of distance education itself is also important.

Nowhere has the pandemic-fueled rise in distance education been more apparent or more discussed than in American higher education, an area that has also found itself the increasing object of general scrutiny in recent years. To a generation for whom the campus experience had become increasingly debated, the loss of that experience and the ability of parents to see firsthand, at home, a new remote academic experience, provided a new perspective on an increasingly expensive educational model and raised very real doubts about what they were paying for. The pandemic also coincided with a national dialogue and debate over race and the inequities that have long been a part of almost all education—distance and otherwise.

The introduction of distance education as a possible and credible alternative both changed the nature of the discussion and also put a spotlight on just what modern distance education entails (Craig 2020b). If it is just the standard lecture over the computer screen, the issue of value becomes a very big one. Indeed, the computer-savvy generation on the receiving end of the initial pandemic response efforts was soon demanding more, as some of their older professors struggled to adapt to the new technology and the demands of the transition. The changed dynamic has forced a much-needed fuller and broader consideration (Roe 2020).

Before we parse specific issues and concerns in venturing beyond a world bound to brick-and-mortar, classroom-based education, there is a fundamental question that must be addressed: "Why distance education?" Do we, as a society, need or want the approach, and what does it really offer? And in fact, what does it really entail?

Basic Elements of Distance Education

First, we need to identify the core aspects of distance education, after which we will take deeper looks at the more controversial areas, consider the pros and cons, and pose possible ways in which the obstacles can be overcome. Throughout, it cannot be forgotten that we are dealing with a comparatively new process seeking to make its way in an educational system that is long on tradition and history and short on open-armed welcomes for innovators and rebels.

By all accounts distance education is flexible in ways that standard education is not. It is certainly more flexible in its ability to offer asynchronous teaching and learning at any time and anywhere. Not just flexible, that is revolutionary. Depending upon exactly how it is structured, a distance education course or program can allow a student to proceed at their own pace, making distance and individual schedules irrelevant. This flexibility and accessibility—at least as far as geography goes—is a major advantage, one that makes distance education particularly attractive for many. At the same time, 24/7 access has the potential to alter the teaching and learning dynamic, putting considerably more responsibility on the student/learner, which may be better suited to some learning styles than others (Clark 2020).

The changed dynamic stemming from asynchronous flexibility inevitably impacts the nature of teacher–student and classroom discussion. Very different from traditional, in-person seminar-style discussions, the efficacy of distance learning interactions can depend in large part on the individual student. For instance, asynchronous discussions allow time for students to reflect on the comments of others in a way that in-person classes do not. Arguably, that opportunity for reflection before response allows for more thoughtful discussions than might occur in the immediacy of an in-person class. A good writer who is not particularly glib or articulate is going to have a very different impact on these discussions. For the quiet introvert, this change may be a good thing, while more extroverted students may find the lack of immediate feedback to be frustrating. In offering physical anonymity, this type of interaction can also be seen as creating a more level playing field, removing the external factors like appearance (e.g., clothing, race, etc.) that can impact in-person class discussions. Like any classroom situation, asynchronous student interaction is a balance, but a very different one from the one that students used to in-person learning are accustomed.

While the flexibility offered by distance learning has generally focused on the way asynchronous learning allows students to take courses on a timetable that is best suited to their daily work lives, this is by no means the only time-related benefit. Sal Khan and Khan Academy recognize that one advantage of their video-based efforts is the fact that, unlike the ponderous process involved with textbook revisions, the videos that he and his organization produce are easily replaced if a better approach is discovered or an error found. Indeed, the group invites such feedback through its website (How do I report mistakes …? n.d.). Making the correction, revision, and updating process open enhances interaction among students, faculty, and the materials they are using, especially foundational texts. Ultimately, such openness and flexibility facilitates the goal of producing a better educational offering for students.

When the pandemic forced almost all educational institutions to adopt some form of online instruction, the strengths and weaknesses that became widely known were for the most part already recognized and being addressed by the distance education community. However, issues like access and equity quickly jumped to the top of the priority list. These often intertwined issues are at once central to the potential of distance education as a game changer while also being no small stumbling block to the achievement of that goal.

Access and Equity

If distance education in the modern world is to fulfill its reported potential to revolutionize teaching and learning as we know it, it can do so only if it is available to as wide-ranging an audience as possible. Unfortunately, from the beginning, and notwithstanding its historic mission to increase educational opportunity, the issue of access has been a challenge for online-based distance education.

In an era in which both private schools and colleges across the nation have sought to increase socio-economic access to their institutions, they have too often made erroneous assumptions about the access of underrepresented populations to the technological tools central to such efforts. These blinders quickly came off when the availability of internet access became a major hurdle for some schools and school districts during the pandemic-induced transition to remote learning.

However, while access issues based in technical capabilities became evident early in the pandemic, the federal government set no speed records in offering a focused response. Fortunately, the use of emergency Covid-19 funds was left mostly up to the states. If only to prepare for the possibility of further extended distance learning efforts, many states quickly directed substantive portions of the funds they received from both the Coronavirus Aid, Relief and Economic Security Act and the American Rescue Plan to broadband expansion projects.

A prime example was Arkansas, in which the Rural Connect program awarded over $275 million in grants to projects that will provide high-speed broadband service to rural areas. In ensuring that these areas had greater internet access, the state government not only opened the door to expanded institutional and school system possibilities, but at the same time also allowed countless individual residents of the newly enabled areas to consider pursuing training and education that were previously all but impossible (Herzog 2021).

Similarly, the states of Virginia and Vermont enhanced the potential for expanded distance learning when they expanded broadband to some of their more distant areas (Smith 2021). The use of the emergency Covid-19 funds to address their broadband shortages and in turn expand the internet access of their residents proved a critical stop-gap measure, especially when the fall of 2020 saw a high level of continued remote teaching and learning (Read and Wert 2021).

It was not until the passage by Congress in November 2021 of the much-touted infrastructure bill that the federal government offered a direct response. That legislation included $65 billion for broadband related spending (News Staff 2021). At the top of the list was $42 billion directed toward the Broadband Equity, Access and Deployment Program, which is managed by the National Telecommunications and Information Administration. Under the program, competitive grants were offered to states for a number of different uses, including broadband deployment in unserved and underserved communities and internet or Wi-Fi infrastructure or low-cost broadband for multi-residential buildings, as well as broadband adoption. Each program directly addresses needs central to eliminating equity and access as continuing concerns in the distance education world (News Staff 2021). While the Federal Communications Commission (FCC) worked to update the nation's broadband maps, states prepared to seek grants appropriate to their needs.

Beyond the critically important funding, the enactment of the Infrastructure Investment and Jobs Act in November 2021 represented a major step forward in another important way, as it designated broadband internet access an essential service. That designation altered its place within the infrastructure landscape, and was in no small part a response to what the pandemic wrought. Indeed, the legislation made clear that Congress recognized that "access to affordable, reliable, high-speed broadband is essential to full participation in modern life in the United States" (H.R. 3684 2021).

For the first time, the federal government acknowledged that, in modern America, broadband access was as important and fundamental as access to running water or electricity. It was also a recognition of its role in the "equitable distribution of essential public services, including health care and education" (Galperin 2021). In fact, in the view of some analysts, the equitable distribution of education was the linchpin in the effort. As one tech writer noted, while decades of academic studies were unable to convince Congress of the importance of this need, the reports and images of teachers in school parking lots and students outside fast-food restaurants seeking to connect with their remote classes during the pandemic did the trick (Galperin 2021).

The new legislation, beyond revealing its understanding of the extent of the problem, also revealed how intertwined access is with the issue of equity. This was apparent when the legislation noted that the "digital divide disproportionately affects communities of color, lower-income areas, and rural areas," while directing the FCC to act against discrimination of access based on a full range of categories (H.R. 3684 2021). The pandemic made clear what had long been assumed, that there is a racial disparity in distance learning access (Cox-Steib 2021). And yet at the same time, and especially with growing awareness prompted by the increase in remote learning, distance education is nevertheless seen by many as the best way to increase college access for minority students (Doak 2022).

Discussions of access to distance education are generally rooted in socio-economic or geographic concerns. Consequently, as more and more standard brick-and-mortar school programs, never mind distance learning ones, have come to rely on at least access to the internet, many analysts are warning about taking full-scale access for granted. Indeed, observers have noted that the long lines to get into local libraries are not based in people rushing to get the latest bestseller but are in fact a product of individuals seeking to take advantage of the public internet access that is increasingly a part of public library offerings. Students forced to rely on that kind of access are at an obvious disadvantage (Werschkul 2022).

Another matter related to the issue of access is the matter of security (Strauss 2020). At the same time that educators and government officials are seeking to expand broadband access, there is a concurrent call to ensure that the expanded internet access is safe and secure. While schools and districts certainly appreciate the greater resources being devoted to broadband expansion, they are no less concerned about seeing the cybersecurity of their new resources improved. While 2020 provided most Americans with an introduction to distance education and online learning, the year also saw an unprecedented number of cyberattacks against US schools. In December of 2020, the Federal Bureau of Investigation (FBI) released a joint report with other federal agencies warning that K-12 schools had become the No. 1 target for ransomware attacks (Nagel 2020). All of this has obvious impacts on both the practical and specific aspects of distance education as well as people's attitudes towards the process.

At the same time, there is growing concern among parents about student privacy and data security. To no one's surprise, the challenges in technology have outstripped the legislative process so that officials are operating under laws and regulations that are substandard, insufficient, and often wholly outdated, thus making it more difficult than ever to protect students' personal data. Happily, such concerns seem to be broad-based enough that there is hope for bipartisan efforts to provide better protection in these areas, a prerequisite to the safe expansion of distance learning opportunities and the access to it. Data security is also an area that has unconsciously pitted two areas of concern against each other, as some software designed to defend against online cheating has been found to be susceptible to data breaches, opening up a whole set of security and privacy concerns (Swaak 2022).

While the issue of equitable access has been one of the leading concerns among opponents of distance education, advocates tout accessibility, in reference to students with learning disabilities, as a selling point. Reflective of the reach and increasing popularity of online options, Landmark College, long recognized as one of the nation's higher education leaders in educating students with learning differences, has embraced the online revolution, quickly emerging as a leader in online education. In 2021, Landmark launched College START, an online learning program that offers "Intentional programming that promotes connection with residential LC students," as well as "Unique course design that fosters student success by reducing barriers commonly found in traditional online learning programs" (LC Online n.d.). In the same spirit as its on-campus program, Landmark's START program seeks to help students understand and develop their own individual learning styles while receiving the same highly personal support from faculty that has always been central to the Landmark educational experience. In that way it serves as a model for how distance education can serve those with learning differences.

Similarly, at a time when private colleges and schools have been focusing on access and equity, they have struggled to ensure that access to distance education is not simply a perk of the privileged. When we speak of equity, finances are a very large factor. A study published by *The Chronicle of Higher Education* right before Christmas 2021 reported that from the start of the pandemic in March

2020 through the beginning of the first semester of the 2020–21 academic year, 41 percent of college students had to purchase items to support their online education, with the largest amount of those (44 percent) buying computers or laptops. Headphones, video cameras, microphones, and other assorted items, as well as internet access, were also important, if less frequent purchases. Combined, these investments could have proven to be serious financial burdens (McLean 2021). The same report, however, noted efforts by schools to make equipment, especially laptops, available, usually via lending programs. Expanded broadband is great and necessary, but often only a start.

The National Digital Inclusion Alliance identified the large and medium-sized cities with the nation's highest share of households that did not have broadband internet subscriptions in 2019. Interestingly, many of the cities on the list (Shreveport, Louisiana; Miami, Florida; Cleveland, Ohio; Gary, Indiana; Trenton, New Jersey; South Bend, Indiana; and Flint, Michigan) are home to at least one college—usually a public, two-year institution but also some full four-year institutions ("Worst Connected Cities …" 2019).

The challenges represented were further crystalized by the findings of a report from a New America and Third Way survey that revealed that, in the summer of 2020, just a little under 60 percent of college students reported that having access to a stable, high-speed internet connection could be a challenge if they were to need to continue their education online (McLean 2021). With most of the nation's largest colleges and universities choosing to go online at least in the early going of the 2020–21 academic year, those concerns were ultimately affirmed by the less than robust enrollment numbers schools experienced that fall.

In considering equity, one must also look beyond internet access and computer hardware and consider the circumstances in which the student is engaging in distance education. While some difficulties families experienced may have been limited to the pandemic-induced transition to remote learning, awareness that the individual settings in which a student undertakes their remote educational experience can play a huge role in their learning experience will be important to discussions about future utilization and expansion of distance learning. Consider the impact of a move to distance education in a household in which both parents work. For them, school plays a major childcare role beyond its academic one. There can be no denying that those families in which both parents work were hit harder by the need to transition to remote learning in the final months of the 2019–20 academic year. Even if one or both parents worked from home, that did not mean they were fully able to supervise or help in their child's school program, attention that was often a necessity for young students and that remote learning attempts assumed was being provided.

While this shortfall may have been a bigger problem for elementary and middle school students and their families, high school students left alone were also affected. With a teacher's presence limited to a Zoom connection, far too many high school students across the country all but dropped out—and many did. Obvious at the time that emergency measure remote learning did not make for an ideal learning environment, subsequent, data-based analysis confirmed the extent of the dropouts ("Nation's ... School Enrollment Did Not Change ..." 2022).

The issue of equity in distance education has, in typical American fashion, found its way into the courts. In early January 2022, as New York City schools struggled to remain open for in-person classes, a Queens mother, in conjunction with five other families, filed suit against both New York City and the state of New York alleging that the school officials failed to provide children—especially low-income students of color—with adequate internet access and working devices (Amin 2022). In the case of the lead plaintiff, the suit was the culmination of an experience that highlighted the full range of problems the pandemic had revealed. Specifically, the young girl had struggled in the early going as she tried to access her lessons via phone or an inadequate computer. The resulting performance earned her a mandated session of virtual summer school, and while she was able to obtain an internet-enabled iPad for the summer program, the child was unable to get the Zoom connection necessary to do her assignments. According to the suit, school officials repeatedly explained that there was nothing they could do. In the end, the young girl was required to repeat seventh grade.

The families allege that state and city officials were fully aware of the scope of the digital divide but did not properly address the issue. Consequently, they failed to provide a "sound, basic education," and as a result, there was a disparate impact on low-income students and children of color (Amin 2022). The suit also asked for appropriate and necessary academic services to allow impacted children to catch up.

The Queens student involved in the suit had continued to learn at home during the 2020–21 school year, plagued by both a faulty device and difficulty accessing websites and assignments. While the school provided a new device in October 2020, it didn't work well, and the student was consistently plagued with internet connection issues. All of this resulted in serious psychological and emotional turmoil, culminating in a suicide attempt that made clear the depth of her despair (Amin 2022).

The case was only one of many, with some being filed as class actions or focused on the failure to provide adequately for students with disabilities. As of the spring of 2024, many cases remained mired in the courts with preliminary rulings offering a range of decisions (Khalifeh 2024). However, the lack of resolution does not diminish the way the lawsuits served to shine a spotlight on many of the challenges that schools, school systems, students, and their families faced with the pandemic-imposed remote learning experience. It also reveals some of the issues that distance education providers have to face as they seek to expand their base among those who choose that educational option. The suit was representative of problems plaguing students and families from coast to coast while reflecting the intersection of access and equity.

While the pandemic-fueled need for remote learning continued in some places into 2022, the Report on School Connectivity released in January of that year offered some evidence of improved access for students across the country, evidence that also bodes well for future forays into distance education by choice. The report indicated that 59 percent of the nation's school districts met the FCC's benchmark for bandwidth. This represented a major increase from the 47 percent that met the standard in 2020, but it was still inadequate, especially when the Omicron surge in late 2021 into 2022 forced many schools to return to virtual teaching and learning (Merod 2022a). Spokespeople for numerous organizations decried the continuing deficit while calling on government at all levels to address the problem, which, as of the end of 2021, still left more than 27 million students lacking the bandwidth necessary to support their digital learning needs (Merod 2022a).

Even when adequate bandwidth is available, and with the median cost per megabit for schools meeting the FCC goal dipping below $1 for the first time, the costs that school districts paid for the all-important access varied widely, a reality that reflected the ongoing inequity as much as bandwidth disparities did (Merod 2022b). Clearly much remains to be done before equity in opportunities for distance learning become a reality.

In addition to issues concerning access and equity, educators continued to worry about the impact of pandemic-fueled distance education and its failure to deliver what the in-person classroom does. These concerns have hounded distance education in the wake of its unasked-for role as an emergency response vehicle, an effort that markedly contrasts with its intended thoughtful, preferred, and pedagogically sound approach. But with the door now open, advocates are determined to take advantage of the opportunity to right the ship (News Staff 2021).

Educational Quality

From its beginnings, distance education has been dogged by questions regarding its quality. Washington State University distance education pioneer Muriel Oaks recalls that from the start of the university's efforts, quality was a constant and consistent faculty concern. Oaks found that helping faculty members understand that different could be good was a central challenge right out of the gate (Nappi 2010).

In many ways, the question of whether the quality of distance education measures up, whether the educational experience one gets in an online course is comparable to what one gets in an in-person class, is the most important question to ask and answer in any consideration of distance education. This is especially true as educators contemplate its expanded use. And yet as anyone in higher education—indeed, in any level of education—will acknowledge, it is also the most difficult question to answer.

Educators have fought for years over the ways people have sought to measure educational quality on both the institutional end and on the student end. Countless efforts and measuring tools having been devised, utilized, embraced, and then discarded, with their effectiveness often more a reflection of an institution or organization's needs and goals than of a true measure of their efforts. And of course, at what point in time that measurement is applied is also no small piece of the equation.

How do you measure the value of lessons that may not really take hold, much less be susceptible to measurement, until years down the road? And even then, the ability to establish and measure a causal relationship between methods and results is often impossible, although that relationship may be the most important factor in evaluating the educational experience. How do you measure the educational product? And, no less important in modern America, how do you market that product? Such uncertainty has done nothing to assuage those who are dismissive of the whole distance education approach in anything other than an emergency capacity. Committed naysayers will never admit to remote learning being anything other than an inferior, short-term, stop-gap measure.

The lack of widespread faculty buy-in to distance learning can be partly traced to their skepticism regarding quality (Kentnor 2015). Despite over two full decades of active degree granting in the online world, this problem remains a real one. Perhaps doubt is to be expected in a higher education system as widely diverse as the United States offers. Or perhaps it is simply a manifestation of the elitism that has long characterized the American higher education landscape. Over the years, educators have sometimes dismissed the efforts and products of those institutions that inhabit the lower rungs of debilitating rankings. This dynamic has increasingly led incoming college presidents to sound like aspirants for higher office when, upon assuming their new post, they proclaim their intention to improve the school's ranking. Indeed, perhaps the skepticism surrounding distance education is partly just another manifestation of the age-old Ivies versus state U. debates that have for so long been part of our educational terrain.

That being said, as the impact of the remote learning experience of the spring of 2020, and in some cases the school year 2020–21 as well, becomes more and more apparent, as more evidence of learning loss is offered, more and more questions have been raised about the quality of the distance learning experience. Among the many factors that have been discussed in evaluating efforts during this time are motivation, isolation, supervision, and a proper learning environment, among others. The studies that came out in the latter part of 2021 raise serious questions about the effectiveness of remote learning among young students especially, but even through high school. There also remain substantive issues beyond the ever-present challenge of measuring effective teaching, including factoring in the way the transition was managed. Certainly no one would maintain that what took place in the spring of 2020 was a scenario designed to bring out the best in the teachers or students who found themselves trying to do the best they could in circumstances no one ever expected. However, as educators faced the strong possibility that remote learning would continue in the fall if not longer, important questions remained about the adequacy of efforts to help teachers adapt their lessons and approaches to the challenges of teaching virtually.

Determining the quality of distance education at this point in its evolution is colored by the many circumstances that shift it from a strictly educationally based analysis to a multifaceted assessment of a whole chapter in a child and family's life. The impressions of those who, through no choice of their own, suddenly became distance education consumers often reflect a combination of feelings and perspectives that can detract from an objective assessment. From the clumsy way schools used virtual learning to the requirements imposed on students, being thrust into a stressful and unexpected situation certainly impacted people's impressions of remote learning in general. Naturally, a parent's view of their child's online experience will be influenced by their own approach to the situation, the impact it had on their lives, and their aspirations for their child's development. With parent, student, and teacher expectations for a traditional school year blown out of the water at short notice, there was little time for training in new methods. In such a situation, what makes for a quality teaching performance may be very different from what makes for a quality educational experience, with a focus on merely surviving and not falling too far behind.

When the March 2020 Covid-19 surge forced a national educational shift, schools at all levels sought to do whatever was necessary to salvage their school years. Considerations of the comparative quality of the teaching and learning were at best secondary to concerns about the basic delivery of the educational product and of continuing the school's operations. The faculty at my school was told over and over again that great should not be the enemy of good— and we were not alone. In pivoting on a dime after the pandemic arrived, questions and concerns were all about technology and little about pedagogy. This made for a first-time experience with distance education for many that was seriously lacking in expectations or expertise. The challenges relating to delivery efforts across the nation were further impacted by the issues of access and equity, themselves affecting the nation's educational experiences in widely varying ways.

Early in the pandemic, to the degree that there was talk, especially at the college level, of students not getting what they paid for, it tended to be aimed at the housing and food plan aspects of a student's tuition bill. Few were focused on academic issues. While some schools moved to a pass/fail system for the semester, the quality of classes was not questioned much as students limped into summer vacation or past graduations that did not take place. The issue became a bigger one the following year, as the realities of the ongoing pandemic and continued virtual learning overwhelmed any real belief that instructors were truly ready to offer polished distance education tailored lessons. Anyone who thought, by fall, instructors could or should have adapted, had little understanding of the factors involved or of the psychic and emotional stress the nation's teachers had experienced in the first run of the pandemic.

Yet the debates started, all too often in unproductive ways. Remote learning often became a political football. Florida became a high-profile battlefield when, in January 2022, while registering a record high number of positive test results, the state's governor, Ron DeSantis, declared that any colleges that went virtual should offer students a full refund (Greenberg 2022). However unintentionally, DeSantis' assertion could also be seen as a comment on the quality of that virtual experience and what kind of value students were getting for their tuition dollars. His declaration certainly highlighted the quality question, even if it did not adequately illuminate it.

This type of negative attention is certainly at least part of why distance education advocates and practitioners have so vehemently sought to distinguish between what they do and what too many people assumed they did when they spoke of remote learning. As advocates emphasized, distance education was not just teaching traditionally but now in front of a screen. While remote learning is at base an offering comparable to any form of telework, distance education online courses involve significantly more planning and preparation, efforts which culminate in a lesson designed for and appropriate to different circumstances.

An EDUCAUSE report indicated that a fully online university course done right usually entailed planning, preparation, and development that typically took from six to nine months. It added that the success of such courses was based not just on the actual instruction but also on having in place other structures and resources that would facilitate student engagement while also providing support. In the best of circumstances, teachers seek to offer such course work in conjunction with an instructional designer who has experience in designing online courses (Manfuso 2020).

Quite simply, distance education is not something done on a whim. The approach of the University of Central Florida (UCF) is more typical of the way a school that is truly committed to this type of learning handles its program. At UCF, which has been offering online courses since the late 1990s, teachers seeking to run such a course are required to not only participate in specific, rigorous training but also to engage in detailed and extensive preparation work when designing their intended course. Indeed, leaders of UCF's online program believe deeply that quality online instruction comes down to three critical words: design, time, and expectations ("Teach Online" UCF n.d.). The end result is clearly a very different type of teaching and learning experience than the remote learning experience of so many pandemic era students. Measurement challenges remain in assessing these programs, but the differences in approach and quality of results are evident.

With the effectiveness of online learning and distance education a central part of the national educational discourse, a report issued in December 2021 by the Center for the Future of Higher Education and Talent Strategy titled "Employers' Post-Covid Business Strategy and the Race for Talent: A View from the C-Suite" added another voice to the discussion. In a survey of 1,000 "C-Suite" (high level) executives about how they viewed online credentials as part of their hiring process, almost half said that their view had been strengthened as a result of their pandemic experience. Forty percent said their view was unchanged, while 14 percent reported a decrease in their regard for online credentials. More importantly, 71 percent of those surveyed said they saw an online credential as being generally equal to or higher than those completed in person (Gallagher and Ferrari 2021). This represented the latest step in a progression that has seen the positive response to this query increase from 40 percent in 2013 to 48 percent in 2014 to 61 percent in 2018 to the now 71 percent (Gallagher and Ferrari 2021). While only one perspective on the value of an online educational program, in an educational world in which preparation for the work force is increasingly a part of the evaluations of educational programs and experiences, the ability of people with online credentials to compete on an almost equal footing with in-person learners represented no small change.

Meanwhile a survey released by the think tank New American in the summer of 2022 found that almost half of American adults, 47 percent, thought that online education "is of roughly the same quality as in-person instruction." This represents a substantial increase over the approximately one-third that held the view in the 2021 survey. At the same time, almost 80 percent of the survey respondents said they thought online education should be less expensive (Seltzer 2022).

As the nation emerged from the worst of the Covid-19 shutdown, the recent experience had for most people rendered the question of the basic efficacy of remote learning moot. But for its true advocates, the focus is on how online education can be best used to serve students, especially working adults. In the forefront of this group is Don Kilburn, the CEO of UMass Online, who began a February 2022 article by saying, "I hope we are, particularly in light of recent events, well past the stage where the value of online learning as a modality is in any doubt" (Kilburn 2022). For Kilburn, we should be past the question of "whether online learning is 'worth it,'" and should instead be focused on examining the nuances of strong online programs and determining how we can make them work even better for the modern student, especially for prospective adult students, already in the workforce (Kilburn 2022).

How effective was the online teaching process of 2020–21? Given the willingness to acknowledge weaknesses inherent in a lack of training or preparation, the jury remains out, with subsequent studies—all with an eye to comparing the effectiveness of different approaches—still very much needed.

Changing the Way We Teach and Learn?

A major issue that the educational world has had to grapple with from the beginning of the distance learning boom has been whether this new approach is simply another way of delivering traditional, lecture-based learning but via a modem and monitor, or whether the developing technology could be used in a way that fundamentally changes the way teachers teach and students learn. As we have seen, the divide between remote learning and distance education is real, but other attendant questions are less easily answered. For instance, how does distance learning impact those skills that educators have long considered central to the educational process? Is posting a comment on a discussion board the same as talking across a table in a seminar room—and if not, are academics dumbing down the process if we still award full credit for a course once based in real-time discussion of in-person students gathered around a table or at least in the same room? Can thinking skills be developed in the same way? Does distance learning have real advantages and represent the future of education?

The way in which distance education went from radio to television and then to a form of virtual education that was essentially an in-person classroom on a screen was, as education consultant Steven Gilbert observed, part of a pattern that has been repeated many times. Indeed, Gilbert recalled watching—and learning from—a TV physics course back in the 1950s. He observed that if you were self-motivated and had some additional resources available, you could learn physics that way (Noer 2012). The same can be said of similar modern efforts, such as those of Khan Academy, whose virtues are many. However, advocates of this approach often fail to recognize that many people either do not like to learn that way or cannot use the method effectively.

This reality was highlighted when the pandemic forced the nation to pivot in a manner that allowed for no real time or opportunity to develop a pedagogically appropriate approach. Teachers quickly recognized how the effort to simply do what they had always done in the classroom did not resonate or connect with students in the same way when it was presented in front of the screen. Initially there was little they could do to make adjustments. The administrative support and the professional development that faculty needed was not readily available during the pandemic, a fact that only reinforced the problem.

Many of the online institutions that were launched, even by established educational institutions like NYU and the University of Maryland, did not survive despite more and more students turning to online and distance-based options for their education (Kentnor 2015). Central to the lack of success appeared to be a lack of understanding about online pedagogy and online learning styles. The efforts were also bedeviled by ongoing tensions among traditional faculty who often were resistant to institutional efforts. But most important was the failure to recognize the differences between teaching and learning in the online environment and the in-person venue. Still open to debate is whether the pandemic had a transformative impact on the world of education and, especially, whether it truly altered the way people view distance education.

Many predicted that the pandemic forcing education to go virtual would be a watershed event. Professor James N. Bradley, the chief information officer at Trinity University in Texas, theorized that the shift could lead to a long-term altering of the educational landscape. With faculty forced to deliver education online and students forced to learn in that same way, Bradley expected that "the resistance to online education is going to go away as a practical matter" (Lederman 2020). The *Chronicle of Higher Education*'s Goldie Blumenstyk went further, positing that it could be a "black swan" moment (unexpected but, in hindsight, seemingly inevitable), serving as more of a catalyst for online education than any number of the pundits and corporate advocates had been over the years. Indeed, she went so far as to assert that the shift would not only be enormously disruptive but would also change the educational paradigm. She saw it as one of those unforeseen events that could change everything (Lederman 2020). In contrast, while acknowledging such possibilities, others noted that since these early—and forced—versions of distance education would, for the most part, be little more than video conferenced lectures, their impact might not be as impactful as others had anticipated.

However unintentionally, the pandemic and its lingering effects sparked debate about another aspect of distance education—how it is combined with in-person instruction. In many cases, the fall of 2020 saw schools only able or willing to have some of their students in attendance, with others at home, an arrangement that led to hybrid learning. Especially for administrators and political leaders under pressure to allow students to end their isolation and return to school, it seemed a way to at least inch back toward normal while at the same time reflecting a sensitivity to continuing health concerns, if not dangers. Yet while it may have satisfied some concerns, for most teachers it was a nightmare. In utilizing hybrid models in which some students attended in person while others were at home watching the class—and hopefully participating—via Zoom or other similar approaches, a whole additional set of challenges were put on teachers' plates (Shah 2021).

If nothing else, the hybrid approach complicated the efforts of teachers to design—or more likely redesign—their lessons, given the split audiences and the distinctive types of interactions that such an arrangement necessitated. Indeed, with some technology, teachers were even given tips about how to move around the room, so, as they would say in Hollywood, they always had their best side facing the camera. By almost all accounts, teachers abhorred the hybrid classroom approach, seeing it as the worst of all worlds and making clear their desire to shelve it at the first opportunity (Shah 2021).

The demands on teachers imposed by hybrid classrooms were largely considered overwhelming. In addition to numerous daily operational challenges, there were psychological feelings of defeat that came at the end of seemingly every day. Dedicated teachers left school demoralized, feeling they had served neither the in-person nor the online student effectively. The experience led to tremendous amounts of frustration, despair, and helplessness. Should the thinning of the teaching ranks that has resulted really be a surprise?

In response, teachers nationwide have sought guarantees that they will not have to manage mixed classrooms again, and in fact, in some districts, teachers have been successful in getting such assurances included in newly negotiated contracts (Shah 2021). And yet many school officials saw things differently during that year. Indeed, the difficulties notwithstanding, they discovered that it really was possible to teach students in person and virtually at the same time. Too, they discovered that there was a definite group of parents and students who preferred the flexibility that at-home learning provided—at least some of the time (Shah 2021).

For many who saw these issues as short-term problems, the continuing realities of Covid-19 coupled with declining enrollments and teacher stress, not to mention ongoing uncertainty about when normal would return, meant that every option was initially on the table. For others, this was simply the first part of a debate about the future of teaching and learning, one in which the role of distance education and technology are front and center. While many saw remote learning as simply a response to a global emergency, others saw it as a way to hasten practices they already saw as the way to the future.

Richard Culatta, the CEO of the International Society for Technology in Education, who worked in the Department of Education under President Obama, argues that, given that technology is not going away anytime soon, we must look for ways to utilize it in the best ways in education, exploring possibilities while addressing downsides revealed during the pandemic. As the author of a book on how to maximize our children's productive involvement in the digital world, Culatta focuses on the importance of helping young people develop and practice the skills they need to be future leaders (Culatta 2021). Of course, such development has always been a part of the broad goals of our educational systems.

Online learning, as the current central form of distance education, seems to be here to stay. Questions now must focus on how it will be maintained and how widespread it will be. While acknowledging the shortcomings and problems made clear by the quick onset of the pandemic, advocates nevertheless are firm in their belief that there is tremendous promise in online teaching for all, but especially for those who historically have suffered from the one-size-fits-all model of education that has so long been the standard approach. Traditional teaching approaches have too often failed students with certain types of disabilities, kids who face bullying or fear for their safety, older students who are both working and going to school, and learners with family responsibilities. For these students, online learning could be a lifesaver. And for that reason, online education advocates do not want to abandon their efforts. While they understand that the switch on a dime to remote learning in the spring of 2020 was not optimal, the potential for the field was nevertheless made evident, and the experience offered a substantive set of examples from which could be developed plans and programs that could change the face of teaching and learning. At the very least, the heightened awareness is leading to wide-ranging efforts at experimentation throughout the United States. Where that leads and what kind of staying power online learning will have remains to be seen.

There is of course a major difference between transitioning to online instruction for individual students in specific, personal, and health-related cases, or emergencies, and making it your basic approach. And how teachers approach those two scenarios is also very different. Aside from the efficacy and the impact of those options, there is also the matter of training and preparation. If online distance learning is to be the norm, then major adjustments, supported by instruction and support for teachers, need to be made. How exactly all of this may play out is at the heart of discussions and negotiations now taking place in school districts across the nation as well as in wider debates about the future of distance education. Distance education will only alter the educational landscape if it is done in a way that maximizes its potential.

Research has made clear that a well-designed, documented, and structured virtual course, one that is dedicated to encouraging and fostering active student engagement, is the key to success. This approach, evident in the principles and guidelines adopted by states and schools that have begun to make distance education a part of their programs, means that colleges and universities need to provide the time, resources, and instruction necessary for faculty to learn how to adapt their longtime in-person practices to these new demands (NY Distance Ed Principles n.d.). But such a move requires an attitudinal as well as a psychological adjustment in both the institutional and the individual approach, and it is not clear that such adjustments have been fully understood.

A question central to all of this is whether distance education properly done will simply impact the way teaching and learning is done in certain offerings or whether its reach will be so great that it ultimately becomes transformative and the norm. Perhaps no less significantly, even if residential higher education as we know it survives or thrives at least in some areas, will the changes derived from the teaching and learning process for distance education also impact the pedagogy, the delivery, and the educational process for in-person teaching and learning?

In the years before the pandemic hit, there was a slowly increasing move within in-person education, in brick-and-mortar schools, towards collaboration, which has itself forced teachers to adjust how they do things. While collaborative techniques are possible in distance education, they are certainly made more difficult with asynchronous learning. Even in synchronous efforts, there can be little doubt that breakout rooms online are not the same as discussions in an in-person classroom. These are some of the issues that discussions about online teaching and learning must include.

While recognizing that the quick transition to virtual learning did not yield the best performances from faculty or students, in the final stages of the 2019–20 academic year, educators held tight to what had worked, identifying the positives things that teachers had accomplished while at the same time trying to determine the best way forward. One article, titled "Crossing the Bridge: From Emergency Remote Teaching to Quality Online Learning," summarized the challenges involved and argued that crossing the bridge involved in part, a shift in mindset, going from the reactive crisis mode that characterized the spring of 2020 to instead looking to move forward (Voelker 2020). Moving ahead would include teachers giving themselves credit for what they had done well despite facing tremendous challenges, and then adopting a more affirmative approach, one that included making the changes necessary to deliver, via distance education, the kind of quality experience that everyone—teacher and student alike—desired. Given that one of the foremost challenges of the remote experience was the reduced connection between teacher and student and the need to bridge that distance, teachers were encouraged to assess their approach and redesign with an eye to better and more effective interaction (Voelker 2020).

One major advantage of distance learning has been the time element, especially the flexibility that allows a student to take a course at their own pace. This approach often relies on project-based programs in which student competency is assessed. A prime example of this approach is the UW Flexible Option offered through the University of Wisconsin's Extended Campus (Mason 2016). This option offers a variety of self-paced, competency-based degree programs, in which the student completes "competency sets" to move forward instead of attending formal classes. The successful completion of a competency set marks the completion of a course. Based on appropriateness for the subject, the make-up of competency sets may vary and include traditional tests as well as projects.

Again, the pace of this type of program is up to the students, who can work it around other aspects of their lives. Students sign up for specific time periods, what some schools refer to as a subscription, and they then have access to the material and the competency sets for a designated period of time (Mason 2016). The UW program uses three-month subscription blocks, while at Northern Arizona University, the subscription is for six months. In both cases, a student's failure to complete the set within the time period does not result in a failing grade as it would in traditional school. Rather, the student may restart the unit (Logan 2014). Completing the tasks and demonstrating competency is the key, as opposed to attending school for a defined period of time.

As previously noted, remote learning can also be a vehicle for providing both professional development and advanced degrees for teaching faculty themselves at all levels. As such, remote learning can help teachers to expand and enhance their own skill sets, enabling them to adjust to the new demands imposed by distance learning and to learn new technology central to those efforts.

An additional benefit and potentially transformative aspect of the online remote learning experience is the wider array of resources available to instructors. These resources open up a wealth of opportunities, for example in the ability to bring in an outsider as a guest lecturer, which otherwise may be too expensive or difficult to arrange.

As we consider the changes that distance education can foment, we can also consider the ways these changes can help move it into the mainstream. In the early going, Sal Khan and his Khan Academy were regularly under siege from critics, especially those with ties to the academic community who questioned his qualifications, especially his lack of any formal pedagogical or teacher training. Khan Academy has clearly weathered that storm to the benefit of many, with its partnership with the College Board serving both as validation and as a vehicle for offering increased access to the College Board's programs (Gorman 2016).

While recent advances and trends in education have sought, in some cases successfully, to reduce "the sage on the stage" approach to teaching, even its successor, "the guide on the side," has never questioned the importance of that lead educator, an expert in their field, as a part of the process. And yet, while most of the formal aspects of distance education discussed in this volume come under formal educational guidelines, in the same way that the field of journalism has in some ways been hijacked by anyone with an internet address and a blog presence, the ability to "share knowledge" is not necessarily tied directly to an educational institution. That reality represents an important element of the technological aspect of distance education. To a generation who are well versed in sharing their own content, the line between experts who expound and posers who post can be blurred in the eyes of the student audience. Indeed, some see yesterday's public intellectual, not to mention formal distance learning instructor, as today's "influencer." As distance education programs continue to expand and grow while seeking to become more fully integrated into the educational establishment, this issue is a factor that cannot be ignored.

A major criticism of online learning programs is that some feel they do not teach people to think in the same way that the interaction among people in a traditional seminar-style learning environment does. While the computer screen can allow an instructor to share information with viewers, there are many educators who do not see the online forum as an effective way to engage in robust and uninhibited discussions (Danisch 2021). Research on this subject is still in its infancy. With the pandemic having offered a skewed introduction to remote learning for most people, there is a great need for extended studies that can assess the effectiveness of engaged, properly prepared and presented distance education courses of study in the years to come. Such work will undoubtedly help bridge the gaps between reality and the impressions based on pandemic-induced necessity.

Protecting and Maintaining Academic Integrity

One thing that has dogged the advent, development, and use of online learning—especially with the quick pivoting necessitated by the pandemic—has been maintaining the security of academic assessments and the integrity of the kinds of testing that have long been a central part of the educational process. From the outset of the pandemic, educators from across the country reported disturbingly high increases in cheating. Officials at Virginia Commonwealth University reported a more than threefold increase in cases of academic misconduct during the 2020–21 academic year, while the University of Georgia saw such cases more than double (Toppo 2021).

The distressingly high upturn even hit the United States Military Academy at West Point. Despite its hallowed Honor Code, a group including over seventy-two West Point freshmen were found to have cheated on the final exam in calculus administered remotely in May of 2020 (Toppo 2021). The largest cheating scandal at West Point in forty-five years featured all of the offending cadets making the same error on a particular part of the exam, an offense that would have been unlikely under standard in-person administrative procedures. The nationwide increase in cheating made clear the need to develop methods, techniques, and technology that could combat the problem if distance education were to grow in the post-pandemic era. Reportedly, that process has begun with a new focus, "cooperative learning" (Toppo 2021).

Numerous online proctoring companies have emerged, offering to stem the tide of cheating, but results have been mixed and concerns have been raised about the security of these products (Swaak 2022). So far, no foolproof response has been offered to the fundamental problem of ensuring the integrity of a test when the students taking it are out of the direct sight or supervision of the instructor.

Students have also found ways to be "present" when they aren't—to check in when they haven't been there, and to offer comments in a class discussion when they are not present. Efforts to prevent students from seeking outside assistance or using additional material that would be forbidden were they in the classroom have also been minimally successful.

But in an interesting split in the education community, a growing number of faculty have not only said that, for all intents and purpose, these trends are no big deal, but that, in a perhaps perverse way, they welcome them, seeing the problems as offering an opportunity for radical change. They argue that these issues are simply one of the many aspects of online learning that requires an adjustment, and that teachers must alter their assessments to better utilize and maximize the value of the online approach (Toppo 2021). These advocates believe the cheating epidemic will force instructors to be more creative, to develop assessments that require more analysis or critical thinking, skills more valued than the simple information regurgitation so often central to traditional tests.

Beyond concerns about academic integrity as it relates to individual assessments is the broader question related to the integrity of the learning process and the students engaged in that effort. Given that distance education has become an increasingly popular option for people seeking to advance their careers, enhancing their résumés through the addition of valuable degrees and certificates, analysts looking at the pros and cons of distance education have noted that in addition to securing the basic integrity of assessments, one cannot overlook the question of whether the person registered for the professional development course or degree program is, in fact, the one actually taking it and earning the professionally valuable degree, certificate, or credential (Fox 2020).

Admittedly such concerns are not limited to distance education forums. In fact, the way "substitutes" have performed in other comparable ways only serves to reaffirm why this is a legitimate concern. Indeed, as the stakes have grown, so too have efforts to circumvent propriety. Anyone old enough to remember the days when signing up for the SAT involved no picture, or more recently when the infamous Varsity Blues admissions scandal involved people taking the SAT and the ACT on behalf of the prospective applicant, should not have difficulty imagining the ways in which similar dishonesty could occur in exclusively online programs where identity and face-to-face recognition are only peripheral aspects of the experience (Korn and Levitz 2020). It is worth noting that, given the vast amount of government funding that can potentially be involved, the legitimacy of the distance learning endeavor becomes a regulatory concern and forms a cloud over the process.

While some approach the problem from a security perspective, others see it as a way to use distance education as a vehicle to reform and refocus the very essence of the educational enterprise. They believe that the nation's educational institutions need to think differently about the very idea of the relationship between learning and assessment, developing methods consistent with the educational approach of distance education. History makes clear that however determined administrators may be to tighten procedures and discipline those who cheat, students will find ways to game the system (Toppo 2021). Advocates of change argue that this game of cat and mouse can be abandoned if educators instead develop vehicles that will both enlighten and engage students while at the same time still requiring them to demonstrate their understanding and mastery of the material at hand. Assessment reformers argue that a shift would not just offer an effective response to the cheating epidemic but also further the learning process.

These ideas reflect the belief that education is changing, entering an era in which academia is increasingly moving away from factual regurgitation and toward teamwork and collaboration. This approach can lead to better online learning methods that go well beyond the posting of a written exam online.

It is also important to look at the context in which modern education, especially distance education, is taking place. On one hand, you have traditional college students, young adults in their late teens to early twenties, whose decision-making abilities, as well as their ability to morally self-regulate, are very much in the developmental stages. On the other hand, you have older, nontraditional students who are far removed from the rhythm of school and who are pursuing their education at the same time that they are balancing family, work, and other responsibilities (Toppo 2021). Decades-old approaches to assessments are not necessarily the best way to serve these different types of students nor are they the best way to assess the distinctive evolving approaches that are distance education.

The longer college instructors work with distance learning, the less they seem to worry about online cheating. A study released by Wiley, the educational publishing company, in January 2022 revealed that faculty concerns about academic integrity in online courses had diminished considerably since the onset of virtual instruction in the spring of 2020 (Carrasco 2022). While 77 percent of respondents to the Wiley survey still believe that students were more likely to cheat in an online course than in an in-person one, that still represented a 16 percent drop from their spring 2020 sampling (Carrasco 2022). Wiley's senior vice president of digital education, Jason Jordan, opined that the decline was attributable to adjustments undertaken by teachers as they became more familiar and comfortable with the online teaching experience. He also noted that, with time, professors had greater experience with a variety of mitigation techniques that were either not yet available or with which they were unfamiliar back in 2020 (Carrasco 2022).

However, educators took little comfort in these improvements, as the 77 percent figure still reflected a faculty belief in an alarmingly high cheating rate in remote learning, as compared to 33 percent for in-person classes. These figures also painted a worrisome picture of the way students approached their work and the learning process (Carrasco 2022). In commenting on the Wiley study, David Rettinger, president emeritus of the International Center for Academic Integrity, observed that much of the early concern seemed to have been based in part on the stress and anxiety that everyone faced back in 2020. Rettinger noted that, while not all online learning is the same, when students are not engaged and when the context for what they are doing is not good, then the risk of misconduct is going to be higher (Carrasco 2022). Distance education advocates emphasize the differences between their focused and pedagogically distinctive efforts to engage students and remote teaching and learning efforts that do not take this careful approach.

The Wiley survey also revealed another change in faculty attitudes. Once faculty came to realize the challenges to academic integrity that were a part of the online experience, they began to crack down (Carrasco 2022). Over 50 percent of surveyed instructors began to use online proctoring software in an effort to stem the cheating. In addition, over a third simply began to use different types of assessments, moving away from the more traditional fact recitation type formats and replacing them with more open-ended approaches. Projects also became a more popular form of assessment. Those who continued with testing employed new strategies like mixing up questions so that while everyone in the class had the same questions, they were in different order and as a result were not as easy to copy or share (Carrasco 2022).

Interestingly, the issue of cheating and academic integrity reflected the divide between remote learning and distance education. The lack of direct supervision made cheating a much greater concern for practitioners who simply moved their in-person class to in front of a computer screen. In contrast, those steeped in distance learning pedagogy, instructors who had designed their courses recognizing that the distance component required a different type of approach, understood that meant differences in assessments too, and having responded accordingly, had fewer concerns (Carrasco 2022).

Financial Costs

Distance education advocates have long hailed the approach as a low-cost option. And as noted previously, that fact has been no small part of the equity discussion, for the highly touted lower costs may allow offerings to be distributed on a far more equitable basis. And yet full-scale discussions of the cost of distance education inevitably remind us of the old adage that "the devil is in the details" (Venable 2023).

Before we examine how and why distance education might differ, we must first look at the costs involved in traditional higher education. What is a student paying for? There are schools where the tuition payment is a flat fee and the academic piece is only part of the total bill that includes room and board. Other schools separate these costs, and how they divide costs can vary widely. Some schools charge by course, some by credit. And schools can charge other assorted student fees.

The pandemic forced virtually all institutions that had tended to bundle their services into one lump sum to consider how their costs were actually split after students who were sent home in March 2020 started to call for refunds, particularly for housing and food that was no longer being provided (Whitford 2020). Yet, for the most part, the academic program, now an online remote learning enterprise, was still deemed worthy of full cost (Anderson 2020).

Notwithstanding the national debates over the nature and quality of online teaching and learning, major colleges generally refused to refund tuition in the still Covid-19-impacted fall of 2020. Their reasoning was perhaps encapsulated in a comment by Brown University president Christine Paxson, who noted that "a Brown degree retains its value and ... students are still learning" (Lieber 2020).

Meanwhile, others saw the pandemic and the move to online learning as having the potential to speed up the unbundling of fees that had increasingly been discussed in higher education circles. The pandemic heightened awareness and concerns about how exactly college costs were allocated and determined, as students learned from home or had hybrid campus experiences, including taking classes online while living in residence halls, carrying out meals from dining halls, and having limited social interaction (Craig 2020a). Consumers (parents and students) also began to look at the situation through a different lens, one that was impacted by the burgeoning number of online offerings, whose value was seemingly validated by increased enrollment. The subsequent low enrollment figures for traditional schools in the 2020–21 school year added credence to administrators' fears that the residential college experience was losing its allure, especially in comparison with established distance options (D'Agostino 2022).

For all the hope and promise of distance education serving as a way for students, especially working adults, to get the additional education and credentials that could further their career at a reasonable cost, the actual experiences of many students have been less than universally satisfactory. One of the most egregious examples was reported by the *Wall Street Journal* in November 2021 following its investigation of the University of Southern California's online social work program (Bannon and Fuller 2021). Students in the program were charged tuition usually seen only for residential programs, leaving them burdened by almost unconscionable debt (Bannon and Fuller 2021).

Whether responsibility lay with the university or the OPM involved, questions regarding the value of the USC program, as well as the fundamental approach and cost of online learning, remained. Was the USC program an aberration, or was it representative of the way business was done? This model would certainly undermine claims that lower costs were one of the major selling points for distance education. Concerns about exactly how distance education programs operated attracted the attention of Washington, where senators were already beginning to look into the relationship between schools and OPMs (Schwartz 2022). In the spring of 2023, graduates of the USC online program filed a class action suit alleging misrepresentation in the school's claims that the program was "exactly the same as the on-campus, in-person program" (Spitalniak, 2023).

Impact on Health: Physical, Mental, and Emotional

For as long as the national experience has included schools, those institutions, in whatever shape and form, have played an important role in the socialization of students, both as individuals and as American citizens. The interactions and shared experiences central to in-person education are particularly important in a democratic society. Consequently, concerns around the isolating aspects of distance education must be addressed, along with related issues of physical, mental, and emotional health.

On the physical side, the sedentary nature of online learning is clear. A less obvious, but no less important issue, is ergonomics. Both doctors and educators have expressed concerns about the impact on a student's physical well-being of spending time in front of a screen in positions that may not be at all good for one's posture. Doctors have expressed particular concern about the potential for injuries and problems related to backs, necks, and shoulders among teens who are suddenly isolated at home in front of a computer screen for a significantly greater amount of time than they had ever previously experienced (Strauss 2020).

The relationship between distance learning and the nation's growing concerns about mental and emotional health among high school and college students also needs continued investigation. Increases in mental health issues in teens and young adults were already recognized before the forced shift to online learning brought on by the pandemic. Experts identify isolation and a lack of interpersonal interaction—both of which are often manifested as a lack of motivation—as major factors in the mental health crisis. Concerns regarding the isolation to which students were consigned during the pandemic was certainly part of the motivation to have students return to class, with masks, in the fall of 2020. While it is important to attempt to separate the effects of the pandemic from the impact of remote learning in general, there can be no denying that mental health is a concern that warrants additional study (Strauss 2020).

When the Omicron-induced surge hit the United States in December 2021, the U.S. Surgeon General issued an advisory on the mental health crisis among the nation's youth. Although she did not blame remote learning in general, she made clear that the pandemic and the isolation that the virtual classroom had fostered had done much to worsen the situation (Richtel 2021). Although some aspects of mental health issues lie outside the realm of providers and developers of distance education, it is important to identify what problems are inherent in the distance education experience, outside of the pandemic's influence, and determine how these problems can be addressed in future distance education endeavors.

While findings regarding a growing mental health crisis are certainly troubling, there is evidence that some students benefited from the experience of learning remotely. One study showed that the transition to remote learning both reduced stress and improved the sleep habits of college students (Ewing

2021). By most accounts, distance learning is best suited to those who are highly motivated to obtain a degree, certificate, or training. However, even among driven students, distance learning can lead to additional stress and pressures that are not as easily addressed as they might be in an in-person class with a more personal, supportive environment. Although academic stress and pressure are factors that predate and transcend distance education and remote learning, they are concerns that educators at all levels must recognize and reevaluate as they seek to integrate distance education into their programs.

Distance Education and the Corporatization of Higher Education

As distance education assumes a more prominent place in the higher education landscape, it finds itself right in the middle of ongoing discussions and heightened concerns about the increased corporatization of higher education. While the earliest wide-scale forays into internet-based distance education were by for-profit institutions like the University of Phoenix, nonprofit educational institutions soon entered the potentially profitable fray, creating subsidiaries and developing partnerships that seemed focused on increasing revenue and expanding their brand. It was, in the eyes of some observers, an endeavor that ran counter to some of the fundamental principles of higher education, specifically, educational quality, institutional governance, and project planning. Former Harvard president Derek Bok spoke for many when he noted that, while new technologies had the potential to greatly improve teaching and learning, schools should be careful about the way in which seeking profit and commercializing the educational process could undermine the credibility and integrity of the institutions central to higher education (Kentnor 2015). In the aftermath of the pandemic, as opportunities to expand distance education emerge, how programs are developed and implemented and their impact on universities becomes an ever-greater concern (Seltzer 2021).

As mentioned, distance education programs were offered largely through for-profit educational institutions at first, a departure from tradition and an approach that has always made the higher education establishment leery, if not downright suspicious. The University of Phoenix is the most obvious example. Although its early success had the higher ed community abuzz, it has also served as the poster child for the dangers and downsides of that approach (Hanford 2012). Doubts and concerns raised by its experience, as well as that of other institutions have led to calls for federal intervention and regulation, an area that is evolving along with distance education (Knott 2023).

Another way in which distance education has helped further the corporatization of higher education has been through the development of Online Program Management (OPM) companies whose partnerships with traditional colleges and universities have proven critical to schools' efforts as participants in the online world of distance education. But these partnerships have not come without a cost. In 2020, Senators Elizabeth Warren (D-MA) and Sherrod Brown (D-OH) raised concerns about the business practices of some of the largest OPMs, companies whose profits often total between 40 and 65 percent of the revenues achieved by their partnering institutions. The senators' inquiry is still ongoing (Vasquez 2022).

As remote learning and online education have increased the trend towards the corporatization of modern education, especially in higher education, new suppliers and new program developers have emerged to provide virtual course content as well as tech support. With successes leading to high finance initial public offerings (IPOs), the educational world has been thrust into a whole new big money sector. This has forced at least the online sector of the educational world to reassess its approach and perhaps its business model as well.

Changes in marketing strategies reflect the increasing corporatization of higher education as well. The University of Phoenix was at the forefront of this trend, but Southern New Hampshire University's push to become a leader in the distance education field was also fueled by a highly successful marketing campaign. The school's marketing efforts raised eyebrows among some, as distance learning offerings were far removed from the roots of the university, but the campaign paid off, enabling SNHU to grow from approximately 8,000 online students to 135,000 over the course of two decades (McKenzie 2019).

As colleges and universities have waded into the world of distance education, they have usually had to go outside to get help to create, develop, and facilitate their newly launched programs. In fact, a whole industry has developed to facilitate these efforts to make the process ultimately easier and more successful for teachers who, courtesy of the outsides services, are allowed to focus on their content and teaching. At the forefront of these efforts are Course Management System (CMS) software programs which are designed to help individual courses make the transition to online teaching and learning. Even more important are the Online Program Management (OPM) companies that help colleges and universities actually take their academic programs online, the necessary precursor for the CMS work with individual courses. While costs to students are generally seen as less with distance education, the start-up costs for institutions can be steep. It is important, then, to make the transition as competently and efficiently as possible. Organizations like CMS companies and OPMs can help with these efforts, increasing the likelihood of a smooth launch (Kronk 2019).

Online teaching is in many ways more onerous and demands more from instructors than traditional in-class teaching, as they provide feedback, responses to assignments, and answers to questions from students who are spread all over and are taking the class, asking questions, and posting comments at all hours. With these additions to the existing array of responsibilities for the course instructor, outside assistance can be very helpful. Indeed, while traditionalists decry the increased corporatization of higher education, distance education advocates point out that the trend is simply a product of a changing world and that those changes have helped make higher education more accessible than it has ever been (Kronk 2019).

Increased corporatization has also manifested through the development of additional products to market. For example, in the aftermath of the spring 2020 transition, Wake Forest University developed and now offers its Online Immersion Program. Available to students aged thirteen and older, the program offers high school students a chance to explore possible career directions, with course options including business, psychology, cancer medicine, women's medicine, and bioscience. Offered in two- or four-week sessions at any time all year, the students are offered a flexible, if pricey, opportunity to gain some insight into what their interest may really entail. The course is significantly more flexible than similar in-person summer programs that are standard offerings at college and universities. Revenue and admissions benefits are obviously part of the goal for schools. While the flexibility of a year-round option makes programs like Wake Forest's more accessible in one way, the approximately $1,000 tuition is out of reach for many students, a fact that is representative of the socio-economic divide that characterizes much of the higher education world (Online Immersion—WFU n.d.). While such programs may be the latest iteration of the traditional summer program that aimed to utilize empty dorms during the lull of the summer months, given the financial figures attached to some of the OPM/school relationships, they do not necessarily have the same level of accessibility.

The Conundrum of OPMs

As noted, the development and delivery of modern distance education has proceeded along two tracks: the pedagogical and the technological/corporate. While the educational side has been working to adapt decades, if not centuries-old teaching practices to this new approach, technological gurus and financiers have worked to develop the technological infrastructure and financial support necessary to deliver the new educational content. The emergence of Online Program Management (OPM) companies that work with colleges and universities to bring their academic programs online has been central to these efforts. OPMs have played no small part in the increased corporatization of higher education.

From the outset, OPMs were controversial (Kim 2018). While there has been little doubt that the educational sector has needed practical assistance in turning their formerly cloistered academic courses into effective and profitable distance education offerings, the pushback from the academic side has been significant. Unsurprisingly, it has mirrored the reluctance of the academic realm to embrace distance learning as a whole, unable to shake its concerns about the credibility and quality of online teaching and learning. In contrast, advocates and supporters of OPMs argue that they have been instrumental in helping colleges and universities quickly and effectively establish and then substantively expand their online offerings, helping them become cohesive programs in a timely fashion.

OPMs have benefited from the fact that they already possess the resources to assist with both the financial and staffing needs central to developing and expanding an online program. With OPMs able to offer both the expertise and the financing models that promise a positive return to a college, it has made sense for the academic side to take advantage of their experience, even if the cost is generally higher than if the schools did it all themselves (Kronk 2019).

At the same time, concerns have been raised about whether OPMs have blurred the line between providing technical and management support and undertaking work related to actual academic instruction. This becomes problematic, given that OPMs have avoided regulatory oversight. The lack of oversight represents a marked contrast from the accreditation requirements of traditional educational institutions (Knott 2023). These concerns and loopholes have led to calls for closer scrutiny of OPMs, with some arguing that greater transparency could do much to increase faith in a facet of distance learning that has long been shrouded in secrecy and distrust (Schwartz 2022).

Given their central role in the expansion of distance education programs in traditional colleges and the lucrative nature of OPM partnerships with higher education, the practice has drawn increasing governmental interest. In early 2020, before the onset of the Covid-19 pandemic, Senators Elizabeth Warren (Democrat from Massachusetts) and Sherrod Brown (Democrat from Ohio) expressed official interest in the business practices of some of the largest companies in the business. In a letter addressed to the five largest OPMs in the country (2U, Academic Partnerships, Bisk Education, Pearson Learning, and Wiley Education Services), Warren and Brown sought copies of all the contracts the companies held with colleges, samples of presentations they made to the schools, and detailed reports of their expenditures and revenues. The letter stemmed from concerns about the influence these companies were having on higher education, especially given the millions of dollars of federal aid potentially involved (Schwartz, 2020).

While this initial inquiry seemed to stall during the 2020 campaign season, the issues did not die. Rather, the growth experienced by the OPMs in the two years following Warren and Brown's letter, partly fueled by the pandemic, did nothing to assuage the senators' concern. In January 2022, Warren and Brown, now joined by Senator Tina Smith (Democrat from Minnesota), wrote the CEOs of those same five companies, as well as three others (Kaplan, Inc., Grand Canyon Education, Inc., and Zovio), seeking updates on the online degree programs they operate for higher education institutions that receive federal financial aid. The senators noted that since their previous January 2020 inquiry, "We continue to have concerns about the impact of OPM partnerships on rising student debt loads," and then added, "The responses to our previous letters confirmed that OPMs often have tuition-sharing arrangements with universities, which commit an ongoing percentage of tuition revenue to the OPM to finance the start-up and ongoing costs of operating online degree programs" (Finn 2022). They concluded by observing that "Online Program Management (OPM) companies appear to have significantly expanded, becoming a more integral part of American higher education," while adding that they sought updated data, with an eye to "inform[ing] effective policy towards this growing sector of higher education" (Finn 2022).

Analysts have said that Warren and Brown's interest in the influence of OPMs is in large part based on a high-profile case reported by the *Wall Street*

Journal. Investigators found that students who took a two-year, online master's degree program in social work at the University of Southern California (USC) were paying almost $115,000 in tuition, an expenditure that left them deeply in debt while preparing them for a career in a field where they will likely earn barely $50,000 a year within a couple of years of graduating. *The Wall Street Journal* put much of the blame on OPM giant 2U, and the article led to debates about accountability for student financial outcomes (Bannon and Fuller 2021). For Warren, a longtime advocate of reducing, if not outright forgiving, student debt, this high-profile program raised serious red flags about the remote learning/distance education experience, for which a supposed benefit is greater affordability. With more and more colleges expanding their online program, usually in connection with an OPM, Warren and Brown are continuing their investigations.

Remote Learning, Distance Education, and the Dangers of First Impressions

There can be no denying that the global Covid-19 pandemic had immediate and immeasurable impacts on the worlds of remote learning and distance education. By the end of the 2019–20 academic year, millions of students who had never given the idea a thought had been exposed to the practice, with varying degrees of success and acceptance. Its sudden arrival at the heart of the national teaching and learning process represented no small shift from its longtime residence on the margins, a place from which distance educators were mounting a methodical campaign to achieve a spot in established mainstream educational circles.

The rapid, unanticipated first-time exposure to the process yielded experiences that could not help but impact people's impressions and opinions of the whole idea of remote learning. Too, however unintentionally, the process quickly became caught up in the national political and cultural divide that marked the nation's response to the pandemic. As if the very nature of remote learning were not controversial enough, its emergence in the midst of a worldwide emergency only added to the challenges, especially for advocates who saw a nation of often desperate students, teachers, and families trying to quickly adapt. The unanticipated arrival also served to highlight many of the issues surrounding the long time, if very different, modern practice of distance education. It remains important to distinguish between those challenges specifically tied to the pandemic and those central to distance education.

Identifying those aspects that are the greatest stumbling blocks for distance education is critical in the effort to make it a wide-ranging and effective approach for those who *choose* to pursue it, while distinguishing between their experience and the forced remote learning that most students have experienced. Any assessments of effectiveness must clearly distinguish between the remote learning that is a product of emergency measures and the educationally sound, pedagogically based distance education offerings pursued willingly. As we have seen, this distinction plays out on two levels—the psychological and the structural—and resulting experiences can vary widely. The foremost challenges identified for distance learners in the aftermath of the pandemic included distractions, motivation, technical issues, some students being left behind, and the impact of diminished social interaction. While these are legitimate concerns, an objective observer must acknowledge that some part of these results reflects circumstances related to the pandemic and not necessarily distance education.

So quickly did the pandemic force schools and their families to switch to online learning that there was little opportunity to create home settings properly suited to the learning process. Too often, the kitchen table, right in the middle of the household traffic flow, was the place of choice for learning, and with it came the obvious attendant distractions. Even if a student had a room of their own, which may provide some comfort as a cherished personal space, being surrounded by the kinds of things (games, books, music, etc.) that someone not fully engaged might turn to did not make for an ideal learning venue. Students, teachers, and families all learned that the situation was unlikely to allow the students to focus on their studies in the most productive way. Indeed, as the pandemic lengthened, educators and psychologists began offering advice about creating schedules, paying more attention to time management, and trying to create physical areas for class and study that would minimize distractions. Of course, just because someone chooses to pursue a distance education program does not mean that these issues will not impact their experience. However, one would hope that those who make the choice would address at least some of the concerns before making the decision to pursue this type of program, a luxury that students in 2020 did not have.

Technological issues have been a challenge since the introduction of technology as an important component in the educational process. Whether it has involved the development of school-wide internet networks or supporting the heightened needs placed on school networks during the pandemic, providing access to proper, working technology is a huge responsibility. It proved to be especially difficult when schools quickly transitioned to distance learning. As some schools make bigger commitments to the kind of teaching and learning in which distance education plays such a major role, they will need to invest in the necessary technology and technical support. Those students who choose online classes will obviously also have to ensure that they have the technology capabilities needed for the demands of the program they are pursuing.

As to the issue of students falling behind, the quick transition to virtual learning in the spring of 2020 did not allow schools the time to adjust their existing program adequately. Student performance is also intertwined with issues like motivation and distraction. Now more aware of these problems, schools can hopefully better address future comparable challenges. Meanwhile, the fundamental attractions of virtual learning, potential benefits like flexibility and lower costs, may help to offset some of the social concerns regarding voluntary distance education, particularly given that many distance education students are older and looking for needed academic credits or professional certifications.

The social aspects of schooling were upended by the pandemic and brought to the forefront of discussions regarding distance learning. Although the pandemic fueled concerns about the effects of isolation on remote learners, given the increasing nature and importance of social media on modern student lives, distance learning may not be as much of a shift in that area as one might expect. Anyone who has observed chemistry and culture at work in a school knows that the important social interactions of a student's school day are usually not focused on the discussion in English class. The more informal interactions that occur between classes, in study halls, at lunch, or during advisory time are equally, if not more, important than in-class social experiences. For older students, social media allowed for some of that interaction, certainly more than similarly situated students of a pre-social media generation would have experienced. For distance learners who pursue a program of their own accord, the lack of social interaction is a recognized factor in their choice of that educational approach. The impacts of isolation, particularly in the longer term, merit further study.

Not surprisingly, as students and families have gotten over the initial hesitation about distance education, the bar has shifted as to how to assess the distance education experience. The quick transition to online during the early days of the pandemic left many with a new-found feeling that this could work, but it also made clear that quality was not a given. The realization that there was a difference between simple remote learning and well-designed and executed distance education ultimately began to penetrate the national psyche. Resonating on numerous levels, it was particularly an eye-opener for those schools just beginning to consider jumping into the distance education pool and not wholly aware of the nuances involved. Most schools that were already looking to add distance learning options to their institutional offerings recognized the technological issues to be addressed and were ready to utilize the newly developed resources available to make that happen. However, there was a new recognition that the actual course presentation was no less a concern, and that in a competitive market, the quality and creativity of presentation of the course, the way the teacher connected and communicated with students, were also very important on numerous levels. Suddenly there was a recognition that the *quality* of the online student experience mattered and could not be addressed as an afterthought.

These concerns over the effects and effectiveness of remote learning were front and center in embattled Michigan Governor Gretchen Whitmer's 2022 State of the State message: "I want to be crystal clear. Students belong in school. We know it's where they learn best. Remote learning is not as fulfilling or conducive to a child's growth. In-person learning is critical to social development and mental health. And that's why we will do everything we can to keep kids in the classroom" (Neher and Roth 2022). As the pandemic receded, it became clear that distance education as an option was something worthy of consideration but that mandatory remote learning was something very different.

Conclusion

Beyond the issues we have addressed in this chapter, there are many others that could be included in a truly comprehensive discussion of distance education. The topic is constantly evolving, with new issues coming to light and new controversies developing. Indeed, in thinking about the shifting nature of the subject, I am reminded of the rumpled and ever curious TV detective Lieutenant Columbo, whose investigations always found him seeking to learn "just one more thing." Any consideration of either the evolution or the future of remote learning and distance education requires no less dogged an approach or open a mind.

For years countless talented, dedicated, and determined educational innovators had been working in the trenches to make widespread distance education and remote learning not just a reality but potentially a revolutionary part of the educational landscape. But neither they nor the millions of us who in the spring of 2020 were suddenly introduced to remote learning would have wanted the field's expansion to have been forcefully accelerated the way it was, with so little preparation. Millions of people in the United States and across the globe were introduced to this potentially revolutionary process in a way that ran counter to any business marketing plan one could ever imagine. It was like a new highly touted musical that was denied its preview tour and instead had its premiere on Broadway, opening before an audience that had no idea what to expect but whose initial impressions could never be erased and would continue to inform all future considerations.

Discussions and debates about the future of remote learning and distance education are continuing. Yet while advocates of distance education continue to work hard to help people understand that what we saw in the spring of 2020 should not be confused with what thoughtful, pedagogically appropriate distance education lessons can offer, there can be little doubt that those early impressions and memories will continue to be part of the dialogue that will determine the future path. The far-reaching influence of the pandemic-fueled expansion of distance education cannot be forgotten.

References

Amin, Reema. 2022. "NYC Schools Failed to Provide Students with Adequate Remote Learning Access: Lawsuit." *Chalkbeat New York*, January 6. https://ny.chalkbeat.org/2022/1/6/22870943/nyc-schools-remote-learning-lawsuit

Anderson, Nick. 2020. "College Students Are Rebelling against Full Tuition after Classes Move Online." *Washington Post*, April 16. https://www.washingtonpost.com/education/2020/04/16/college-students-are-rebelling-against-full-tuition-after-classes-move-online/

Bannon, Lisa, and Andrea Fuller. 2021. "USC Pushed a $115,000 Online Degree. Graduates Got Low Salaries, Huge Debts." *Wall Street Journal*, November 9. https://www.wsj.com/articles/usc-online-social-work-masters-11636435900?mod=djemedu

Carrasco, Maria. 2022. "Concerns about Online Cheating Decline." *Inside Higher Ed*, January 27. https://www.insidehighered.com/news/2022/01/28/instructors-express-fewer-concerns-about-online-cheating#:~:text=Instructors%20expressed%20a%20range%20of,be%20prepared%20for%20the%20future

Clark, Amanda. 2020. "What Are the Advantages of Distance Education?" *Classcraft*, July 14. https://www.classcraft.com/blog/advantages-of-distance-education/

Cox-Steib, Joshua. 2021. "Racial Disparity in Digital Education: How We Got Here and What We Can Do." allconnect.com, September 2. https://www.allconnect.com/blog/racial-disparities-in-digital-education

Craig, Ryan. 2020a. "The Great Unbundling of Higher Education Starts Now." *Forbes*, July 24. https://www.forbes.com/sites/ryancraig/2020/07/24/the-great-unbundling-of-higher-education-starts-now/?sh=74ed1d1e6ed2

Craig, Ryan. 2020b. "What Students Are Doing Is Remote Learning, Not Online Learning. There's a Difference." *EdSurge*. April 2. https://www.edsurge.com/news/2020-04-02-what-students-are-doing-is-remote-learning-not-online-learning-there-s-a-difference

Culatta, Richard. 2021. *Digital for Good: Raising Kids to Thrive in an Online World*. Cambridge, MA: Harvard Business Review Press.

D'Agostino, Susan. 2022. "A Surge in Young Undergrads, Fully Online." *Inside Higher Ed*, October 13. https://www.insidehighered.com/news/2022/10/14/more-traditional-age-students-enroll-fully-online-universities

Danisch, Robert. 2021. "The Problem with Online Learning? It Doesn't Teach People to Think." *The Conversation*, June 13. https://theconversation.com/the-problem-with-online-learning-it-doesnt-teach-people-to-think-161795

Doak, Mol. 2022. "Online Learning Can Lead to Increased Success for Minority Students in Higher Education." *EdTech Magazine*, March 7. https://edtechmagazine.com/higher/article/2022/03/online-learning-can-lead-increased-success-minority-students-higher-education

Ewing, Robert. 2021. "Transition to Remote Learning during Pandemic Reduced Stress, Improved Sleep in College Students." ASU News, August 16. https://news.asu.edu/20210816-discoveries-transition-remote-learning-during-pandemic-reduced-stress-improved-sleep

Finn, Teaganne. 2022. "Senate Democrats Probe Impact of Online Degree Programs on High Student Debt Loads." NBC News, January 16. https://www.nbcnews.com/politics/congress/senate-democrats-probe-impact-online-degree-programs-high-student-debt-n1287578

Fox, Alice. 2020. "What Are the Advantages and Disadvantages that Distance Education Can Offer You?" elearning industry, July 4. https://elearningindustry.com/advantages-and-disadvantages-distance-education-offer

Gallagher, Sean, and Michael Ferrari. 2021. "Employers' Post-Covid Business Strategy and the Race for Talent: A View from the C-Suite." Northeastern University Center for the Future of Higher Education and Talent Strategy. December. https://cps.northeastern.edu/wp-content/uploads/2022/01/NUReport_CFHETS_EmployersPostCovid_12-22-2021.pdf

Galperin, Hernan. 2021. "Infrastructure Law: High-Speed Internet Is as Essential as Water, Electricity." *Government Technology*, November 17. https://www.govtech.com/opinion/infrastructure-law-high-speed-internet-is-as-essential-as-water-electricity

Gorman, Nicole. 2016. "College Board Says Khan Academy Partnership Has Led to 19 Percent Fewer Students Paying for SAT Prep." *Education World*, March 7. https://www.educationworld.com/a_news/19-percent-less-students-pay-sat-test-prep-thanks-college-board-khan-academy-partnership

Greenberg, Susan H. 2022. "DeSantis: Colleges That Move Online Should Refund Tuition." *Inside Higher Ed*, January 4. https://www.insidehighered.com/quicktakes/2022/01/05/desantis-colleges-move-online-should-refund-tuition

Hanford, Emily. 2012. "The Story of the University of Phoenix." American Public Media. September. https://americanradioworks.publicradio.org/features/tomorrows-college/phoenix/story-of-university-of-phoenix.html

Herzog, Rachel. 2021. "32 Broadband Projects Approved for Arkansas Locations for Nearly $125M in Government Grants." *Arkansas Democrat Gazette*, November 17. https://www.arkansasonline.com/news/2021/nov/17/32-broadband-projects-approved-for-arkansas/

"How Do I Report Mistakes in Videos?" n.d. Khan Academy Help Center. Accessed July 5, 2023. https://support.khanacademy.org/hc/en-us/articles/212934867-How-do-I-report-mistakes-in-videos-

H.R.3684. 2021. "Infrastructure Investment and Jobs Act. 117th Congress (2021–2)." https://www.congress.gov/bill/117th-congress/house-bill/3684/text

Kentnor, Hope. 2015. "Distance Education and the Evolution of Online Learning in the United States." *Curriculum and Teaching Dialogue* 17, nos. 1 and 2.

Khalifeh, Ramsey. 2024. "Judge: Lawsuit over Pandemic-era Services to NYC Students with Disabilities Can Proceed." *Gothamist*, March 31. https://gothamist.com/news/judge-lawsuit-over-pandemic-era-services-to-nyc-students-with-disabilities-can-proceed

Kilburn, Don. 2022. "President Speaks: Stop Asking Whether Online Learning Is 'Worth It.' Start Focusing on How It Helps Working Adults." *Higher Ed Dive*, February 7. 2022. https://www.highereddive.com/news/president-speaks-stop-asking-whether-online-learning-is-worth-it-start/617705/

Kim, Joshua. 2018. "5 Misconceptions about Online Program Management Providers." *Inside Higher Ed*, July 10. https://www.insidehighered.com/digital-learning/blogs/technology-and-learning/5-misconceptions-about-online-program-management

Knott, Katherine. 2023. "Oversight Coming for Online Program Providers." *Inside Higher Ed*, February 15. https://www.insidehighered.com/news/2023/02/16/education-department-review-rules-online-program-providers

Korn, Melissa, and Jennifer Levitz. 2020. *Unacceptable: Privilege, Deceit & the Making of the College Admissions Scandal*. New York: Portfolio/Penguin.

Kronk, Henry. 2019. "What Do OPMs Do?" *eLearning Inside*, March 13. https://news.elearninginside.com/what-do-opms-do/

"LC Online." n.d. Landmark College. Accessed July 6, 2023. https://lconline.landmark.edu/College-START/

Lederman, Doug. 2020. "Will Shift to Remote Teaching Be Boon or Bane for Online Learning?" *Inside Higher Ed*, March 17. https://www.insidehighered.com/digital-learning/article/2020/03/18/most-teaching-going-remote-will-help-or-hurt-online-learning

Lieber, Ron. 2020. "Colleges Won't Refund Tuition. Autumn May Force a Reckoning." *New York Times*, May 1. https://www.nytimes.com/2020/05/01/your-money/college-tuition-refunds-coronavirus.html

Logan, Julianne. 2014. "NAU Touting Success with 'Competency-based' Education Program." *Cronkite News*, July 25. https://cronkitenewsonline.com/2014/07/as-congress-eyes-competency-based-degrees-nau-already-claims-success/index.html

Manfuso, Lauren Glenn. 2020. "From Emergency Remote Teaching to Rigorous Online Learning." *EdTech Magazine*, May 7. https://edtechmagazine.com/higher/article/2020/05/emergency-remote-teaching-rigorous-online-learning-perfcon

Mason, Kyla Calvert. 2016. "UW Flexible Option Program Sees 800 Students, 26 Graduates 2.5 Years After Launch." Wisconsin Public Radio, September 2. https://www.wpr.org/uw-flexible-option-program-sees-800-students-26-graduates-2-5-years-after-launch

McKenzie, Lindsay. 2019. "Marketing for a Massive Online University." *Inside Higher Ed*, October 7. https://www.insidehighered.com/news/2019/10/08/how-marketing-helped-southern-new-hampshire-university-make-it-big-online

McLean, Danielle. 2021. "Failed Connection: The Broadband Gap." *The Chronicle of Higher Education*. https://connect.chronicle.com/rs/931-EKA-218/images/FailedConnectionInisghtsReport.pdf

Merod, Anna. 2022a. "K–12 Connectivity on the Rise, but Work Still Needed." *K–12 Dive*, January 13. https://www.k12dive.com/news/report-k-12-connectivity-on-the-rise-but-work-still-needed/617122/

Merod, Anna. 2022b. "District Outreach Critical as 10M Households Benefit from Affordable Connectivity Program." *K-12 Dive*, February 16. https://www.k12dive.com/news/district-outreach-critical-as-10m-households-benefit-from-affordable-connec/618954/

Nagel, David. 2020. "K–12 Has Become the Most Targeted Segment for Ransomware." *The Journal*, December 11. https://thejournal.com/articles/2020/12/11/k12-has-become-the-most-targeted-segment-for-ransomware.aspx

Nappi, Rebecca. 2010. "Wise Words: Retiring WSU Dean Helped Pioneer Distance Learning." *Spokesman-Review* (Spokane, WA), December 4. https://www.spokesman.com/stories/2010/dec/04/going-the-distance/

National Council for Online Education (NCOE). 2022. "Emergency Remote Instruction Is Not Quality Online Learning." *Inside Higher Ed*, February 2. https://www.insidehighered.com/views/2022/02/03/remote-instruction-and-online-learning-arent-same-thing-opinion

National Digital Inclusion Alliance (NDIA). 2019. "Worst Connected Cities 2019." https://www.digitalinclusion.org/worst-connected-cities-2019/

"Nation's Total Public School Enrollment Did Not Change from Fall 2020 to Fall 2021." 2022. National Center for Education Statistics. August 16. https://nces.ed.gov/whatsnew/press_releases/08_16_2022.asp

Neher, Jake, and Cheyna Roth. 2022. "Why Whitmer's Call for In-person School Matters." WDET 101.9FM, January 31. https://wdet.org/2022/01/31/why-whitmers-call-for-in-person-school-matters/#:~:text=Remote%20learning%20is%20not%20as,the%20beginning%20of%20that%20quote

"New York State Education Department, Distance Education Program Principles of Good Practice." n.d. Accessed July 5, 2023. https://www.nysed.gov/college-university-evaluation/distance-education-program-principles-good-practice

News Staff. 2021. "Infrastructure Bill Allots $65 Billion for Broadband Expansion." *Governing*, November 10. https://www.governing.com/finance/infrastructure-bill-allots-65-billion-for-broadband-expansion

Noer, Michael. 2012. "One Man, One Computer, 10 Million Students: How Khan Academy Is Reinventing Education." *Forbes*, November 18. https://www.forbes.com/sites/michaelnoer/2012/11/02/one-man-one-computer-10-million-students-how-khan-academy-is-reinventing-education/?sh=17000d3244e0

"Online Immersion Programs for High School Students." n.d. Wake Forest University. Accessed July 5, 2023. https://wfuonline.precollegeprograms.org/

Read, Ann, and Kelly Wert. 2021. "How States Are Using Pandemic Relief Funds to Boost Broadband Access." Pew Trusts, December 6. https://www.pewtrusts.org/en/research-and-analysis/articles/2021/12/06/how-states-are-using-pandemic-relief-funds-to-boost-broadband-access

Richtel, Matt. 2021. "Surgeon General Warns of Youth Mental Health Crisis." *The New York Times*, December 7. https://www.nytimes.com/2021/12/07/science/pandemic-adolescents-depression-anxiety.html

Roe, David. 2020. "Why Remote Learning and Online Learning Are Not the Same." Reworked, May 13. https://www.reworked.co/learning-development/why-remote-learning-and-online-learning-are-not-the-same/

Schwartz, Natalie. 2020. "Democratic Congressional Inquiry Targets OPMs," *Higher Ed Dive*, January 28. https://www.highereddive.com/news/congressional-inquiry-targets-online-program-managers/571275/

Schwartz, Natalie. 2022. "The Chess Game behind Senators' Inquiry into OPMs." *Higher Ed Dive*, February 7. https://www.highereddive.com/news/the-chess-game-behind-senators-inquiry-into-opms/618441/

Seltzer, Rick. 2021. "Can Colleges Compete with Companies Like Coursera?" *Higher Ed Dive*, September 28. https://www.highereddive.com/news/can-colleges-compete-with-companies-like-coursera/607324/

Seltzer, Rick. 2022. "Online Education's Reputation Jumps, Survey Says." *Higher Ed Dive*, July 26. https://www.highereddive.com/news/online-educations-reputation-jumps-survey-says/628064/

Shah Nirvi. 2021. "'I Feel Half as Successful': Teachers Push to Ban Hybrid Instruction, but Districts Want to Keep It." *Politico*, December 29. https://www.politico.com/news/agenda/2021/12/29/teachers-districts-hybrid-education-526214

Smith, Carl. 2021. "Stimulus Funds Help Virginia, Vermont Build Broadband Equity." *Governing*, October 27. https://www.governing.com/now/stimulus-funds-help-virginia-vermont-build-broadband-equity

Spitalniak, Laura. 2023. "USC Graduates Sue over Online Social Work Program, Alleging False Advertising." *Higher Ed Dive*, May 4. https://www.highereddive.com/news/graduates-of-uscs-online-social-work-masters-sue-alleging-misrepresentat/649509/

Stauffer, Bri. 2020. "What's the Difference Between Online Learning and Distance Learning?" Applied Educational Systems (AES), April 2. https://www.aeseducation.com/blog/online-learning-vs-distance-learning

Strauss, Valerie. 2020. "Five Concerns about the Mass Rush to Online Learning That Shouldn't Be Ignored." *The Washington Post*, March 30.

Swaak, Taylor. 2022. "A Vulnerability in Proctoring Software Should Worry Colleges, Experts Say." *The Chronicle of Higher Education*, January 6. https://www.chronicle.com/article/a-vulnerability-in-proctoring-software-should-worry-colleges-experts-say

"Teach Online." n.d. Center for Distributed Learning, University of Central Florida. https://cdl.ucf.edu/teach/course/

Toppo, Greg. 2021. "Hybrid Learning Sparks New Worries about Cheating. Can Assessment Evolve?" *Higher Ed Dive*, December 22. https://www.highereddive.com/news/hybrid-learning-sparks-new-worries-about-cheating-can-assessment-evolve/616476/

Vasquez, Michael. 2022. "Online Program Management Firms Are Thriving. And These Democrats Want Answers." *Chronicle of Higher Education*, January 22. https://www.chronicle.com/article/online-program-management-firms-are-thriving-and-these-democrats-want-answers

Venable, Melissa. 2023. "Comparing the Costs of Online vs. On-Campus Programs." *Best Colleges*, March 23. https://www.bestcolleges.com/blog/comparing-costs-online-on-campus-programs/

Voelker, Christine. 2020. "Crossing the Bridge: From Emergency Remote Teaching to Quality Online Learning." *Equity and Access*, August–October. https://www.ace-ed.org/crossing-the-bridge-from-emergency-remote-teaching-to-quality-online-learning/

Werschkul, Ben. 2022. "White House Says 20 Internet Companies Will Provide Effectively Free Internet to Millions of Americans." *yahoo!finance*, May 9. https://finance.yahoo.com/news/white-house-says-20-internet-companies-will-provide-effectively-free-internet-to-millions-of-americans-094812381.html

Whitford, Emma. 2020. "Colleges Continue to Churn Through Refund Plans." *Inside Higher Ed*, April 5. https://www.insidehighered.com/news/2020/04/06/colleges-announce-room-and-board-refund-plans-students-are-asking-more

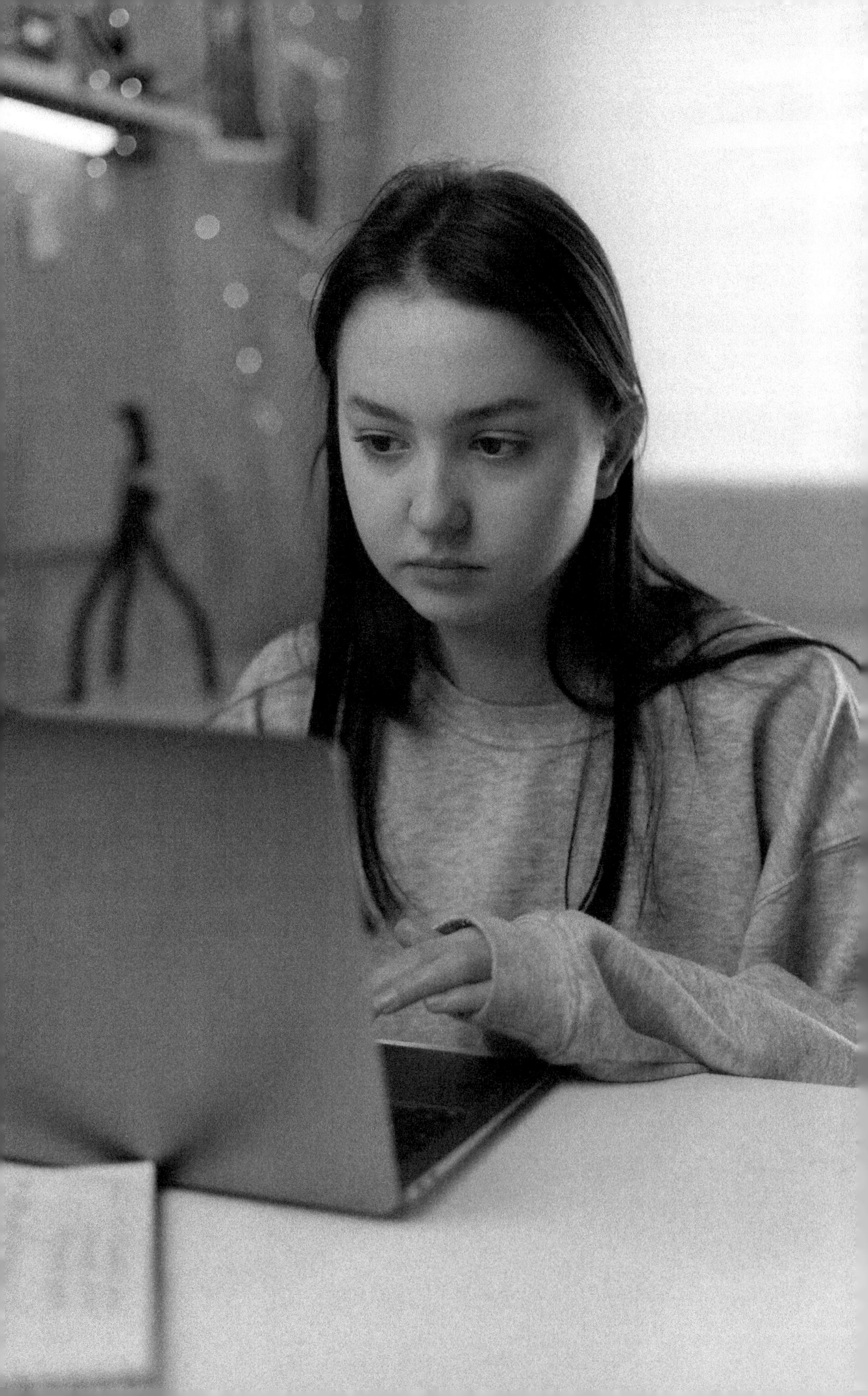

3

Perspectives

This chapter consists of six essays by a range of people whose direct but varied experiences with remote learning and distance education offer a window into the pluses and minuses at the heart of the debates about the value and efficacy of this type of teaching and learning. The testimony and impressions of this group of teachers and students, including a teacher whose two teenage children had very different reactions from each other to the experience as well as one individual who has experienced remote learning from both sides of the desk, offer an informative window onto the most critical aspect of the distance education experience: the human dimension of teaching and learning.

Lindsey Barrett

Class of 2026, University of South Carolina, Columbia, SC, Majoring in Business Administration

The Covid-19 pandemic had a profound impact on my life in many ways, most specifically the type of student I am now. Throughout the first year and a half of the pandemic, I was a fully remote student due to my mom's immunocompromised health status. Remote learning completely transformed the ways in which I approached being a student. In broad terms, it seemed as if I was no longer a high school student, but a college student. By this, I mean that my academic success was now entirely up to me. I made the decisions as to whether or not I attended class, paid attention in class, completed the homework, and overall how much effort I put into school. There were no teachers collecting homework and

---

Some students flourish under the flexibility and freedom of remote learning and distance education, while others struggle to find focus and have difficulty engaging with teachers and classmates. (© Andrii Lysenko/Dreamstime.com)

giving me a disapproving glance if I had nothing to turn in, or teachers roaming the hallways looking for students who were not in class. If I was struggling with a certain concept, I had to take the initiative and find time to schedule a meeting with my teacher, which was a startling concept for a new high school student who was now faced with many new challenges. While navigating the long roller coaster that is researching and visiting potential colleges, AP coursework, extracurriculars, and being a teenager is difficult, adding the remote learning layer made my learning experience more difficult and forced me to alter the way that I learned and how I approached being a successful student.

I believe that remote learning forced me to become a better student by learning crucial skills and concepts early in high school, which would better prepare me to later take on and manage more difficult classes and extracurriculars. One of the most valuable lessons that remote learning taught me is the importance of time management. As a current college freshman, I cannot stress how important it was for me to learn this lesson earlier rather than later. Time management is something that makes a huge difference in terms of reducing my stress, boosting my grades/GPA, and allowing me to take on more activities or have more leisure time. Because of remote learning, my schedule was very open and I was able to choose when I was going to complete homework, when I was going to hold meetings for different organizations I led, when I could have downtime, etc.

At the beginning of the pandemic, I procrastinated quite a bit as I was learning how to manage my class schedule with the amount of free time that I had. However, as time went on I learned that I had to start managing my schedule in a more effective manner instead of leaving assignments and studying until the last minute because it added unneeded stress into my life, on top of a global pandemic, and the work that I turned in wasn't my best because I wasn't giving myself enough time for each assignment. I am so glad that I learned this lesson during high school instead of college because since my schedule now is so similar to my schedule during the pandemic, I was prepared for freshman year when I found myself with plenty of down time and I could choose how I spent it. And while time management was an important aspect of remote learning for me, there were other parts of my life that were significantly altered as well.

Personally, the pandemic had an almost bigger influence on my life socially than it did academically. A major part of remote learning is interacting with other students and teachers in new ways. While being isolated in my home, I found myself becoming more creative regarding the ways in which I socialized with others. In every class I had there were at least four other completely remote students, and oftentimes our remote-learning status was common ground that brought us closer together.

We started off by forming virtual study groups and peer-editing workshops in order to have some form of social interaction, and then those later turned into virtual hangouts where we bonded over the struggles of being isolated from the outside world. This was a unique situation because I most likely would not have spoken much to these people if we had all been in person. By forcing myself to reach out to people I've never met and make friendships via Zoom, I pushed myself out of my comfort zone. This portion of social isolation has served me well because I am now much more comfortable with striking up conversations with random students in my classes, and if I have a remote class, I am the person who takes charge and forms the online or in-person study sessions because of the experiences that I had during remote learning. However, as with every technological barrier, there are definitely some difficulties that come along with remote learning, both from the technological standpoint as well as from the human use standpoint.

While there was a definite learning curve for me with regard to remote learning, I found that my teachers also had a somewhat difficult time transitioning into a hybrid teaching environment. There was a big stereotype amongst high schoolers that it was significantly easier to get a good grade in online classes, and yes, that was true for a couple of classes; however, for the majority of my classes, this was not true due to the unique teaching styles that each of my teachers had and how their expectations changed once we switched to remote learning.

Because of the pandemic, all of my teachers were thrown into a hybrid teaching environment with little to no prior experience. On top of my junior year being the most stressful year of high school, this made remote learning all the more difficult because there was no longer a "standard" for teaching anymore regarding the expectations that we as students had for each class, and the expectations that the teachers had from us.

There was a lot of disarray and disorganization as neither the students nor the faculty knew how to approach this new and unprecedented situation. Each teacher was learning on the fly while having to adjust their coursework and teach with both in-person and remote students like myself. This was probably one of the most difficult challenges in the hybrid-learning environment because teachers no longer had to adhere to the school's set of rules regarding accommodations, absences/tardies, due dates and late work, illnesses, paper *vs.* online tests and quizzes, etc. Teachers were thrust into a whole new world virtually overnight and some adapted well to the new environment, while others struggled.

Different teachers had different expectations of what they wanted their remote students to do and how much participation they expected from their remote students. Although, as time progressed, there seemingly became a two-way street of understanding and constructive criticism between some of the teachers and students. Some teachers were very open to how they could make their classes better for their remote learners and strived to implement these measures into their classroom environment. On the other hand, the students had to learn to be patient, speak up when necessary and appropriate, and even accept that some aspects of their previous school life were not going to be that way anymore, specifically regarding the types of assessments given, due dates, online assessments, etc. It was a huge learning experience for both sides that is not only applicable to the pandemic, but throughout the rest of high school into college, I found that many more of my teachers are much more approachable and open to constructive feedback about ways to make their class, material, and/or teaching style better or more understandable to more students.

Remote learning had a profound impact on who I am as a student as well as who I am as a person and taught me a lot about interacting with others in unique ways, both friends and faculty.

Eleanor Campbell

Class of 2024, Columbia University, New York City, Majoring in Economics

March 13th, 2020 is a date forever seared in my mind. Not because it was particularly traumatic or exciting but because it was the day everything changed. It was a Friday, and just like any other Friday, my peers and I felt energized and excited for the weekend. We were seniors in high school at the time, and each weekend of freedom brought us one step closer to what we viewed as that ultimate freedom: graduation. But there was something else in the air that day. An element of unknown. Our head of school had recently declared we would spend the next two weeks attending our classes virtually, moving online due to the spread of the novel coronavirus. We knew little about the virus at this point. I'd read about it for an assignment in AP Biology but hadn't given it much thought since. I remember thinking of the film *Contagion* but only transiently; for now the virus was a remote problem, a saga we watched unfold across the

Pacific Ocean. Few cases had been detected in the United States, and it was not yet clear how quickly and dangerously the virus would spread. Moving our classes online, a strategy I had never heard used in my lifetime, seemed an overreaction to a problem I felt confident public health experts could contain. My friends and I laughed over making the most of our "last day of school," but it never dawned on us our jokes might come true. We felt certain we would return to the same familiar halls a couple of weeks later.

Then, over that weekend even, the news began pouring in. It became apparent not just our school but the entire nation, the entire world, was on pause. Cases spread like wildfire, and my family's television was always turned to the news, reporting death and desperation in hotspots such as New York City. Weeks, days, hours before, it seemed the pandemic would end before it even started; now, it seemed the pandemic might just end the world as we knew it.

Through the chaos of the next few months, school seemed remarkably calm. I attended a small, private, non-residential, college preparatory school in the suburbs of Raleigh, North Carolina. Our school had an emergency digital learning plan, on which all of our teachers received training the week of March 9th, and which was fully operational by March 16th.

The first couple of weeks of online high school felt like just that: high school, but online. No one understood yet the importance of the medium and the impact attending a full day of school online had on students' and educators' well-being. After those first two weeks, our school adapted the schedule: our classes met less frequently, and we completed more of our work independently. For me, this change was a welcome one. I had always thrived off of scheduling, and the extrinsic motivation of honoring teachers who had poured so much into me over the past four years and the intrinsic motivation of finishing my senior year strong kept me on track. I know, though, that for students who thrived on the communal aspect of school, the dynamic nature of full classrooms and bustling hallways, it was difficult to stay motivated and energized in this new environment.

Come fall, I began my studies at Columbia University in the City of New York. Thanks to Covid-19, however, I did not actually study in New York. This seemed like a relatively unusual experience: although all schools experienced some level of disruption due to the pandemic, most of my classmates from high school at least lived on their colleges' campuses, even if some or all of their classes were conducted online. For me, a fully remote first year was not as distressing as one might expect. Having not been to college yet, it seemed like merely another transition along the way. My life and routine would have changed drastically either way, even if I had physically gone to school, actually even if there hadn't been a pandemic at all. I found virtual classes very conducive to my learning style: I've always been a slow note-taker, so recorded classes were a welcome way by which I could make sure I didn't miss a single detail of a lecture. I considered it fortunate, actually, to adjust to the academic novelty of college before the social novelty. Having always lived a fairly busy and structured life, the free time offered by a college schedule left flexibility I simply hadn't had in the preceding years. A year of disconnect from our usually bustling world only made me more inspired to fill that free time with the lively culture of the city to which I was to relocate. It made me prioritize not only the formal artistic and cultural opportunities of New York but also the informal, transient connections and conversations that take place on any college campus.

I had no pre-pandemic college experience to which to compare my experience over the past two years, but it seems the nature of college learning has changed. Our first year back was an odd one: with quarantine and isolation policies still in place, professors tried their best to balance the value of in-person classes with flexibility for students who could not attend. Some came closer to striking that balance than others. I, at least, found classes retaining as many of the pandemic procedures as possible preferable. Zoom and recordings, to me, were an excellent implementation regardless of the circumstances. Of course I would always prefer attending a lecture in person: the remote option substituted not for in-person classes but for missing lectures altogether under unavoidable circumstances such as illness, travel. Not all of my classmates agree, and in response to empty lecture halls, many professors have stopped offering Zoom altogether. I understand why they do this: not to punish students but to disincentivize skipping lectures and thus to help students help themselves. However, I hope more instructors will come to recognize the value of their flexibility in helping those students who truly need accommodations. I believe education is by its very nature what you make of it, and new pandemic policies simply provide a new arena for this truth.

Aidan Carroll

Instructor in Computer Science, Deerfield Academy, Deerfield, MA

The most prevalent question I was asked leading up to the 2020–21 school year was, "How are you feeling?" I have found this question relevant every year, but in 2020 it carried an extra significance. It was my first year teaching after four years working in the technology industry. It was my first year at a New England boarding school, having spent most of my life in North Carolina. However, to most people the question referred to the ongoing Covid-19 pandemic and the prospect of starting the school year with online classes.

My answer was always, "I actually feel pretty good." While I was certainly naive, I had a number of perceived advantages over other teachers.

I was new to teaching, so I had been prepared to make new materials for all my classes. There was nothing I had to change or remake. I could design my class for the challenges ahead, rather than adapting in-person material to a virtual or hybrid classroom.

I was teaching Computer Science, so, of course, Computer Science was going to be easy to teach on the computer. I intended to de-emphasize lectures and emphasize project-based learning. Students could share their screens as they programmed, and computer literacy was a skill I wanted them to practice.

And lastly, boarding school offered a number of advantages not shared by day schools. The school was able to isolate, provide testing, and heavily limit the number of close contacts for both students and teachers. All of this allowed us to primarily teach in person for the entire year.

The first week of class was entirely virtual because students quarantined after traveling to school. We then switched to a hybrid model, as some students were unable to make the trip to campus for a variety of reasons. For the remainder of the school year I had 10–20 percent of my students online and the rest in person.

Before the school year started, I focused my preparation around myself and my material, not on the thing that every teacher should focus on: the students. The inherent issue was not that I had to present my material differently, but that the students had to consume it differently. More precisely, students had to rely on their ability to communicate, something that teenagers tend to struggle with.

Teachers communicate ideas to students, and students communicate their understanding to teachers. Students spend their schooling practicing how to consume and express complex ideas through different modalities. Adding the additional layer of technology, changes that. It is like changing the weight of a basketball after years of practice; shooting percentage is inevitably going to drop.

Imagine a traditional classroom from the perspective of a student. The teacher has just explained something the student does not understand. Students have developed strategies for coping with that situation. It could be to raise their hand, ask a neighbor, approach the teacher after class, or simply look confused.

Now assume the same situation in a virtual setting. The teacher has given the same explanation and the student has the same understanding (or lack there-of) as before. How does the student get the teacher's attention? How do they ask a classmate for help? How do they stay after class, or express confusion over a digital connection?

While there are solutions to these issues, my mistake was not being explicit with my students and not giving them ample time to practice. How should they interrupt me? When should they ask questions? When should they talk to classmates about what they learned?

For some students this was not a problem. Those more extroverted had no problem interrupting me. Students who were more independent had no issue supplementing lectures with readings or other resources. However, too many faded into the background. Zoom made it all the easier by automatically deprioritizing silent participants.

This polarized my class. Strong students coped with the challenges, and weak students slipped through the cracks. While this is not a problem unique to distance education, the added medium of the internet exacerbated the problem. I could not easily tell when a student was distracted during a lecture, or when they were not contributing to a breakout room discussion. I could not watch their process as they attempted to solve a problem. I could not take advantage of daily interactions outside of class, an especially effective tool at a boarding school.

My interactions with my online students were confined to class time, with the occasional email or scheduled meeting. My other students were able to ask me questions in passing. Even a passing question in the halls like "How is your project going?" was a check-up that my online students didn't get.

I didn't realize the impact of these check-ins until my second year of teaching, when all of my students were in person. My first year I had no reference for where students should be, and I was so concerned with preparing each class that I simply assumed my students were keeping up.

Ultimately, distance learning and distance education live by the same principles as everything else. If you want to be good at it, you need to practice. Students need years to develop strategies for learning, and instructors need years to develop strategies for teaching. No matter how much we prepare, no substitute exists for experience. I experienced a year of hybrid education, but I have spent over half my life in traditional classrooms.

Independent of the Covid-19 crisis, no one expected me to be as effective a teacher in my first year as the thirty-year veterans (and I dare say their expectations were spot on). A freshman shouldn't be expected to absorb the same amount of information as a senior. In 2020, everyone was a first-year teacher with a classroom full of freshmen. Students found their learning strategies less effective, and teachers weren't much better.

As we continue to move forward into the new normal, students and teachers must take time to practice the skills of virtual communication. Technology is evolving, and so is the world around it. Virtual meetings are becoming more frequent in many industries, and students who are comfortable with different online mediums will be better positioned to succeed. The best way to build this competency is still unknown. Schools could offer additional classes to students from organizations like Global Online Academy. Teachers could try flipped classrooms, and focus on asynchronous learning. Whatever the solution might be, it would be a disservice to everyone if we did not continue to develop our hard-won experiences with distance education.

Laura Kovalaske

Math Instructor, Green Hope High School, Cary, NC

Being catapulted into the world of remote learning in the spring of 2020 with no preparation felt like an overwhelming challenge. As both a high school math teacher and a parent, the standard items like content and technology were not the issue. The biggest obstacle to overcome for me in remote learning were the things you can't create on a computer screen or through a camera. Human interaction and collaboration were severely lacking. I can learn how to create interactive websites and videos and I can put my students in breakout rooms, but these things cannot replace the impact of being together in a physical space and sharing ideas. While remote learning was an unexpected way to broaden myself both as an educator and a parent, the process and outcomes did not meet my expectations.

The initial jump into remote learning in March 2020 felt more like academic survival. How can I make sure I give my kids the content they need to finish out the school year and not be too far behind for the next? I became a fast expert on all things Google and found new ways to utilize the features of my Canvas site. At home we set up individual learning areas for my sixth and ninth grader. I created my own little virtual classroom on the dining room table. I fully anticipated that the Covid threat would pass and things would return to normal the next school year.

In the fall of 2020 when it was apparent we would not be returning to the classroom, I initially didn't have a problem with the idea of remote learning. Students log into a Google Meet, I teach, they pay attention, take notes, and ask questions when they don't understand. I upload my lesson to Canvas as additional support, they do homework, check answers online, and come to class the next day with questions. How hard can this be? I felt that if I could do it every day in the classroom, I could handle it in the virtual world. I started the 2020–21 school year excited and ready to go. I had a perfect picture of what I envisioned for the upcoming semester.

In my desire and push to create the most "normal" environment for my kids, what I didn't think about was the fact that this situation was not normal. What worked for me in a regular classroom, was not going to work online. I expected teenagers to behave like responsible adults. My district did not enforce the use of cameras so most days were spent staring at a black void of thirty or more silent squares on a screen with no feedback. It was rare to hear a student's voice and instead questions and answers were communicated through a chat box. The relationships I cherish and rely on with my students during the first few weeks of school weren't developing. By the end of the first month, I knew very little about the kids in my class and the students that started the semester with their cameras on were dwindling. One student was kind enough to send an email apology stating she felt like everyone was staring at her during class so she was going to turn her camera off. I was losing them. I found myself manifesting ideas about who my kids were based solely on their choice of avatar for their Google Meet, if they chose one at all. Each day was more stressful and lonelier than the one before.

I was forced to rethink my approach. We had just made it through a major shutdown during the spring semester of 2020, and this was an opportunity to put time and thought into the new skills I had acquired during that time. I reimagined my approach, but still kept everything centered around me and my teaching of the content. I flipped my classroom and created video recordings of the lessons that students could watch before class instead of after so we could utilize our time together for practice. I still encouraged verbal responses during live class time, but I added surveys and polls in Google Meet to gather feedback and hopefully inspire a few more students to participate. By tracking Canvas video access, poll data during and after class allowed me to form a better picture of who my students were and what they were capable of. I was able to edit my lessons and to reach out to students and families and offer support like I would have in a regular classroom. It provided a way for me to connect with my kids and their families and develop those relationships that I had been lacking earlier in the semester. In-person lunch tutorials were replaced with one-on-one video chats and, surprisingly, most students were willing and even eager to meet. The one thing I avoided was using multiple websites and platforms as a replacement for delivery of content. Everyday my inbox included multiple emails about a new app or website that promised to enhance the remote learning experience. The whole online environment was still confusing and difficult enough so I kept things simple. Interactive sites and online practice resources all have their individual strengths for student learning, but if I wanted to develop that human interaction and collaboration I was missing, they needed to see and hear me every day.

Assessments changed as well. In math nothing can replace the power of putting pencil to paper and reasoning your way through an equation or proof, but the challenge of ensuring academic integrity became the main concern. Online apps that provide answers with steps to anyone who uses them forced me to rethink how I assessed students. The traditional ninety-minute test wasn't going to work. I had to find a way for the students to show me they understood the content, but in a way that worked in the virtual world. I realized this was the one place where I could take a step back and let the students shine. Their creativity and collaboration in recording teaching videos and designing artistic presentations allowed their personalities to emerge while still showing me their comprehension of content. I was learning and connecting with my students and they were connecting with each other, but in a different way than before.

As a parent, I also wanted the remote experience to be positive for my own children. At the start, we purchased bulletin boards, calendars, organizers, laptops and upgraded Wi-Fi routers. Everyone was given a quiet space to work in different rooms in the house. The hardest part was making sure work was getting done. The hours that I put in to making sure my own students were engaged were sometimes lost to my children. The balance was not there. I didn't need to be an expert at social studies or science, I just needed to be present and that was difficult. I found I was putting a lot of trust in them and hoping that they had a strong work ethic. My oldest thrived in the remote learning environment. She enjoyed the flexibility it provided her to work at her own pace, but she had always been good at prioritizing and planning out her time effectively. She's also a person who enjoys the company of a few close friends and despises the politics of high school, so remote learning removed the burden of having to physically go to school for her. I could see the relief she felt each day as she happily climbed the stairs to her room to start class. My younger son needed more structure. To him, school had become boring and the fun was gone. Every day was a battle to complete his assignments, turn things in on time and to put effort into the work he was doing. There was no learning, just doing. I found myself praying every night that he would make it through and I lost sleep worrying that he would leave sixth grade with about as much knowledge as he entered.

The most unexpected challenge was knowing when to stop. My home was my classroom and I had everything I needed to do my job right in front of me. It was a welcome convenience, but also a hazard. It was too easy to get up in the morning, grab a cup of coffee, go right to the dining room table and work. After class, it was easy to sit at the table and keep working. I didn't have to pack up and go home to meet my kids because I was home and my kids were upstairs. There was no separation of work and family life and I never looked at a clock. For all of that time, I can honestly say I don't know if I accomplished any more or less than I did when we were in person.

Does remote learning have its place? In some cases, yes. Do I want to go back to remote learning? No. I appreciate the things I gained during my experience ... new ways to reach and assess students, flexibility, but those do not compare to what I felt I lost during that time. I missed the ability to talk face to face or high-five a student as they entered my room because they earned a high score on the last test. I missed being able to pull someone out in the hall to give a pep talk because while they may be having a rough time, I see their potential. For my own kids, I missed the structure that a school day can provide. I wanted them to feel that they were connected to their teachers, their classmates and their school outside of a computer screen. At the end of the semester, most of my students met their learning goals and my own children passed their classes, but I feel the gains would have been greater had the year not been remote. No amount of technology can replace the benefits and growth that come from in-person interaction and collaboration in the classroom.

Guy Lancaster

Editor, CALS Encyclopedia of Arkansas, Little Rock, AR

Between 2016 and 2020, I taught, as an adjunct professor, a fall semester graduate-level seminar titled, "Power, Privilege, and Oppression," for the University of Arkansas Clinton School of Public Service. The class entailed an interdisciplinary exploration of the historical and present day dimensions of oppression based upon class, race, gender, etc., with an eye toward the potential of ameliorating these—or at least being aware of them—in future public service work. During the five years I taught it, my class typically varied between half a dozen and a dozen students, some Arkansans but many from the far corners of the United States and the world at large. My full-time public history job offered me flexible enough hours to teach this three-hour seminar one morning a week, especially as the building containing my classroom was just right next door.

Not long after the first reported case of Covid-19 in Arkansas on March 11, 2020, many state universities began moving classes online. Early during the summer break, I was informed that fall classes would also be online, with video instruction occurring through some combination of Blackboard and Google Meet. I had never used Blackboard before, but my university offered both remote instruction and additional money for the added trouble, which was a luxury many adjunct professors did not experience. By this time, my full-time job had also shifted to remote work. However, despite the relative convenience of this, the training necessary to learn Blackboard necessitated burning through a lot of my paid time off.

In addition, as the university had to juggle the schedule a bit to accommodate the shift to online, my class became the final refuge for a number of students who needed that last second-year elective, and so the limit on students was expanded to twenty, which increased my grading workload dramatically throughout the fall. Typically, my semester started with some more structured lectures to lay down general concepts but would shift, about halfway through, to much more in the way of general discussion centered upon the books, as the students became comfortable with the subject matter and the format. However, rather than a relaxed three-hour seminar with a nice break in the middle, I was asked to turn my lecture outlines into more detailed notes that the students would access beforehand via Blackboard, and then we would have a ninety-minute general discussion via Google Meet.

Although my institution was gracious and accommodating and truly did their best, there was no way to make this a truly immersive intellectual experience. Some of my students were parents whose own children were doing remote instruction from home at the same time and so would have to disappear for small stretches of time. Some of my students were from various parts of Africa or the Middle East, and while they were certainly capable of conversational English, there is a palpable difference between conversing in person, where one has access to the broader range of body language that helps so much to convey meaning, and conversing through a computer, especially over an occasionally ratty internet connection. Moreover, the whole set-up simply did not facilitate organic conversation, did not lend itself to that dynamic whereby individuals, through the shared experience of this class, start to coalesce as a group.

More than everything else, however, the remote experience simply flattened our conversation. With a title like "Power, Privilege, and Oppression," and with a reading list that has included such books as *The Racial Contract* by Charles W. Mills and *Down Girl: The Logic of Misogyny* by Kate Manne, my class regularly touched upon some of the most sensitive issues under scrutiny in the United States today. My students regularly came from an array of philosophical, religious, and political backgrounds with their own unique body of experiences—including both Iraq War veterans and antiwar activists in the same semester one time—and not only had I worked to challenge the easy orthodoxies of both Right and Left, but I also worked to make my classroom a place where "dumb questions" were permitted, where people could share their own stories or preconceptions without judgment.

However, all of that fell apart in the attempt to teach online. The fact that we were requested to record classroom discussions for those who may be unable to attend made people much more unwilling to ask those dumb questions or share anything that might reveal some kind of ignorance, lest it be broadcast beyond the bounds of the class. Second, that format was much less welcoming for my international students, who became increasingly shy due to the challenges of communication. Third, people would regularly, during the discussion, drop links to various articles into the chat, and while this was meant to be helpful, it nonetheless meant that all of us were often simply not on the same (web)page while the class was going on.

As Leonard Cohen once sang, "I did my best—it wasn't much." I feel the same way about that semester. But there was one thing I did succeed in doing. My previous student evaluations regularly praised my grading, namely the fact that I added extensive comments to student papers before returning them. I was determined to keep this up despite having twenty graduate students in my class, and so I did. And then, when I submitted my final grades, I told my university that this was the end of the line for me as an adjunct. That plague year was my last year, and I have not looked back.

Sarah Swain

*Dean of Innovation and Experiential Learning at
The Field School, Washington, DC*

It is Monday, March 9th, 2020. Talk of a global pandemic has spread rapidly and resulted in school being canceled. We have one day of professional development to prepare for a possible remote school transition in the coming days. Teachers are quickly briefed on using Google Meet, making sure all assignments and resources are posted in the digital classroom and given the guidelines to do direct instruction for the first twenty minutes of the schedule and then have their virtual room open for help and questions. This experience exemplified the term "crash course."

Education plunged headfirst into the biggest transition of the past century with the Covid-19 pandemic. Schools where students did not have access to personal computers were forced to quickly adapt and ensure students could connect to virtual classes. Those schools that could not find a solution in the first year could no longer ignore the critical importance of students developing digital literacy. Beyond making it irrefutable that all students need to have access to a computer for a complete education, the pandemic drove innovation in pedagogy and programs that would have taken years under different circumstances. As we emerge from the depths of this crash course it is critical to assess the lessons learned and uplift the most valuable to transform education for the better of all students.

On March 12th, 2020 we got the memo that the following Monday we would start remote learning "for two weeks." My AP Environmental Science had just visited the Wake County North Carolina Habitat for Humanity building site as part of a three-week project. The final product challenged them to propose more energy-efficient home designs to panelists from that organization and an energy efficiency engineering firm. As the world shut down, their team-based research and preparations for the final presentation (which moved to Zoom) flowed seamlessly into the virtual learning environment. The routine of feedback sessions, collaborative Google docs, and evidence gathering gave students a foundation even as everything around them shifted.

As two weeks turned into two months, I had to shift my perspective to accommodate an extended remote learning paradigm. The project served as a smooth transition but now I had to use many different strategies to keep students engaged and motivated. I found that what worked best were active, student-driven strategies. To learn the dangers of air pollutants, pairs of students worked together to research and present to their peers. To make it relevant, students conducted a home air pollution audit and worked together to determine the leading concerns. As I worked to make each day more interesting and help students be accountable for their own learning, I left behind traditional direct instruction and employed many other strategies. On days when I couldn't keep up with the changing pace, I employed programs like Pear Deck and Kahoot to gather data about each student's ability to apply information to a new situation or problem.

The following year I started a Master's in Education Entrepreneurship from the University of Pennsylvania. What was supposed to be an executive-style, low residency, in-person program became a fully remote journey. This program curates a cohort of forty diverse educators and business-minded folks to build new platforms, programs, and pedagogies to help transform education at scale. Even at a prestigious university, the professors were learning in real time how to craft exemplary remote learning experiences. From the other side of the screen, I got to observe some real Masters at work.

From the beginning, I knew the professors were ready to guide us through a pivotal process. First, the final Capstone was a practical application of all our skills in service to designing our own business model. This work-focused approach to earning a degree resonated and felt relevant to the work and a future I wanted for myself and to help build for students. The initial Design Thinking class engaged us in a series of exercises to enact the method. We also began to explore the landscape of our eventual business model, testing ideas as we progressed.

Master remote learning designer Dr. Susan Yoon led the fall semester course Designing for Learning Environments. The course sequence was expertly planned for maximum student engagement and application. The introductory class skillfully showcased the use of discussion breakouts, survey question functions, and activity-based assessment to maximize our understanding of the material and course direction. In further weeks, teams of students worked prior to each meeting to facilitate activities and discussions about the assigned readings. As we read about best practices in engaging pedagogy, teams were tasked to create exemplary learning experiences for our peers. With built-in opportunities for reflection and critique, this format of student-designed learning experiences provided the best way to apply and test pedagogical designs. For the final project in this course, each student designed a unique learning experience for their Capstone business model, a practical and relevant application of the work in class.

Reflecting on the pandemic transition to remote learning solidifies my commitment to helping teachers develop pedagogies that engage students and connect them to their world in compelling ways. The best practices in remote learning are best practices in the in-person classroom and vice versa. In my current role in education leadership, I'm helping teachers build out problem-solving projects in their classrooms. To immerse teachers in this style of learning, I planned the first week of new faculty training to engage interdisciplinary faculty teams with the community, developing ways to use the city in their curriculum. The final team products were resources and curriculum ideas presented to each other and the whole faculty.

As education navigates a world transformed by the pandemic, there are key takeaways from remote learning that can inform and enhance all learning. Develop thinking routines. Limit passive student experiences. Be intentional about class, small group, and individual activities to further learning and engagement. Design lessons with a variety of pedagogical approaches and activities. Last, and most important, ensure a relevant and compelling driver of learning, preferably a community connected problem.

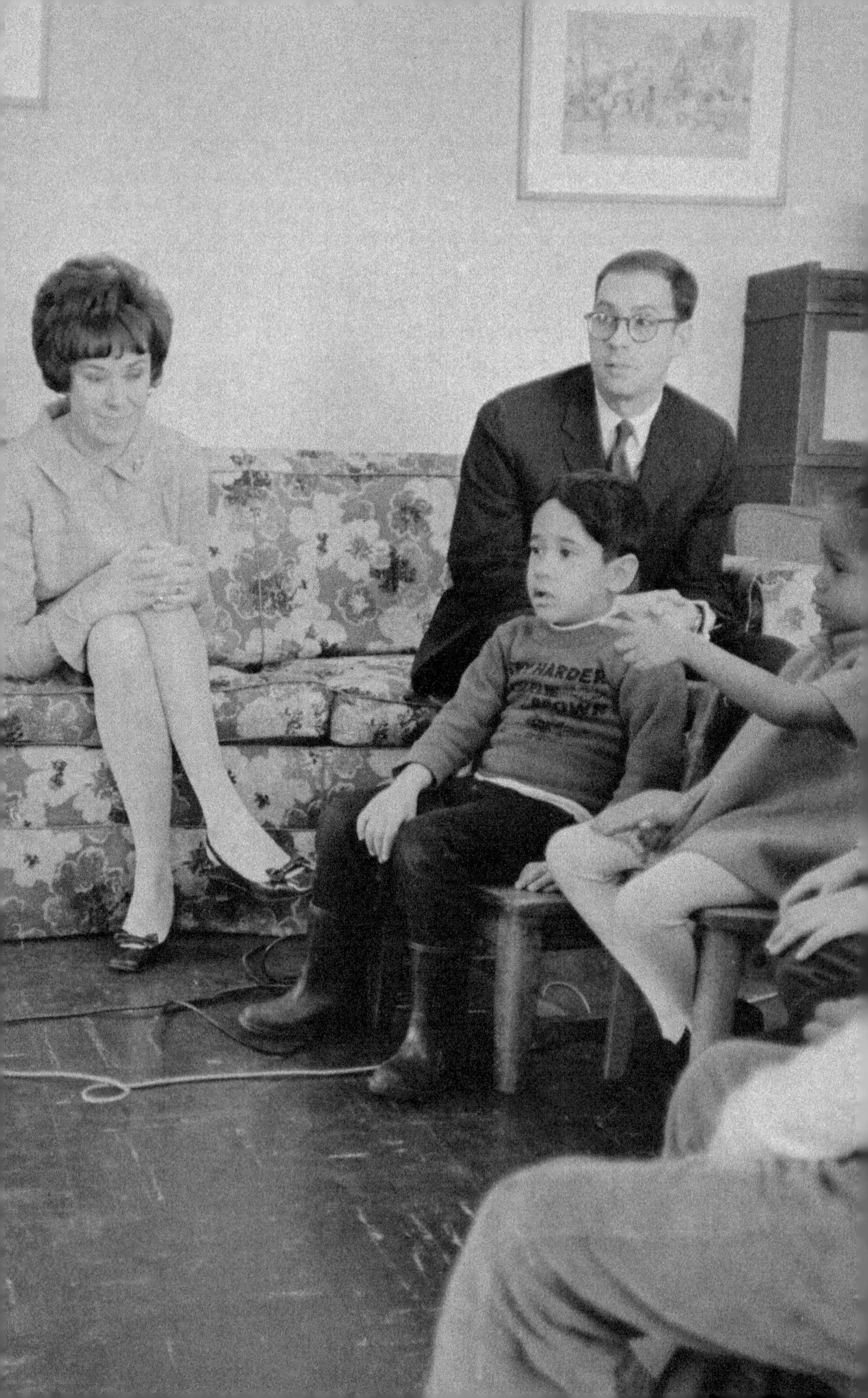
HARDER

4
Profiles

Given its long history, not to mention the speed of its most recent evolution, there are countless individuals and organizations that could be spotlighted in a collection like this. The diverse group presented here seeks to offer the reader a historical sense of the changes central to the development of distance education, as well as the multiple aspects and perspectives from which one can view this potentially transformative approach to learning. The following selection of profiles includes people and organizations whose efforts and vision have and will continue to shape this dynamic field of education.

People

Joan Ganz Cooney (1929–)

Joan Ganz Cooney is a television producer and writer. One of the founders of the Children's Television Workshop (CTW), she is best known for creating the *Sesame Street* educational program for children. Cooney's own career mirrored the evolution of TV as an educational tool, and her pioneering work not only added another dimension to the efforts to educate the nation's youth, but also helped further discussions about how best to reach a new generation of American young people.

Joan Ganz was born on November 30, 1929. An Arizona native, she moved to Washington, DC after earning her bachelor's degree in education from the University of Arizona in 1951. She initially worked in a clerical position in the US State Department (Zane 1998). Inspired by Father James Keller's Christopher

---

Joan Ganz Cooney, creator of the groundbreaking educational children's television show *Sesame Street*, observing children watching the show, 1969. (Photo by Charlotte Brooks. LOOK Magazine Photograph Collection, Library of Congress Prints & Photographs Division)

Movement and its emphasis on the power of the individual to make an impact, she decided to become involved in television and media (Watson 2023).

After a brief stint as a reporter with the *Arizona Republic*, Ganz returned to the East Coast in 1953 where she worked as a publicist in the television industry, first for David Sarnoff at RCA, then at NBC, and finally at CBS with the *United States Steel Hour*. When a colleague left to work for WGBH-TV, Boston's educational television station, she had an epiphany, realizing that she wanted to work in educational television as well (Riechers 2003).

Ganz soon secured a job as a producer with WNDT Channel 13, the New York area's non-commercial public television station (and precursor to PBS station WNET). For the next half-dozen years, she was a documentary producer while also producing a wide range of issue-oriented debate shows that covered topics like poverty, United States–Cuba policy (which aired just a week before the Cuban Missile Crisis), race relations, and many of the other subjects dogging the nation in the tumultuous 1960s. Her efforts were well received, and she earned a number of local Emmy awards as she helped develop Channel 13 into a vehicle for engaging and informing the public (Zane 1998). During this time, she also married Timothy Cooney, a political aide with the New York City's mayor's office.

At an informal gathering at the Cooney home in February 1966, a guest speculated about whether television could be used to teach young children (Zane 1998). It was a question that changed the trajectory of her life. After further discussions, Cooney agreed to undertake a feasibility study on the possibility of creating an educational television program for preschool-age children. Taking a leave from WNDT in the summer of 1967, Cooney traveled around the United States and Canada using a grant from the Carnegie Corporation, talking to experts in television, education, and child development. The result was a 55-page document titled, "The Potential Uses of Television in Preschool Education," and it became the impetus for the launching of Children's Television Workshop as well as the outline for the show that would become *Sesame Street* (Watson 2023). Cooney and Carnegie executive Lloyd Morrisett spent the next two years raising $8 million, developing the show, and founding CTW (Riechers 2003).

Cooney was named executive director of CTW in February 1968, becoming one of the first female executives in American television. *Sesame Street* hit the airwaves on November 10, 1969. The show Cooney was instrumental in creating changed the very nature of children's television. Its tremendous critical reception was made clear by the three Emmys, the one Peabody, and the *Time* cover story the show garnered in its first year ("Who's Afraid …" 1970). It was a smash hit.

Sesame Street and *The Electric Company* were phenomena representative of a new frontier in education in general and distance education in particular. From the start, educational television was an offering that worked, having a major and measurable positive impact on its viewers. Indeed, early research indicated that small children from poor and middle-class families who watched *Sesame Street* did better on cognitive tests than those who did not. Similarly, frequent viewers performed better than those who watched less often. Too, children who started watching at age three learned faster than those who started watching at four (Adler 1972).

By 1972, 80 percent of the nation's 12 million preschool children had watched *Sesame Street*. By developing animated characters and puppets with whom the youthful audience could engage and combining them with adults who reinforced various lessons, the innovators at CTW created a distance education platform of a sort. CTW emphasized interactive programming for children rather than content that turned children into disengaged "zombies," as one researcher stated, who were less likely to retain the lessons contained in the broadcasts (Adler 1972).

Cooney's efforts offered new insights into the power of television as a teaching tool, while also laying groundwork for the future education endeavors of generations to come. The extent of her accomplishments was recognized anew when the Covid-19 pandemic made teachers across the spectrum recognize just how much effort and creativity it took to make teaching and learning in front of a screen an effective and developmentally appropriate enterprise.

Michael Grahame Moore (1938–)

Michael Grahame Moore is a leading figure in the development of distance education. He was one of the early voices to assert that distance education was not just about geographical separation, but that it also involved and required a different pedagogical approach. He is acclaimed as a founding father of modern distance education, with the *Routledge Encyclopaedia of Educational Thinkers* calling him one of the "most important, innovative, influential, and interesting thinkers on education of all time" (Cooper 2016).

Born on February 28, 1938, Moore's longtime interest in and advocacy for distance education has its roots in an even older commitment to adult and continuing education. After earning an undergraduate degree from the London School of Economics, he got his first taste of teaching in the early 1960s, serving as a high school history and geography instructor in Horley, Surrey, in England (Moore, PhD n.d.).

Moore followed that stint with a seven-year sojourn to rural east Africa where from 1963 to 1967 he was an education officer in Kismu, Kenya. That position included a mix of administrative responsibilities and teaching high school economics classes. In addition, Moore helped develop a correspondence radio course in economics—one of the first distance education programs in Africa. Moore moved from there to the University of East Africa in Nairobi, Kenya in 1967. For the next three years, he was responsible for the university's continuing education programs in each of Kenya's four major cities—Kisumu, Mombasa, Nairobi, and Nakuru. His responsibilities included the planning and the delivery of a range of courses for the military, professions, and labor unions. He also worked with the health, literacy, and agricultural agencies to help ensure the delivery of basic education programs in the country's rural communities (Moore, PhD n.d.).

In 1970 Moore returned to the United States and the University of Wisconsin-Madison, where he earned a PhD in 1973. In 1972, he made his initial mark in the academic world when, drawing upon his dissertation research, he introduced the term "distance education" into his work (Moore—HoF 2013). During the same period, he came under the tutelage of Charles Wedemeyer, assisting the revered innovator while teaching and researching about the use of communications media (Saba 2014b).

Wisconsin proved to be the jumping off point for a career of teaching, research, and advocacy of distance education and its role as a vehicle for his longtime interest in adult education. With his PhD in hand, Moore headed to Canada, where he became an assistant professor at St. Francis Xavier University in Nova Scotia. He taught courses in adult education while also conducting research on the cognitive style of adult learners (Moore, PhD n.d.).

In 1977, Moore began an almost decade-long stint at the Open University in the United Kingdom. During this time at Britain's foremost distance teaching university, he had both administrative and teaching responsibilities, and he was particularly involved with the university's first non-credit continuing education courses. As a member of a number of design teams, he helped with the development of the first university-level distance education course in adult education. He also taught Open University course E201, "Personality in Learning," a pioneering 30-week distance education course in educational psychology (Moore, PhD n.d.).

During his time in the United Kingdom, Moore also returned to the University of Wisconsin for a few summers, where he taught graduate seminars in distance education in the United States, courses that are believed to have been the only graduate distance education courses in the world at the time. In 1985, Moore returned to the United States to begin a long-term tenure on the faculty of Penn State University where, in 1986, he co-founded the American Center for the Study of Distance Education. The following year he founded the *American Journal of Distance Education* for which he served as editor (Barbour and Reeves 2006).

Moore's lengthy stay at Penn State coincided with the beginnings of the serious movement towards expanded distance education. Moore's research, advocacy, and leadership played an important, if often overlooked, part in that effort. As the technology needed to make what came to be known as online learning came to the fore, much of the research about learning that helped shape its pedagogy had its roots in work Moore had originally done relating to applied adult learners. Many of his findings and theories were equally applicable to children.

The earliest major efforts at marketing distance education targeted adult learners interested in earning their degrees or exploring professional opportunities for growth and advancement for credentials and certifications accessible online. Moore's research and advocacy were critical to the advancement, growth, and development of these education opportunities (Saba 2014b).

Moore's tireless efforts did a great deal to advance the cause of distance education. He also did his own research and produced both articles and books, including the *Handbook of Distance Education*, which first appeared in 2004 and was updated with new editions in 2007, 2012, and 2016. In 1989, he founded and supervised the Distance Education Online Symposium which he oversaw until 2001, an effort that ran parallel to the founding in 1988 of the American Center for the Study of Distance Education, for which he served as director until 2001 (Moore, PhD n.d.).

Moore's decades of advocacy for distance education alternatives earned him numerous awards and accolades. He was the recipient of honorary degrees from universities in the United States and Canada as well as Mexico and Brazil. He has been inducted into numerous education-related halls of fame and has been a visiting professor at universities around the globe. An innovative and creative thinker, one deeply committed to serving adult learners and others for whom the normal brick-and-mortar set-up does not work, Michael Grahame Moore has been an instrumental figure in the development of modern distance education.

Muriel Oaks (1943–) and Janet Ross Kendall (1945–)

Given its close ties to Silicon Valley and the tech industry, distance education has often been seen as an overwhelmingly male preserve. But over the course of two and a half decades, the pioneering partnership of Muriel Oaks and Janet Ross Kendall not only made Washington State University's distance education program a standard bearer in the fast-developing field, but also demonstrated that commitment to excellence, openness to innovation, and dedication to expanding educational opportunities are not limited by gender.

By the time they retired from Washington State in 2010, Oaks and Kendall, who were the Dean of the Center for Distance and Professional Education and WSU Online's director of academic programs, respectively, had combined for over fifty years of service at Washington State, and for forty-six of those years they had worked together developing the university's distance education capabilities ("Pioneers ... to retire" 2010). But they had taken very different paths to the university and to the partnership that would add a distinctive dimension to the institution's identity.

Muriel Oaks was born in 1943 and grew up in Caldwell, Idaho, earning her bachelor's degree in medical technology from the University of Idaho in 1965. She then worked as a medical technologist for ten years at hospitals in California, Washington, DC, and Pullman, Washington, before earning a master's of education and a PhD in education from Washington State University. She began working for the university in 1979 and in 1983 joined what would become the Center for Distance and Professional Education (Oaks CV n.d.).

When Samuel H. Smith assumed the presidency of Washington State University in 1985, he brought with him a vision for using video technology to teach students in the university's new branch campuses in Spokane, Tri-Cities, and Vancouver, Washington. It was an ambitious goal, and when Oaks assumed the position of program director for Washington Higher Education Telecommunication System (WHETS) in 1988 (a post she held until 1993), it fell to her to make Smith's vision a reality (Oaks CV n.d.).

Fortunately, Oaks found a kindred spirit in Janet Ross Kendall. Kendall had earned her bachelor's degree from Occidental College and her PhD in Educational Psychology from the University of Iowa. Before she arrived at WSU in 1987, Kendall taught undergraduate and graduate reading courses at a number of different universities in both Canada and the United States ("She's the 'Boy Scout'" 2009). But her arrival in the same year that Oaks became director of WHETS marked the beginning of a new era, as Kendall joined with Oaks to begin to make Smith's vision a reality.

Their initial assignment was to find a way to deliver courses from the main campus in Pullman to the recently established Spokane, Tri-Cities, and Vancouver campuses. "At first, we didn't have faculty or staff," Smith said, and the new campuses consisted of little more than a spare room in a high school or bank building ("Pioneers … to retire" 2010). With the creation of WHETS, and through the use of two-way audio video conferencing using microwave transmissions, they were able to do it. By 1992, they were able to offer asynchronous instruction through videotaped lectures and a sophisticated voice-mail system, and in 1998 they moved online ("Pioneers … to retire" 2010).

None of this was easy. Indeed, as one writer observed, "distance education was a lonely place" in the early 1990s, with very few colleges or universities making the effort ("Pioneers … to retire" 2010). Oaks herself remembered that "It was a huge leap of faith for us—and for the university" ("Pioneers … to retire" 2010). But they were willing to experiment and unafraid of failure in the pursuit of success. Oaks once said her work in medicine, where decisions were often a matter of life or death, gave her a perspective on their venture that made her more willing to try—and fail—and then try again, if that was what was needed (Nappi 2010). It was an approach that paid off handsomely.

In 1993, Oaks assumed the position of director of Extended University Services (EUS). Later, as WSU's efforts expanded, she became Dean of the Center for Distance and Professional Education (CDPE), which has recently become the program for Academic Outreach and Innovation (AOI) as well as the home of the Global Campus (Oaks CV n.d.). In these posts Oaks became widely recognized for her work in distance education, a field she saw as providing the opportunity to use learning technologies to support the land grant mission to both expand access to WSU programs and to improve the student experience.

Under Oaks' leadership, and working with Kendall, WSU became one of the nation's first universities to deliver video-based distance education courses. With a determination to provide expanded access to quality education globally, Oaks also oversaw the transition from online courses to full online program offerings, and the progress was impressive. At the time of their retirement, WSU Online—renamed to reflect its modern evolution—offered seven undergraduate degree majors and four graduate degrees ("Pioneers … to retire" 2010).

In her role as Director of Distance Degree Programs (DDP) at WSU, Oaks oversaw the coordination of the university's distance learning degree-completion programs, while also working with departments and colleges to develop additional programs and courses. DDP is noteworthy for its efforts to offer students a complete set of services. It was in that domain that Kendall, who was the primary overseer of student services, really made her mark, developing a program recognized as a national leader for the comprehensive services available to its distance learning students (Oaks Award n.d.).

Kendall's efforts also included launching the Northwest eTutoring Consortium, and she built partnerships with academic and administrative units across both WSU and with other institutions ("She's the 'Boy Scout'" 2009). These efforts helped earn her numerous honors, including the 2009 Professional Contributions to Continuing Education award from the University Continuing Education Association Region West ("Pioneers … to retire" 2010). Laird Hartman, the dean of Continuing Education of Weber State University, observed, "I view Janet as the continuing education 'Boy Scout' for the West region. She is so courteous, kind, trustworthy, punctual, informative, thoughtful, insightful and energetic" ("She's the 'Boy Scout'" 2009).

At the same time that Oaks and Kendall were establishing WSU Online as a model for inclusive distance education, they were actively sharing the message both domestically and in international appearances. Both women were active contributors to the broad-based development of the world of distance education, speaking and writing on numerous facets of the developing concept. Each contributed numerous articles to professional journals and presented at many conferences. The 2008 article, "Building Communities within a Diverse Adult Population," which they co-wrote with peers from New York University for *Continuing Higher Education Review*, was particularly noteworthy for the way it reflected their longtime efforts to make distance education more of an educational experience, and not just a means to a diploma or professional credentials, for their diverse clientele (Gossett et al. 2008).

Both women earned numerous awards and accolades for their work over the course of the years. WSU honored Oaks by establishing the Oaks Academic Technology Award, which recognizes the innovative use of technology to transform teaching and learning. Kendall's devoted efforts to the UCEA, where she was chair of UCEA Region West and for which she led various committees and task forces, were rewarded with the organization's Elizabeth Powell Award for contributions to research in distance education ("She's the 'Boy Scout'" 2009).

Upon their retirement at the end of 2010, one article noted that while in hindsight the path from WHETS to WSU Online looks clear, in fact, it was not at all so. Indeed, when the two women undertook their assignment "the future was shrouded in fog." They now acknowledge that, like all true innovators, they had "made a lot of it up as [they] went along" ("Pioneers ... to retire" 2010). But former WSU president Samuel Smith gave the pair far more credit, observing, "People who change the world don't always realize it at the time. That's what these two did" ("Pioneers ... to retire" 2010).

Sir Isaac Pitman (1813–97)

Sir Isaac Pitman was arguably the first truly successful distance educator, as he turned his correspondence course in shorthand writing (a method that uses symbols and abbreviations to shorten writing time) into a global enterprise. His original English language lessons were translated into numerous other languages, facilitating their distribution to a wide audience of eager students.

Pitman was born on January 4, 1813, in Trowbridge, Wiltshire, in England. He initially attended the local school, but ill health forced him to continue his schooling at home, beginning when he was thirteen. Interestingly, he had great difficulty pronouncing words, a fact that may have played a role in the development of his shorthand system (Rabina 2013).

While Pitman continued his education at home, he also served as a clerk in a cloth factory. In the mid-1830s, in response to the request of a friend, he sought to develop a new system of shorthand writing. After a couple of unsatisfactory attempts, in 1837 he developed Pitman's shorthand system, a new approach based in phonics that was notable for its simplicity and practicality. He published it later that year as Stenographic Soundhand, and he taught it at Wotton-under-Edge, where he had served as a master since 1832 (Reed 1890). Just as Pitman's pioneering approach began to gain attention, he converted to Swedenborgianism in 1839. This controversial religious system, based on the teachings of Swedish philosopher Emanuel Swedenborg, emphasized the divinity of Christ and the spiritual interconnectedness of the universe (Coleman 2014). In response to his conversion, Pitman was fired from his teaching position at Wotton-under-Edge.

The setback did not stop the innovative entrepreneur. He rebounded from his firing by opening his own private school at Bath, where he taught until 1843. He subsequently moved to London where he started a new school in 1845. Throughout this period, Pitman dedicated himself to perfecting his system and looking for ways to publicize its usefulness. To facilitate that effort, in 1840 he founded the Phonetic Institute and published both a book and a phonetic journal, *Phonography* (Reed 1890).

The journal, which included full instructions in his shorthand method, was familiarly known as "the Penny Plate" because Pitman was able to send it in the mail through Great Britain's inexpensive and countrywide "penny post" postal system established in 1840. Pitman initially offered the publication free of charge, an approach that reflected his democratic beliefs about education. Indeed, at the outset he made clear that he was interested in educating people of any class and any location. All they needed was the ability to read and a desire to learn (Reed 1890).

After a time, though, Pitman recognized the commercial potential of his system, and he soon started to sell the journal, as well as its subsequent revised versions. Beginning in the 1840s, Pitman began to teach his system of shorthand directly to students by mailing texts that had been transcribed into shorthand on postcards. He would then receive transcriptions from his students in return for correction. The inclusion of this student feedback element was an important innovation that helped improve and refine Pitman's system (Reed 1890).

While it has since been overtaken in many areas (especially the United States) by the Gregg System, at one point the Pitman system was the most commonly used shorthand system in the entire English-speaking world. It was eventually adapted into over thirty languages including French, Spanish, Afrikaans, and Hindu. Historians believe that part of its enduring success can be traced to its roots as the first subject taught by correspondence course (Rabina 2013).

Isaac Pitman was a perfectionist who continued to revise his system until his death, ultimately publishing twelve editions. He was married twice, the first time in 1835 to Mary Holgate, who died in 1857 (Reed 1890). In 1861 he married Isabella Masters, with whom he had two sons, Alfred and Ernest. His contributions to shorthand writing, as well as his successful and innovative business and publishing ventures undertaken in partnerships with his brothers, were widely recognized, and he was knighted by Queen Victoria in 1894. Sir Isaac Pitman died in Somerset, England, on January 12, 1897.

Charles A. Wedemeyer (1911–99)

Charles A. Wedemeyer was a central figure in the development of distance education. Indeed, many consider the longtime education professor at the University of Wisconsin-Madison the father of modern distance education.

Born in Milwaukee, Wisconsin, in 1911, Wedemeyer received a Bachelor of Science degree in Education with a major in English and later pursued a master's degree in Education, studying at both the University of Wisconsin-Madison and Northwestern University (Saba 2014a). A career educator, one of the things that makes Wedemeyer's role in the development of distance education so distinctive is the fact that he was the first to develop a modern pedagogy specifically intended for distance education. Wedemeyer's efforts reflected a clear recognition that distance learning was different from that done in a traditional school setting and was not something achieved by simply looking to overlay the existing materials and approaches to the distance mode (Saba 2014a).

Another part of Wedemeyer's legacy in the world of distance education is the way he deconstructed the teaching process, breaking it down into parts that would be worked on by the specialists who made up the teaching team. They would then work with a wide array of communication media who would deliver the completed program. Wedemeyer believed that the overall quality of this completed program would exceed that of individual teachers working on their own or that could have been delivered by a single communications media. This approach helped make possible the system theory of distance education (Saba 2014a).

In many respects, these beliefs were evident as far back as the early 1930s, when, while an instructor at the University of Wisconsin, Wedemeyer had used the university's radio station to broadcast English lessons. This effort made his instruction accessible to listeners who were unable to take advantage of the formal education system (Diehl 2012).

From the beginning of his career, Wedemeyer displayed an abiding interest in removing educational barriers from those who wanted to learn (Moore 2009). His determination to remove these obstacles and encourage learning became a lifelong cause. Indeed, his longtime study of nontraditional learners did much to inform his effort to develop forms of instruction that could meet their needs. Distance learning became one of those ways.

Wedemeyer served as a naval instructor during the Second World War. Further experimenting with some of the approaches he had pioneered back in Madison, he created a number of effective teaching methods for "classes" that included sailors stationed around the world (Wedemeyer—HoF 1998). The experience provided him with an unparalleled laboratory in which to experiment with different learning tools and methods. As a result, when the war ended, he was ready to embark on programs that ushered in a whole new approach to education, albeit one utilized by only a small part of the burgeoning post-Second World War university population.

Wedemeyer served as the Director of the University of Wisconsin's Correspondence Study Program from 1954 to 1964. During that time, Wedemeyer and his graduate students initiated numerous research projects focused on learning theory and the sociology of independent learners. Their efforts helped develop and foster a new discipline in the field of education as they helped integrate adult, distance, open, and independent learning with instructional system design to which they then applied instructional technology, organizational development, and evaluation (Diehl 2012).

Wedemeyer's career was based in his lifelong association with formal educational institutions, most prominently, the University of Wisconsin. Yet the work he did in the university's labs and with its graduate students was focused on freeing the learning populace, especially those he would come to call his "back door learners," from the physical constraints of attending classes at the nation's colleges and universities (Diehl 2012).

Indeed, in the aftermath of his pioneering efforts, Wedemeyer predicted the rise of modern distance learning. As he declared in 1965, "the extension student of the future will probably not attend classes; rather, the opportunities and processes of learning will come to him. He will learn at home, at the office, on the job, in the factory, store, or salesroom, or on the farm … the teacher will reach students in his own state or region but nationally as well, since the media and methods employed by him in teaching will remove barriers of space and time in learning" (Saba 2014a).

Wedemeyer's place in the distance learning revolution stemmed at least in part from his passionate belief that technology could be an invaluable tool to the expansion of educational opportunities while also furthering democracy in education (Diehl 2012). A lifelong advocate of access to learning, he saw distance learning as a way to spread the experiences and opportunities that were too often hoarded by elite institutions. He worked to ensure that access to education was open to all, regardless of age, race, gender, job, income, socio-economic status, or place of residence (Moore 2009).

Central to these efforts was his dedication to using technology to provide learning opportunities on an equitable basis. According to friends, Wedemeyer's deep-seated commitment to those at the back door was evident in a picture he posted in every office he occupied. The image portrayed a pre-Revolution Russian child, dressed in ragged clothes, peering through a school room door at the privileged peers welcomed in the schoolroom (Moore 2009). Wedemeyer, who died on August 1, 1999, in Huntsville, Alabama, was unflagging in his determination to end such inequities in access to education.

Organizations/Institutions/Corporations

ASU Online

After Arizona State University (ASU) named Michael M. Crow its president in 2002, the university became a dynamic player in the American higher education landscape. At his inauguration, Crow announced his intention to make ASU a "comprehensive public research university, measured not by whom it excludes, but rather by whom it includes and how they succeed; advancing research and discovery of public value; and assuming fundamental responsibility for the economic, social, cultural and overall health of the communities it serves" (Crow 2002). In that vein, he announced his intention to transform ASU into a single university that would educate in many places, a goal that ultimately resulted in the development of ASU Online. This distance learning option offers courses developed by the same faculty who teach on campus but with an eye to engaging students in ways appropriate to the online experience.

After laying the groundwork and beginning to develop the program, the university first began to offer an online bachelor's degree program in 2006. By 2022 it boasted more than 150 undergraduate and graduate degree programs, as well as hundreds of additional courses unrelated to degrees. These are all available to its almost 40,000 students through the university's online platform. In an effort to facilitate student efforts and to make the programs more flexible, all of the university's online classes are recorded and archived, thus allowing students the ability to access lecture material at their convenience (Global at ASU n.d.).

The ASU Online program is an integrated part of the university experience, allowing online students the same opportunities for interaction with the university's faculty as students attending classes on campus. As a centerpiece of president Crow's effort, ASU Online, which is headquartered in Scottsdale, Arizona, at the school's SkySong campus, has quickly established itself as one of the nation's leading distance education providers. Its programs have earned high rankings from *U.S. News & World Report* as well as other analysts ("ASU, UArizona ranked ..." 2023).

In 2015 ASU Online partnered with ed tech leader edX to create a first of its kind program called the Global Freshman Academy. Open to all potential students, applicants need only to submit a high school transcript or GPA in order to register for a course. The courses, which cost $600 per credit, are paid for only after they are completed and only if the student wants the credit (Lewin 2015). ASU Online programs are designed to enable students to learn in highly interactive environments, working collaboratively with their peers and through the school's technological personalized learning environments.

At the same time, recognizing the increased need and desire of working adults to complete their undergraduate studies or pursue additional degrees or credentials, ASU Online has developed programs with companies and junior and community colleges over a wide-ranging area. An early effort that got considerable attention was the 2014 launch of the Starbucks College Achievement Plan. The plan, representing a partnership between ASU Online and Starbucks, offers full tuition coverage to all benefits-eligible employees upon their enrollment in any of ASU Online's undergraduate degree programs (Nietzel 2023).

In January 2022, the university announced a new initiative to reach 100 million learners worldwide by the year 2030. The free program, backed by an initial gift of $25 million, offers an online global management and entrepreneurial certificate. The credits earned towards the certificates will be transferable for those who seek to pursue a graduate degree at ASU and other affiliated institutions. Reflective of its proposed international reach, the program will be translated into forty different languages (Belkin 2022). Some analysts see the effort as the latest attempt to use massive open online courses (MOOCs) to reach a larger audience, something that had been long tried but had usually fallen prey to low completion rates. While program developers expect to eventually open it up to undergraduates, ASU hopes the initial focus on college graduates will result in a higher completion rate (Belkin 2022). The initiative represents an intriguing next step in the advancement of distance education, an effort in which ASU has played a leading role.

Coursera

As distance education became more formalized and the availability of online instruction expanded, many students, faculty, and educational institutions expressed a desire for something more than a mere duplication of the content and experiences of in-person classes. One of the most notable companies to accept the challenge is Coursera, based in California's Silicon Valley. Founded in 2012 by Stanford University computer science professors Andrew Ng and Daphne Koller, the company quickly developed into a massive open online course (MOOC) provider. Coursera partners with higher education institutions and other organizations to provide courses, certifications, and degrees in a range of subjects. As of 2021, it was estimated that Coursera, through its partnerships with over 200 colleges and universities, offered more than 4,000 courses. The company has also developed a wide range of professional development offerings for online students ("Coursera"—Success n.d.).

Ng and Keller began offering their Stanford classes online in 2011, but the following year they left Stanford and founded Coursera. With Princeton, Stanford, the University of Pennsylvania, and the University of Michigan among the first schools to offer content on the Coursera platform, the company achieved immediate credibility. Once established, they were able to expand to include collections of courses that allowed students to develop skills in specific subjects. They also began to offer degrees and a workforce development product for government and business organizations (Lewin 2012).

Coursera originally competed with edX, a nonprofit provider of open courses developed jointly at Harvard and MIT for offering courses on their own platform. However, in recent years, as distance education has become more acceptable, Coursera has changed its approach. It now partners with universities and companies in helping them stage and market their online programs.

The standard Coursera course can last from four to twelve weeks and includes one to two video lectures a week. Each course includes a combination of quizzes, weekly exercises, and peer-reviewed and peer-graded assignments as well as an optional honors assignment. Many courses culminate with a final project or exam. Coursera also offers on-demand courses where the participants can receive all the materials at once and then are able to take their time to complete the work. The company also has shorter, guided 2–3 hour projects that one can do at home ("Coursera courses" n.d.).

In March 2014, after a 20-year tenure as president of Yale University, Richard Levin assumed the role of Chief Executive Officer of Coursera, adding academic cachet and credibility to the company (Snyder 2014). And in 2020 the company established a partnership with the University of North Texas, an arrangement that enabled the platform to offer its first online bachelor's degree from an American university. The program, which offers a bachelor of applied arts and sciences degree, is aimed at nontraditional students—long a fertile market for online learning—and offers multiple paths to the degree (McKenzie 2020).

The number of online degree programs at both the bachelor's and master's levels offered by Coursera is ballooning (Schwartz, 2021). Coursera has also developed courses for specific niche groups, launching Coursera for Government & Nonprofits and announcing partnerships with the Institute for Veterans & Military Families in the United States as well as in a number of other countries ("Coursera courses" n.d.). In conjunction with corporations like Google, Facebook, and IBM, Coursera has launched a variety of professional development courses culminating in professional certificates that can facilitate a student's professional placement and advancement ("Coursera"—Success n.d.).

Coursera's increasing presence in the world of higher education and professional certification have given it considerable visibility in the distance education world. It remains active in developing programs that offer the opportunities for upskilling that modern companies need, but it has also become an increasingly important player in the effort to develop alternative ways to offer the more traditional courses at the heart of the collegiate experience. The company's public offering in March of 2021 reflects the profitability that the OPMs so central to the development of distance education are enjoying (Young 2021). In that way, it is a poster child for the intersection of distance education and the corporate world.

Khan Academy

The world of distance education has many forms and many approaches. There is no denying that what Salman Khan and his Kahn Academy offer is a singular form of distance learning, offering a combination of courses and academic discipline-based support as well as test preparation. In an educational landscape that is changing quickly and often in unintended ways, Khan Academy has established a distinctive niche, attracting countless struggling students desperate for help wherever they can find it, while also enduring the ire of those parts of the educational establishment that sometimes seem more concerned with procedures and process than with the travails of the students they purport to serve. Criticisms about his lack of a proper pedagogical background or educational credentials notwithstanding, Sal Khan has also been hailed as "the world's first superstar teacher" (Noer 2012).

Khan Academy had its genesis in family tutoring sessions. In 2006, Khan was working as a hedge fund analyst when he began tutoring a cousin in math aided by a service called Yahoo! Doodle Images. One cousin led to another, and he soon found himself working with multiple younger cousins on their schoolwork. Demand increased to the point that Sal started making YouTube videos to more effectively reach his expanding audience (Oremus 2011).

Khan worked in this way for three years until 2009 when an email made him realize that this family-based tutoring project could be something more. The email was from a young man who credited Kahn's YouTube videos with helping him address deficits in his own schooling: "I can say without any doubt that you have changed my life and the lives of everyone in my family" (Noer 2012).

The message resonated in a powerful way for Khan. Growing up poor and raised by a single mother, he had used education to build a better life. Born in the American south, the child of Bangladeshi and Indian immigrants had, by virtue of his own intelligence and work ethic, earned degrees at both MIT and Harvard and become well established in the world of finance (Adams 2013). With the popularity of his YouTube tutoring, Khan decided to change direction and undertake a project that he hoped would smooth the road to greater educational opportunities for children across the country (Noer 2012).

By 2009, approximately 100,000 people were using Kahn's videos, and he decided to quit his job to devote himself to the fledgling Kahn Academy on a full-time basis. He locked himself in a walk-in closet office and began to churn out new videos. He also undertook efforts to raise the project's profile with appearances on CNN and feature stories in national media like *USA Today*.

However, despite the media attention, Khan Academy soon fell into dire financial straits. Khan was reluctantly preparing to return to his old job when he received his first major contribution, a $5,000 grant from Silicon Valley's Ann Doerr, who later became the Academy's Board Chair (Noer 2012).

Doerr later explained she simply wanted to offer support for Kahn's efforts. She assumed that he was well off financially and was shocked to find out that she was his first major donor. In looking back, she recalls being frightened upon learning that Khan had been on the brink of abandoning the project and going back to getting a "real" job. But with Doerr's contribution and advocacy in hand, the Academy's fortunes quickly turned around (Adams 2013).

Kahn Academy is now officially a 501 (c) (3) nonprofit, and it has been the beneficiary of sizeable donations from Google, the Bill & Melinda Gates Foundation, Elon Musk's foundation, and AT&T. Expanding significantly, Khan

Academy has moved a long way from its family-based tutoring roots and its walk-in closet production site (Thompson 2011). In 2014 Khan founded Khan Lab School in Mountain View, California. In 2017 Khan Academy officials released the Financial Literacy Video Series, aimed at a prospective audience of young job seekers, especially college graduates and young professionals. Khan Academy videos have been translated into numerous languages that allow them to be used around the globe. The subtitled translations are primarily a product of volunteer driven efforts as well as international partnerships (Ungerleider 2012).

Khan Academy's more traditional academic offerings include all basic subjects covered in schools, from kindergarten through high school. In addition, it offers online courses that help students prepare for a range of standardized tests, including the SAT, AP Chemistry, the MCAT, and the LSAT. Since 2015 Khan Academy has been the official SAT preparation website (Madda and Corcoran 2016). In 2017, building upon its longtime collaboration with the College Board, Khan Academy was named the official practice partner for the organization's Advanced Placement program ("Khan … Partner for AP" 2017). More recently, Khan Academy has introduced new programs to make it easier for teachers to integrate Khan offerings into classrooms while also working to put a greater focus on mastery learning (an educational approached based on a student achieving proven mastery of a subject before advancing) (Young 2021).

Online Learning Consortium

The Online Learning Consortium (OLC) is a nonprofit organization created to encourage collaboration among leaders of the higher education community to enhance the quality of digital teaching and learning. OLC utilizes a wide range of resources including quality benchmarking, leading edge instruction, practitioner-based research, and best practice publications to inspire and encourage quality and innovation. Reflecting the wide range of interests and resources it seeks to draw upon, the consortium's membership includes faculty members, administrators, trainers, and other learning professionals, as well as education institutions, professional organizations, and corporate interests ("What is the Online …" n.d.).

The organization was founded in 1992 with funding from the Alfred P. Sloan Foundation, a respected philanthropic not-for-profit grant making institution. It initially formed as the Asynchronous Learning Network (ALN), with members seeking to develop educational alternatives for those who were unable to attend traditional schools (Kentnor 2015). As online education grew, the organization took a new name, the Sloan Consortium, and began funding institutions offering online education programs (Kentnor 2015). As the organization itself stated, it wanted to be "a vehicle for engaging other institutions and supporting them to build successful and quality online programs." In 2008 the organization was incorporated as a nonprofit before becoming a member-supported organization in the 2015 fiscal year (Straumsheim 2014).

In the aftermath of the name change, the organization's leaders made clear that online education and not advocacy would continue to be their primary focus. That continuing emphasis is evident in the conferences the organization sponsors and the resources it shares with its many members (Straumsheim 2014). Organizational leaders said that rather than seeking to become the voice of higher education on matters relating to distance education, they hoped to instead serve as the representative of its members in discussing relevant issues with other higher education associations. They hope to be able to ensure that distance education voices are heard as educators across the country continue to wrestle with a wide range of challenges in modern higher education (Straumsheim 2014).

The Consortium also touts guidance and resources for its members through regional and national conferences and professional development opportunities. Recognizing the fluidity of the educational landscape, OLC seeks to ensure that its members are fully apprised of the developments in the ever-changing landscape and thus able to pursue the paths best suited to their institutions while also helping their own members become comfortable with the many evolving facets of distance education ("What is the Online ..." n.d.).

At the heart of OLC's effort is a commitment to making distance educators better, and that is evident in the range of learning opportunities it offers as well as the programmatic efforts it facilitates and supports. It also offers annual awards for excellence in Online teaching, Research and Leadership, and effective practice (OLC Awards n.d.). Other OLC offerings include workshops and professional development programs for teachers seeking to adapt their instructional practices to the online platform. Members can also earn online teaching certificates or advanced certificates through the organization (OLC History n.d.).

Institutional membership in OLC allows institutions to draw upon expert consultants who can assess the needs and capabilities of a school's programs.

OLC's workshops include synchronous webinars and self-paced workshops at numerous levels. They also provide access to articles from the *Journal of*

Asynchronous Learning as well as reports and networking opportunities for faculty members at all points in their digital teaching development ("What is the Online ..." n.d.).

OLC also has an active publications program. In addition to *Online Learning: A Journal of the Online Learning Consortium*, the organization includes publications that highlight best practices, inspire innovation and quality in online learning environments, and increase the competence and confidence of online educators. In addition, OLC also offers annual reports that offer statistical reports on online learning in American higher education ("What is the Online ..." n.d.).

While online education was growing before the Covid-19 pandemic altered the whole educational landscape, the impetus provided by the pandemic has not only increased the demand itself, but also heightened the need for ever more up-to-date research and information as more and more teachers and educational institutions seek to use distance education to do their job. OLC's basic mission is to respond to that need, and it seeks to do that by providing the research-based ideas for teaching and learning as well as the networking opportunities that will allow faculty to navigate the learning curve that every individual and institutional move to distance education entails ("What is the Online ..." n.d.).

Southern New Hampshire University

Southern New Hampshire University (SNHU) is a private university located between Manchester and Hooksett, New Hampshire. Accredited by the New England Commission of Higher Education, some of its programs in hospitality, health, education, and business have received accreditation from national organizations. For over half a century, it offered a traditional residential collegiate experience. However, in 1995, the college began to offer an online program that would, in a comparatively short time, transform the overall university's place in the higher education landscape. Indeed, SNHU's enthusiastic embrace of online learning has made it one of the nation's fastest-growing universities, with its more than 135,000 online students dwarfing the 3,000 that take courses on campus (McKenzie 2019). And yet the vibrant in-person identity enhances the attractiveness of the online program.

Founded in 1932 as the New Hampshire School of Accounting and Secretarial Science, its original focus was on teaching business. Its fortunes ebbed and flowed and by the time founder H. A. B. Shapiro died in 1952 there were only twenty-five students enrolled. In 1961, the school was incorporated and renamed the New Hampshire College of Accounting and Commerce, and two years later the state of New Hampshire granted the college its charter, providing the school with the authority to grant degrees. The college granted its first associate degrees in 1963 and its first bachelor's degrees in 1966. In 1968, the status of the school changed again when it became a nonprofit institution under a board of trustees. The following year the name was shortened to New Hampshire College (SNHU Zippia n.d.).

The 1970s saw continuing change with new programs, including a Master of Business Administration that was launched in 1974, being added to the curriculum. Human services programs were adopted from Franconia College, which closed in 1978. In the early 1980s the college expanded its offerings to include Master of Science degrees in business-related subjects (SNHU Zippia n.d.).

The mid-1990s saw the college undertake a major building boom. In addition to a new residence hall, new homes for the School of Business, the Hospitality Center, the student-run restaurant and culinary arts programs, the Institute for Language Education, the School of Education, and several university offices sprouted up during the decade. Another major innovation came in 1995—though its significance would only later be fully recognized—when New Hampshire College began offering distance learning programs through the internet (SNHU Zippia n.d.).

Befitting its growth and development, the twenty-first century also brought a name change when New Hampshire College became Southern New Hampshire University on July 1, 2001. That same year saw the completion of another new residence hall, while a new academic facility (incorporating the McIninch Art Gallery) opened in 2002 (SNHU Zippia n.d.). Under the leadership of Paul LeBlanc, who assumed the university presidency in 2003, the school weathered the recession of the early 2000s and began a campus transformation. In 2004, the university commissioned a revitalization plan which was initially funded by bonds. At the same time, the school's leadership began to put an increased focus on the College of Online and Continuing Education (SNHU Zippia n.d.).

Utilizing both the rapidly increasing revenue stream generated by the online program as well as the bond dollars, SNHU worked to stabilize declining enrollment on the main campus and then engineered a virtual makeover of its online curricula to meet the needs of the working adult population that was at the heart of its online student body (SNHU Zippia n.d.). Fueled by the increased online revenues, the college has remade the campus with new buildings and renovations that made SNHU New Hampshire's first carbon-neutral university. In another sign of the school's deep interest in environmental sustainability, LeBlanc signed the American College & University Presidents' Climate Commitment (SNHU Zippia n.d.).

The next decade saw additional building efforts featuring the Learning Commons, a 50,000-square-foot structure that houses the library, the information technology help desk, a café, and media production services. In 2016, the university purchased naming rights to the downtown Manchester Civic Arena. In addition to the arena carrying the name SNHU Arena for at least a decade, the agreement also provided for student internships as well as university use of the facility for athletic events and graduation. All of this has made the university a vibrant part of the Manchester community. In 2017, the university announced plans for a $100 million project that was slated to include a 1,700-space parking garage as well as an additional 500 jobs at the university's downtown Manchester offices that support the online college (McKenzie 2019).

Today SNHU offers a full-scale college experience to its residential students, while at the same time providing online students with a full slate of digital coursework to pursue any degree offered by the school. At around 135,000 annually, SNHU has the third-largest online enrollment in the nation making the university a major player in the remote learning world (McKenzie 2019). The transformation of the SNHU campus into an attractive small liberal arts college has enabled the school to mesh its established and still growing brick-and-mortar residential liberal arts college with a robust online distance education program. These assets have made SNHU the nation's largest nonprofit distance education provider.

Like a number of the distance learning programs, including most prominently the Western Governors University, SNHU's College for America (CfA) offers degrees that rely on competency-based learning rather than the traditional earning of credit hours (Grush 2013). In a reflection of the university's pioneering and innovative approach, CfA in 2013 became the first school of its type to achieve federal approval from the U.S. Department of Education ("SNHU's College for America ..." 2013). Four years later, in 2017 SNHU formed a partnership with the U.S. Office of Personnel Management under which all federal employees were eligible for CfA courses (Keane 2017).

From the outset, growth has been the hallmark of the SNHU online programs, and the enrollment figures tell an impressive story. In fact, enrollment in the College of Online & Continuing Education (COCE), based in downtown Manchester, grew from 8,000 students in 2001 to 34,000 in 2014 to over 135,000 in 2021. Not surprisingly, the rapid increase in students has translated into an increase in faculty hiring, and in fact, the university has become one of the top twenty employers in the state (McKenzie 2019). While many of the new faculty have been full-time instructors, befitting the nature of distance learning, many are part-time and located across the United States and also abroad.

The school's aggressive recruiting efforts as well as its nationwide advertising campaigns have led to criticism from both alumni and outside educators, who have derisively compared the efforts to those of the University of Phoenix, a for-profit pioneer in online higher education. But president LeBlanc has unhesitatingly defended the efforts, asserting that SNHU has "borrowed the best of operational practices from the for-profits (customer service, data analytics, a sense of urgency and accountability) while eschewing the practices that cast them in such a poor light" (LeBlanc 2014).

Telelearning Systems and the Electronic University Network

In 1983, Ron Gordon, former Atari president and chairman of Telelearning Systems, Inc., launched the Electronic University Network (EUN). The goal of the venture was to use modern technology to make education more accessible. Under the plan, anyone with a Commodore 64, IBM PC/PCjr, or Apple II series computer, a modem, and an enrollment packet from the Electronic University Network would have access to all EUN had to offer (Darling 1985). Those offerings were made up of an initial 170 courses, as well as another 300 scheduled to be developed by the end of 1984 (Euchner 1983). The menu included subjects ranging from personal improvement classes to university level offerings. In Gordon's announcement press conference, he said that students could get one-on-one instruction from some of the instructors and that they would be able to progress at their own pace (Special to *NY Times*, 1983).

The initial announcement was met with mixed reactions. Secretary of Education Terrell H. Bell hailed the idea, offering praise for the flexibility it appeared to offer as well as the potential broad reach of the effort (Euchner 1983). Vice President George H. W. Bush was equally enthusiastic, calling it a breakthrough that would "provide education on an unprecedented scale" (Smith 2019). Other observers, however, voiced concerns about accreditation for the university, not to mention whether people would in fact be willing to "purchase" their education through an electronic network as opposed to the more customary means.

When it launched, the Electronic University Network represented the latest effort to take advantage of the growth in computer-based services and networks. These included banking and shopping services, as well as news and video games, and while none had made a major commercial impact, EUN had higher aspirations. Touted as a "A School Without Walls," as a 1985 *PC Magazine* article termed it, the initial cost undoubtedly impacted its early reach since a personal computer went for about $150, while TeleLearning was selling modems for $100 to those who did not have them (Pearlman 1985). Meanwhile, the tuition EUN charged ranged from $12 for one of the program's seminars to just under $300 for courses leading to a degree. In addition, students had to pay connect-time so they could participate in seminars as well as being able to access any of the network's more than sixty databases (Pearlman 1985).

The university's roots are somewhat mixed. An early motivation for the development of EUN was Gordon's desire to develop an MBA program for employees at Fortune 500 companies. Gordon even secured commitments from 40 Fortune 500 companies to pay the tuition for employees to an MBA program offered by Gordon's soon to be launched EUN. While some individual colleges and universities, including Stanford, had begun to experiment with the idea of individual courses, Gordon wanted to offer a full MBA program and he had the built in-clientele for the effort (Darling 1985). In an effort to fully develop the curriculum, Gordon met with John F. Ebersole, an early leader in adult education who had a particular interest in the developing area of distance education (Ebersole 2015).

But as the university was developing its own identity, it also saw that some sectors of the educational community were not prepared for online learning. EUN soon decided to take advantage of that, changing its focus to take advantage of the large but untapped market of adult learners seeking flexible offerings that were more amenable to the other demands of their lives, including job and family obligations (Darling 1985).

When Telelearning had first approached universities with its idea of computer-based courses beyond the initial MBA program, the schools were reluctant, but over time its potential began to be recognized. By the end of 1985 close to 15,000 students were taking courses in subjects ranging from economics to the subtleties of California wines. More impressive and significant was the fact that over 1,700 colleges and universities—including institutions like

Cornell University, American University in Washington, DC, Virginia Tech, and Brigham Young, as well as the California State University system and the State Universities of New York—were participating (Darling 1985).

The early success was impressive and by 1986, Gordon hoped to have the enrollment up over 50,000 students. That was only a beginning, however, as he talked of ultimately having the world's largest system. But despite being first out of the gate and recognizing the market, implementation efforts were unable to match Gordon's vision. In fact, the pioneering online learning network was plagued by technological and pedagogical bugs. After taking three courses in 1985, a writer for *PC Magazine* described the company's offerings as onerous for many students (Pearlman 1985). The writer asserted, among other criticisms, that communication with instructors was difficult and that its technological infrastructure needed to be shored up (Pearlman 1985). In the end, EUN was unable to fully address these shortcomings (Etherington 2018). In 1992 what remained of EUN began to collaborate with internet service provider America Online (later AOL), serving as its coordinator for higher education.

While the Electronic University Network did not last, it nevertheless left an indelible mark and an enduring legacy. Gordon and EUN helped pave the way for many of the modern iterations of technology-based distance education (Etherington 2018).

2U, Inc.

Central to the advent of modern distance learning has been the development of a range of companies playing different roles and offering different services as part of institutional efforts to deliver online education. One such company is 2U, Inc., which was initially 2tor Inc (2U Zippia n.d.). An American educational technology company, it contracted with nonprofit colleges and universities to offer online degree programs. But unlike some that focus solely on course content, 2U supplies institutions with a cloud-based, software-as-a-service platform, as well as coursework design, infrastructure support, and capital while also assisting with the development of course content.

The specifics of its products depend on the specific needs and desires of the schools it works with. Its initial foray into the online world came with the launch of an online teaching degree at the University of Southern California (USC) in 2009. Two years later, the company established an online degree program in conjunction with Georgetown University's School of Nursing, as well as an

MBA program at UNC–Chapel Hill's Kenan Flagler School (2U Zippia n.d.). That same year, it returned to help USC establish an online degree program in social work. In 2015, the company entered into a partnership with Yale University to introduce a master's of science degree (2U Zippia n.d.).

2U was founded in 2008 by John Katzman, whose previous work in the education field included cofounding *Princeton Review* (2U Zippia n.d.). Katzman secured Chip Paucek, the one-time CEO of Hooked on Phonics, as well as Jeremy Johnson, to help develop the company. In 2013 Katzman left the company, and Paucek took over the reins as CEO. Shortly thereafter, Paucek earned an MBA from UNC–Chapel Hill through the online program developed by the 2U–UNC partnership (2U Zippia n.d.).

2U quickly sought to establish itself as an organization that worked to bring online education to some of the nation's most highly ranked colleges and universities. Seeking to develop relationships and partnerships with these more prestigious institutions, the company intentionally refused to adopt the low-cost, low-quality business model then prevalent in the online education world.

Building upon its initial efforts with the University of Southern California (USC) and Georgetown, it assembled partnerships with highly ranked colleges and universities including Amherst, Columbia, Johns Hopkins, Harvard, MIT, and Rice (2U Partners n.d.).

Reflective of the fact that growth and expansion was a central part of the online learning game on both the business side and the enrollment side, in 2019 2U announced the start of a partnership with the EGADE Business School at the Tecnologico de Monterrey to offer an online MBA program. That program is complemented by the partnership Coursera and Tecnologico de Monterrey have with the Washington University School of Law to offer an online master's of law program (2U Zippia n.d.).

The Covid-19 pandemic proved to be a boon for 2U. With schools scrambling to move in-person lessons into online operations, 2U experienced rapid growth. The company secured numerous new partners while also expanding its relationship with existing ones.

In the fall of 2021, 2U purchased edX, the nonprofit online platform started by Harvard and MIT, as part of its effort to expand its reach. When the planned acquisition was initially announced, many in academia expressed concern that edX's stated mission to expand access to learning would be undermined with the nonprofit being taken over by the for-profit U2 (Blumenstyk 2021). Although, at the formal announcement of the sale in November 2021, leaders of both companies claimed the new organization would offer a huge range of educational opportunities, these assurances did not quiet critics of the acquisition. EdX's nonprofit roots had always been part of edX's attraction to the academic community—and a notable contrast with Coursera. At the same time, there was a recognition that the academically based edX had long "struggled to find a sustainable business model," and that through the new deal it "will receive the capital injections it needs to continue its work and potentially expand its impact through research and improved technology" (Whitford 2021). Indeed, defenders of the acquisition asserted that 2U's move gave a much-needed financial lifeline to edX, while making 2U a formidable competitor with Coursera (Whitford 2021), as both companies prepared to compete in a changing educational world.

University of Phoenix

The University of Phoenix (UoPX) is a private, for-profit university headquartered in Phoenix, Arizona. Founded in 1976, the university's driving force was John Sperling, aided by John D. Murphy (Schulzke 2015). The school's first class consisted of eight students (Hanford 2012). Now owned by Apollo Global Management, an American private equity firm, the university offers certificates, as well as associate, bachelor's, master's, and doctoral degrees. Accredited by the Higher Learning Commission, its open enrollment admission policy accepts all applicants with a high school diploma, GED, or its equivalent. It earned regional accreditation in 1978. While the main campus remains in Phoenix, in 1980, UoPX expanded to San Jose, California.

While it began as a traditional brick-and-mortar institution, in an effort to increase enrollment, it launched its online program in 1989, a move that made the university both a leader in that developing field as well as a source of controversy (Hanford 2012). As the online program grew, the University of Phoenix described itself as an innovator in the field of higher education for working adults, and it became a symbol of what online education could be. However, it soon also became a reflection of the challenges of that world. Indeed, the University of Phoenix has had to pay hundreds of millions of dollars in fines and settlements concerning its student recruiting practices and education programs. In particular, it has come under fire for allegations of deceptive advertising practices (Halperin 2023).

In its early years, the school derived much of its revenue from businesses that subsidized higher education for their managerial employees, but in

1994 the university's leaders took its parent company, Apollo Group, public (Hanford 2012). Critics charged that after this change, the University of Phoenix abandoned its founding mission of providing continuing education for working adults and increasingly focused its admission decisions on whether the applicant was eligible for federally funded loans (Murphy 2013).

One thing that became clear was that as its online enrollment grew—reaching a peak of 470,000 in 2010—the university became less dependent upon corporate-based tuition payments and more reliant on government funding. Nowhere was that more apparent than in the huge payments the school received over the years in G.I. Bill payments and Pell Grant assistance, which regularly dwarfed those received by any other school in the United States. This drew the attention of Washington policymakers (Hanford 2012).

In 2010, the University of Phoenix operated more than 500 campuses and learning sites. Despite this success, the university's numerous controversies and high-priced legal battles, not to mention the frequent focus on its extensive and high cost marketing efforts, have often relegated discussion of its academic programs and results to the backburner (Quintana 2023). The school still serves around 100,000 online students annually and maintains its residential campus in its namesake city. It offers a large number of undergraduate degrees from its many colleges and schools, including the School of Business, College of Education, School of Nursing, and College of Social Science. It also offers master's degree programs in Business, Criminal Justice, Education, Healthcare, Nursing, Psychology, Technology, and Behavioral Science (Degrees and Courses n.d.).

Yet for all these offerings, the school's academic reputation has been dogged by reports of poorly performing teachers and inadequately rigorous courses. Criticism have targeted the high percentage of part-time faculty—almost 95 percent, twice the national average—and a lack of faculty engagement. In addition, the school has long had below-average graduation rates, although school officials assert that their focus on older students who seek the flexibility Phoenix offers skew these numbers (Dillon 2007).

To combat these negative perceptions, Phoenix has scaled back and reorganized. With the overwhelming percentage of its students now being online, the university is putting a new emphasis on opening resource centers to serve those students. These centers are being developed with an eye to providing space for alumni to network while also offering current students a venue where they can seek help from professors and their peers (Support and Resources n.d.).

Such services have been increasingly in demand by online students, and schools need to address these demands as the distance education landscape becomes more competitive and schools seek to differentiate themselves.

As it looks to the future, the University of Phoenix continues to face legal troubles as well as damaging metrics such as low graduation rates (often below 20 percent) (Dillon 2007). Equally disturbing have been the high debts incurred by students, debts made all the more troublesome by some students' failure to complete their degree (Hill 2015). The one-time success story of a place that was seen by many as the future of high education has become a sobering cautionary tale.

In the spring of 2022, the university announced it was closing down all of its remaining campuses outside of Phoenix, focusing on bolstering its reputation as a leader in online education (Anderson and Edgemon 2022). In another effort to address its financial challenges, the for-profit giant was sold to the University of Idaho in 2023. The deal came after months of discussions between the University of Arkansas and Phoenix came to naught. Although accreditors still had to review the deal, the Idaho acquisition called for the University of Phoenix to be converted to a nonprofit that Idaho officials were calling "New U." (Vasquez 2023). But that was not the end of the saga. As of spring 2024, Idaho political leaders and University of Phoenix officials were engaged in discussions involving a restructuring of the deal that would make it more "more palatable" to the Idaho legislature (Guido 2024). The still-to-be-finalized transaction certainly represented an interesting new chapter in the University of Phoenix's star-crossed history.

Western Governors University

Western Governors University was envisioned as an online educational institution from the outset. Founded in 1997, the university can trace its roots back to a time when a bipartisan group of governors sought an answer to the increasingly pressing question of "How can we ensure more of our residents have greater access to a college education that fits their schedule?" (Schindelheim 2020). As they sought to answer that question, the governors recognized that the emerging technology of the internet had the potential to radically change the educational landscape. Indeed, recognizing that the internet offered the possibility of allowing people to take classes "anytime, anywhere," they began putting together the institution that would eventually become Western Governors University (Cortez 2022).

It was a unique institution from the start. With the governors of nineteen American states as its founders, the school's initial start-up costs were underwritten by governmental sources (each participating state government committed $100,000 to the institution). And yet when the idea, first proposed in June 1995 by Utah Governor Mike Leavitt at the annual meeting of the Western Governors Association, became a reality, it quickly became established as a self-supporting, private, nonprofit institution (Cortez 2022).

Beyond its technology and distance learning aspects, as well as its determination from the start to provide opportunities and access to that part of the country's population that geographically had long been on the margins of the higher education community, the most radical aspect of the WGU program was its approach. A WGU education was to be rooted in competency-based learning, an approach under which each student would progress toward their degrees not by simply accumulating credits but by demonstrating competency in the field they were studying (Cortez 2022). It was an approach that reflected some of the central tenets of distance education, including flexibility and the opportunity for students to proceed at their own pace.

The university was one of the first to receive accreditation from the National Council for Accreditation of Teacher Education (NCATE) ("Western Governors University History Timeline," Zippia). It includes four different colleges: Business, Information and Technology, Teacher Education, and Health Professions. Each of the four colleges offers both undergraduate and graduate degrees, as well as post-master's certificates (WGU History—Plexuss n.d.).

Despite its status as a relative newcomer to the world of higher education, WGU has established itself as an institution on the cutting edge in preparing students for an ever-changing and evolving work world, offering courses and degrees in cybersecurity and information assurance, data analytics, and IT management. Too, WGU offers programs in the education and health fields, as it helps to prepare the next generation of providers in these critically important areas that impact all of society. In fulfilling its goal of providing flexible educational opportunities for working adults, the university has made itself a tremendously popular option. Indeed, since granting its first degree in December of 2000, WGU has grown in leaps and bounds. In 2020, the university reported enrollment of just over 147,000 (Schwartz 2021).

Many of these students make use of WGU Academy, a personalized transition program. The Academy provides personal coaching, one-on-one interaction, and an introduction to competency-based online learning while also providing other support aimed at ensuring that students are ready for their university experience (WGU Academy n.d.).

Helping to spur WGU's growth has been the continuation of the bipartisan spirit that characterized the university's original founding. Drawing upon that historical legacy, WGU has continued to work with state leaders to expand and improve its educational offerings in a way that serves the state's distinctive populations. One result of these efforts has been the development of affiliated state-based programs. Beginning with Indiana in 2010, a number of states, including Texas and Washington in 2011, Missouri and Tennessee in 2013, Nevada in 2015, North Carolina in 2017, Ohio in 2018, and Utah in 2021, have established state-based affiliates of the central WGU (WGU History—Plexuss n.d.).

Each of these state-based WGU off-shoots shares the basic WGU academic model, as well as its faculty, services, accreditation, tuition, and curricula. The individual entities benefit from having the official backing of their state while at the same time increasing the WGU name recognition. Students in these programs are often eligible for state-based aid. In addition, the state affiliations make it easier for students to transfer local state or community college credits they have previously earned, a fact that can allow them to complete their WGU degree more quickly. At the same time, each of the affiliated schools has a distinctive identity since WGU itself has no physical campus at any of the state affiliates. The state affiliates are another way that WGU furthers its original mission (WGU History—Plexuss n.d.).

Student success is made more achievable as a result of cooperative arrangements with many junior colleges and policies that make transferring credits easier than is often the case in traditional higher education programs. The university's competency-based advancement also allows students to start a program at WGU or any of its affiliates at the beginning of pretty much any month. Along with the obvious flexibility inherent in a distance learning program, these additional options make it much easier to fit the pursuit of additional courses, degrees, or certificates into the lives of working adults, including rural residents, military students, minorities, and first-generation college students. This, of course, is exactly what WGU set out to do from the beginning (WGU History—Plexuss n.d.).

References

Adams, Richard. 2013. "Sal Khan: The Man Who Tutored His Cousin—and Started a Revolution." *The Guardian*, April 23. https://www.theguardian.com/education/2013/apr/23/sal-khan-academy-tutored-educational-website

Adler, Renata. 1972. "Cookie, Oscar, Grover, Herry, Ernie, and Company: The Invention of Sesame Street." *The New Yorker*, June 3.

Anderson, Mark, and Erin Edgemon. 2022. "University of Phoenix to Shutter Campuses Nationwide, Go Remote." *Phoenix Business Journal*, April 21. https://www.bizjournals.com/phoenix/news/2022/04/21/university-of-phoenix-remote.html#:~:text=University%20of%20Phoenix%20to%20shutter%20campuses%20nationwide%2C%20go%20remote&text=The%20University%20of%20Phoenix%2C%20Sacramento,student%20preference%20for%20remote%20learning.&text=The%20University%20of%20Phoenix%20is,students'%20preference%20for%20online%20courses

"ASU, UArizona ranked among nation's top 10 online programs by US News and World Report." 2023. KTAR.com. https://ktar.com/story/5427354/asu-uarizona-ranked-among-nations-top-10-online-programs-by-us-news-world-report/

Barbour, Michael, and Thomas C. Reeves. 2006. "Michael Grahame Moore: A Significant Contributor to the Field of Educational Technology." *Education Faculty Publications*. Paper 86. https://digitalcommons.sacredheart.edu/cgi/viewcontent.cgi?referer=&httpsredir=1&article=1089&context=ced_fac

Belkin, Douglas. 2022. "Arizona State University Looks to Enroll 100 Million More Students by 2030." *Wall Street Journal*, January 20. https://www.wsj.com/articles/arizona-state-university-looks-to-enroll-100-million-more-students-by-2030-11642674604

Blumenstyk, Goldie. 2021. "The Edge: What This Week's $800-Million Deal Means for the Future of Online Education." *The Chronicle of Higher Education*, June 30. https://www.chronicle.com/newsletter/the-edge/2021-06-30

Coleman, Brent. 2014. "A Missionary of Education and Decorative Arts." *The Enquirer* (Cincinnati), March 1. https://www.cincinnati.com/story/life/2014/03/01/a-missionary-of-education-and-decorative-arts/5937703/

Cooper, Joy Palmer. 2016. *Routledge Encyclopaedia of Educational Thinkers*. New York: Routledge

Cortez, Marjorie. 2022. "Western Governors University at 25: How a Group of Governors Disrupted Higher Education." *Deseret News*, August 5. https://www.deseret.com/utah/2022/8/4/23288039/western-governors-university-anniversary-higher-education-online-wgu

"Coursera courses." n.d. Coursera.com. Accessed July 6, 2023. https://www.coursera.org/courses

"Coursera." n.d. Success Story. Accessed July 6, 2023. https://successstory.com/companies/coursera

Crow, Michael M. Inauguration Address, Arizona State University, November 8, 2002. https://www.youtube.com/watch?v=TwPr40WiNQ0

Darling, Sharon. 1985. "The Electronic University." *Compute*, September. https://www.atarimagazines.com/compute/issue64/electronic_university.php

"Degrees and Courses." Accessed July 6, 2023. University of Phoenix. https://www.phoenix.edu/learn-more.html?alloy_redirect=eyJ2IjoxLCJhZCI6IjU0MDIxMTowOjB8Miw1Nzk0NzU6MTowfDIsNTc5NTA1OjE6MHwyLDU0ODMzNTowOjB8MiJ9

Diehl, William C. 2012. "Charles A. Wedemeyer." In *Handbook of Distance Education*, edited by Michael Grahame Moore. 3rd edition. New York: Routledge.

Dillon, Sam. 2007. "Troubles Grow for a University Built on Profits." *The New York Times*, February 11. https://www.nytimes.com/2007/02/11/education/11phoenix.html

Ebersole, John F. 2015. "Reflections on an Evolution." In *Centennial Conversations: Essential Essays in Professional, Continuing, and Online Education*, edited by Daniel W. Shannon and Robert Wiltenburg. Washington, DC: University Professional and Continuing Education Association.

Etherington, Cait. 2018. "What Happened to the Electronic University Network?" elearninginside.com, January 9. https://news.elearninginside.com/what-happened-to-the-electronic-university-network/

Euchner, Charlie. 1983. "Business Group Announces Creation of 'Electronic University.'" *Education Week*, September 21. https://www.edweek.org/education/business-group-announces-creation-of-electronic-university/1983/09

Global at ASU. n.d. Arizona State University. Accessed July 6, 2023. https://global.asu.edu/

Gossett, Barbara, Anna Condoulis, Muriel Oaks, and Janet Ross Kendall. 2008. "Building Communities within a Diverse Adult Population." *Continuing Higher Education Review* 72. https://www.learntechlib.org/p/55535/

Grush, Mary. 2013. "Blazing the Trail: Competency-Based Education at SNHU." *Campus Technology*, December 18. https://campustechnology.com/articles/2013/12/18/competency-based-education-at-snhu.aspx

Guido, Laura. 2024. "Senate Committee Approved Bill That Restructures University of Phoenix Deal." *Idaho Press*, March 26. https://www.idahopress.com/news/local/senate-committee-approves-bill-that-restructures-university-of-phoenix-deal/article_ac4186e6-eb96-11ee-abd4-93e90ed938cb.html

Halperin, David, 2023. "University of Phoenix Seems to Break Pledge to Avoid Misleading Ads." *Republic Report*, January 17. https://www.republicreport.org/2023/university-of-phoenix-seems-to-break-pledge-to-avoid-misleading-ads/

Hanford, Emily. 2012. "The Story of the University of Phoenix." *American Public Media.* September. https://americanradioworks.publicradio.org/features/tomorrows-college/phoenix/story-of-university-of-phoenix.html

Hill, Catey. 2015. "Student-loan Crisis: 10 Colleges Where Students Owe the Most." *MarketWatch*, September 11. https://www.marketwatch.com/story/10-colleges-where-students-owe-the-most-2015-09-11?page=2

Keane, Lauren. 2017. "First Competency-Based Degree Program to Be Offered to All Federal Employees and Their Families." Newsroom, Southern New Hampshire University, March 14. https://www.snhu.edu/about-us/newsroom/press-releases/competency-based-degree-program

Kentnor, Hope. 2015. "Distance Education and the Evolution of Online Learning in the United States." *Curriculum and Teaching Dialogue* 17, nos. 1 and 2.

"Khan Academy Is the Official Practice Partner for AP." 2017. Khan Academy Blog Post. July 27. https://blog.khanacademy.org/khan-academy-is-the-official-practice-partner-for/

LeBlanc, Paul. 2014. "Setting the Record Straight Again (Sigh)." President's Corner, Southern New Hampshire University, January 3. https://president.snhu.edu/2014/01/setting-the-record-straight-again-sigh/

Lewin, Tamar. 2012. "Universities Reshaping Education on the Web." *The New York Times*, July 17. https://www.nytimes.com/2012/07/17/education/consortium-of-colleges-takes-online-education-to-new-level.html

Lewin, Tamar. 2015. "Promising Full College Credit, Arizona State University Offers Online Freshman Program." *The New York Times*, April 22. https://www.nytimes.com/2015/04/23/us/arizona-state-university-to-offer-online-freshman-academy.html

Madda, Mary Jo, and Betsy Corcoran. 2016. "How Khan Academy Is Shaking Up the SAT." *EdSurge*, April 1, 2016. https://www.edsurge.com/news/2016-04-01-how-khan-academy-is-shaking-up-the-sat

McKenzie, Lindsay. 2019. "Marketing for a Massive Online University." *Inside Higher Ed*, October 7. https://www.insidehighered.com/news/2019/10/08/how-marketing-helped-southern-new-hampshire-university-make-it-big-online

McKenzie, Lindsay. 2020. "A New Player in the College Completion Market." *Inside Higher Ed*, January 23. https://www.insidehighered.com/news/2020/01/24/coursera-launches-college-completion-pathway

Moore, Michael Grahame. 2009. "Editorial: Charles Wedemeyer in Memoriam 1999." *American Journal of Distance Education* 13, no. 4 (September 24). https://www.tandfonline.com/doi/abs/10.1080/08923649909527031?journalCode=hajd20

"Moore, Michael Grahame, Hall of Fame Class of 2013." International Adult and Continuing Education Hall of Fame. Accessed July 5, 2023. https://halloffame.outreach.ou.edu/Inductions/Inductee-Details/michael-grahame-moore

"Moore, Michael Grahame, PhD" n.d. Accessed July 5, 2023. http://michaelgmoore.com/a/

Murphy, John D. 2013. *Mission Forsaken—The University of Phoenix Affair with Wall Street*. Cambridge, MA: Proving Ground Education.

Nappi, Rebecca. 2010. "Wise Words: Retiring WSU Dean Helped Pioneer Distance Learning." *Spokesman-Review* (Spokane, WA), December 4. https://www.spokesman.com/stories/2010/dec/04/going-the-distance/

Nietzel, Michael. 2023. "Starbucks Partnership with Arizona State University Celebrates 10,000 College Graduates." *Forbes*, May 8. https://www.forbes.com/sites/michaeltnietzel/2023/05/08/starbucks-partnership-with-arizona-state-university-celebrates-10000-graduates/?sh=69eab43a6426

Noer, Michael. 2012. "One Man, One Computer, 10 Million Students: How Khan Academy Is Reinventing Education." *Forbes*, November 18. https://www.forbes.com/sites/michaelnoer/2012/11/02/one-man-one-computer-10-million-students-how-khan-academy-is-reinventing-education/?sh=17000d3244e0

"Oaks Academic Technology Award." n.d. Washington State University-Academic Outreach and Innovation. Accessed July 6, 2023. https://li.wsu.edu/teaching-awards/oaks-academic-technology-award/

Oaks, Muriel. CV. n.d. Accessed July 6, 2023. http://phd.mbuisc.ac.th/ajarns_new/Muriel_CV.pdf

OLC – Awards and Recognitions. n.d. Online Learning Consortium. Accessed July 6, 2023. https://onlinelearningconsortium.org/about/awards-and-recognition/

OLC – Our History. n.d. Online Learning Consortium. Accessed July 6, 2023. https://onlinelearningconsortium.org/about/history/

Oremus, Will. 2011. "Salman Khan, Founder of Khan Academy." *Slate*, August 2. https://www.slate.com/articles/technology/top_right/2011/08/salman_khan_founder_of_khan_academy.html

Pearlman, Dara. 1985. "A School Without Walls." *PC Magazine*, April 16. https://books.google.com/books?id=rtmJgtfaxz8C&pg=PA6&lpg=PA6&dq=dara+pearlman+%22a+school+without+walls%22&source=bl&ots=OhFH8xFtci&sig=ACfU3U1uVqNp6SE3eCn4GQ-WjHWQmUKN9A&hl=en&sa=X&ved=2ahUKEwjKrYHcv7v_AhXmFVkFHZsjBf4Q6AF6BAgHEAM#v=onepage&q=dara%20pearlman%20%22a%20school%20without%20walls%22&f=false

"Pioneers of Distance Education to Retire." 2010. *WSU Insider*, November 2. https://news.wsu.edu/news/2010/11/02/pioneers-of-distance-education-to-retire/

Quintana, Chris. 2023. "This Controversial, For-profit College Has Received $1.6B in GI Bill Funds, the Most of Any School." *USA Today*, March 22. https://www.usatoday.com/story/news/investigations/2023/03/22/gi-bill-university-of-phoenix-veterans-affairs/11486672002/

Rabina, Debbie. 2013. "A Brief History of Sir Isaac Pitman & His Legacy." *MiNYstories*, December 10. https://minystories.wordpress.com/2013/12/10/a-brief-history-of-sir-isaac-pitman-and-his-legacy/

Reed, Thomas Allen. 1890. *A Biography of Isaac Pitman (Inventor of Phonography)*. London: Forgotten Books (2013). https://obgin.net/wp-content/uploads/2016/12/Biografia-de-Isaac-Pitman-english.pdf

Riechers, Maggie. 2003. "Joan Ganz Cooney." National Humanities Medal, National Endowment for the Humanities. https://www.neh.gov/about/awards/national-humanities-medals/joan-ganz-cooney

Saba, Fred. 2014a. "Introduction to Distance Education: Theorists and Theories—Charles Wedemeyer." Distance-educator.com, March 16. https://distance-educator.com/introduction-to-distance-education-theorists-and-theories-charles-wedemeyer/

Saba, Fred. 2014b. "Introduction to Distance Education: Theorists and Theories — Michael G. Moore." Distance-educator.com, March 23. https://distance-educator.com/introduction-to-distance-education-theorists-and-theories-michael-g-moore/

Schindelheim, Ramona. 2020. "Access Equals Opportunity: The WGU Higher Ed Model." *Working Nation*, February 18. https://workingnation.com/access-equals-opportunity-the-wgu-higher-ed-model/

Schulzke, Eric. 2015. "The Rise and Fall of the University of Phoenix." *Deseret News*, April 25. https://www.deseret.com/2015/4/25/20563390/the-rise-and-fall-of-the-university-of-phoenix

Schwartz, Natalie. 2021. "Pandemic Fueled Huge Online-only Enrollment Growth, Report Finds." *Higher Ed Dive*, October 20. https://www.highereddive.com/news/pandemic-fueled-huge-online-only-enrollment-growth-report-finds/608522/

"She's the 'Boy Scout' of Distance Education." 2009. *WSU Insider*, September 16. https://news.wsu.edu/news/2009/09/16/shes-the-boy-scout-of-distance-education/

Smith, Ernie. 2019. "Learning at 300 Baud." Tedium.com. May 23. https://tedium.co/2019/05/23/telelearning-electronic-university-history/

"SNHU's College for America Receives D.O.E. Approval." 2013. New Hampshire Public Radio (NHPR), April 18. https://www.nhpr.org/word-of-mouth/2013-04-18/snhus-college-for-america-receives-d-o-e-approval

Snyder, Bill. 2014. "Coursera CEO Richard Levin: Democratizing Learning Takes Time." *Insights by Stanford Business*, November 10. https://www.gsb.stanford.edu/insights/coursera-ceo-richard-levin-democratizing-learning-takes-time

"Southern New Hampshire University History Timeline." n.d. Southern New Hampshire University History—Zippia.com. Accessed July 5, 2023. https://www.zippia.com/southern-new-hampshire-university-careers-1267640/history/

Special to The New York Times. 1983. "Correspondence School Via Computer Is Planned." *New York Times*, September 13.

Straumsheim, Carl. 2014. "Sloan Goes Online: Ahead of Its 20th Conference on Online Education, the Sloan Consortium Renames Itself the Online Learning Consortium." *Inside Higher Ed*, July 6. https://www.insidehighered.com/news/2014/07/07/sloan-consortium-renames-itself-online-learning-consortium

"Support and Resources." n.d. Accessed July 7, 2023. University of Phoenix. https://www.phoenix.edu/student-resources/overview.html

Thompson, Clive. 2011. "How Khan Academy Is Changing the Rules of Education." *Wired*, July 15. https://www.wired.com/2011/07/ff-khan/

"2U Company History Timeline." n.d. 2U History – Zippia.com. Accessed July 6, 2023. https://www.zippia.com/2u-careers-29/history/

"2U Partners." n.d. 2U.com. Accessed July 6, 2023. https://2u.com/partners/

Ungerleider, Neal. 2012. "How Khan Academy Is Going Global." *Fast Company*, June 14. https://www.fastcompany.com/1840263/how-khan-academy-going-global

Vasquez, Michael. 2023. "U. of Phoenix Lands a Buyer." *Chronicle of Higher Education*, June 9.

Watson, Bruce. 2023. "When a Revolution Was Televised." *The Attic*, March 3. https://www.theattic.space/home-page-blogs/2023/3/3/the-woman-who-brought-you-big-bird

"Wedemeyer, Charles A." Hall of Fame Class of 1998. International Adult and Continuing Education Hall of Fame. Accessed July 5, 2023. https://halloffame.outreach.ou.edu/Inductions/Inductee-Details/charles-a-wedemeyer

"Western Governors University History." Plexuss.com. Accessed July 6, 2023. https://plexuss.com/u/western-governors-university/history

"Western Governors University History Timeline." Western Governors University History—Zippia.com. n.d. Accessed July 6, 2023. https://www.zippia.com/western-governors-university-careers-1417538/history/

WGU Academy. n.d. Accessed July 6, 2023. https://www.wgu.edu/admissions/wgu-academy.html#_

"What Is the Online Learning Consortium?" n.d. Top Degrees Online.com. Accessed July 6, 2023. https://www.topdegreesonline.org/faq/what-is-the-online-learning-consortium/

Whitford, Emma. 2021. "2U and edX Merger Benefits Both." *Inside Higher Ed*, June 29. https://www.insidehighered.com/news/2021/06/30/online-learning-giants-2u-and-edx-will-merge

"Who's Afraid of Big, Bad, TV?" 1970. *Time*, November 23. https://content.time.com/time/magazine/article/0,9171,943327,00.html

Young, Jeffrey R. 2021. "Khan Academy Wants to Make 'Mastery Learning' Mainstream. Will Partnering with Schools Help?" *EdSurge*, December 1. https://www.edsurge.com/news/2021-12-01-khan-academy-wants-to-make-mastery-learning-mainstream-will-partnering-with-schools-help

Zane, Sharon, 1998. "Oral History Interview with Joan Ganz Cooney." Carnegie Corporation of New York Digital Archive, January 14. https://dlc.library.columbia.edu/carnegie/cul:pc866t1hsj/details?initial_page=0&title=false

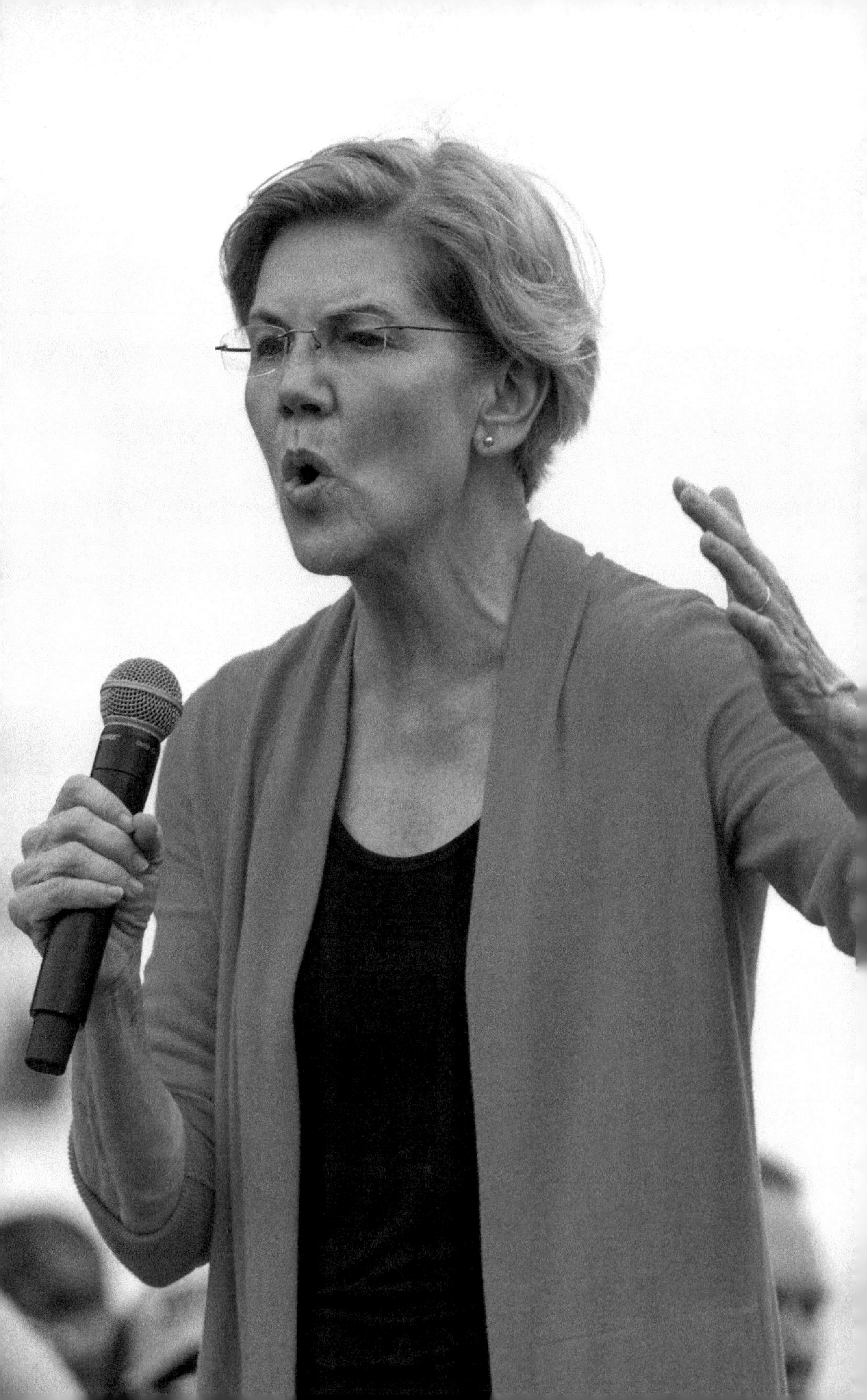

5

Data and Documents

Data

Changes in Higher Education Online Learning Enrollment

Table 5.1 illustrates that remote learning was already growing in popularity pre-pandemic. The largest growth in online learning from 2013 to 2018 was in students who took at least one, but not all, of their classes online. The number of students taking part in online learning grew from about 5.5 million to around 6.9 million during that time. The data is also broken down by 4-year and 2-year schools, as well as public, private nonprofit, and private for-profit status. Growth was particularly strong among private not-for-profit institutions, where students who took all courses online increased by over 54 percent.

Table 5.1 Pre-pandemic Growth of Online Learning, 2013–18

	Total students (#)	No distance-education courses (%)	At least one distance course, not all (%)	All distance-education courses (%)
All institutions				
2018	20,008,434	65.3	18.4	16.3
2017	19,765,598	66.3	18.0	15.7
2015	19,977,270	70.2	15.4	14.4
2013	20,375,789	72.9	14.1	13.1

Senators Elizabeth Warren (pictured) and Sherrod Brown sent letters of inquiry in 2020 to the CEOs of the five largest Online Program Management (OPM) companies in the country, raising concerns about their business practices and use of federal student aid funds. (© Jhansen2/Dreamstime.com)

	Total students (#)	No distance-education courses (%)	At least one distance course, not all (%)	All distance-education courses (%)
All institutions				
4-year (total):				
2018	13,901,011	64.3	18.0	17.6
2017	13,823,640	65.8	17.3	16.9
2015	13,486,342	69.7	14.4	15.9
2013	13,407,050	73.0	12.2	14.8
2-year (total):				
2018	6,107,423	67.6	19.2	13.2
2017	5,941,958	67.5	19.5	13.0
2015	6,490,928	71.2	17.6	11.2
2013	6,968,739	72.7	17.6	9.8
Public:				
2018	14,639,681	66.1	21.5	12.3
2017	14,560,155	67.8	20.8	11.4
2015	14,568,103	72.0	18.0	10.0
2013	14,745,558	74.6	16.7	8.7
Private Non-Profit:				
2018	4,147,604	69.7	10.1	20.2
2017	4,106,477	71.3	9.5	19.2
2015	4,063,372	75.0	8.5	16.5
2013	3,974,004	80.0	6.9	13.1
Private For-Profit:				
2018	1,221,149	41.0	8.6	50.4
2017	1,098,966	29.0	11.1	59.9
2015	1,345,795	35.9	8.6	55.5
2013	1,656,227	40.7	7.6	51.7

Sources: Department of Education. 2020. "Distance Education and Innovation." September 2, 2020. https://www.federalregister.gov/documents/2020/09/02/2020-18636/distance-education-and-innovation; Data from National Center for Education Statistics.

Table 5.2 shows that in the fall of 2021, the percentage of students enrolled in distance education classes went down from its pandemic peak in 2020, as many students returned to in-person classrooms; however, it remained higher than the percentage in 2019. Of the undergraduate students who took distance education courses exclusively, 58 percent did so through private for-profit institutions, 28

Table 5.2 Percentage of Students in Online Learning, 2019–21

	At least one distance course, not all (%)	All distance-education courses (%)
Undergraduate		
2021	61	28
2020	75	44
2019	36	15
Postbaccalaureate		
2021	56	40
2020	71	52
2019	42	33

Source: Data from National Center for Education Statistics. n.d. "Fast Facts—Distance Learning." Accessed March 13, 2024. https://nces.ed.gov/fastfacts/display.asp?id=80

percent through public institutions, and 21 percent through private nonprofits. Of the postbaccalaureate students taking classes exclusively online, 88 percent were at private for-profit institutions, 38 percent at private nonprofits, and 36 percent at public institutions.

K-12 Parent Views on the Impact of the Pandemic on Their Children

The Covid-19 pandemic forced most U.S. students into remote learning. The data in Tables 5.3, 5.4, and 5.5 is the result of a September/October 2022 Pew Research Center survey of the parents of K-12 students regarding their opinions about the impact of the pandemic on their children's education and well-being. The survey included 3,757 parents. As shown in Table 5.3, most parents felt that the first year of the pandemic had a negative effect on their children's education, with a smaller percentage saying the impact on their children's emotional well-being was negative.

Table 5.3 Parent Opinions of the Impact of the First Year of Pandemic on Their K-12 Children's Education and Well-being (Percentages)

	Very/somewhat negative	Very/somewhat positive	Neither positive nor negative
Education	61	7	28
Emotional well-being	48	7	39

Source: Data from Pew Research Center survey of U.S. parents conducted September 20–October 2, 2022. https://www.pewresearch.org/short-reads/2022/10/26/most-k-12-parents-say-first-year-of-pandemic-had-a-negative-effect-on-their-childrens-education/ft_2022-10-26_covidk12_01/

Although studies have generally shown that learning loss was more severe among Black and Hispanic students as well as lower-income students during the pandemic, the Pew Research Center survey showed that white and upper income parents were more likely to say their children were negatively impacted by the pandemic (Table 5.4).

Table 5.4 Differences by Race, Ethnicity, and Income in Percentage of Parents Who Said the Impact of the First Year of the Pandemic Was Negative

	Education	Emotional well-being
All K-12 parents	61	48
White	66	53
Black	50	39
Hispanic	55	41
Asian*	50	40
Lower income	54	43
Middle income	63	49
Upper income	68	57

*English speakers only.

Source: Data from Pew Research Center survey of U.S. parents conducted September 20–October 2, 2022. https://www.pewresearch.org/short-reads/2022/10/26/most-k-12-parents-say-first-year-of-pandemic-had-a-negative-effect-on-their-childrens-education/ft_2022-10-26_covidk12_02/

The survey results show that most parents felt the pandemic's negative impacts on emotional well-being were temporary and that they had seen improvement in their children by September 2022. However, the percentage of Black parents who thought their children's emotional health had improved was considerably lower (Table 5.5).

Table 5.5 Parents Who Said the First Year of the Pandemic Had a Negative Emotional Impact, by Race, and Their Views on Whether It Improved (Percentages)

	Gotten better	Stayed about the same	Gotten worse
All K-12 parents	74	18	8
White	77	15	9
Black	61	30	9
Hispanic	73	18	9

Source: Data from Pew Research Center survey of U.S. parents conducted September 20–October 2, 2022. https://www.pewresearch.org/short-reads/2022/10/26/most-k-12-parents-say-first-year-of-pandemic-had-a-negative-effect-on-their-childrens-education/ft_2022-10-26_covidk12_03/

Teen and Parent Views on Virtual Learning

In a survey conducted by the Pew Research Center in April and May 2022, most teens (thirteen to seventeen years old) indicated that they preferred to return to in-person learning after the pandemic. However, Table 5.6 shows that white students and students from higher income families were more likely to want to return to traditional learning environments than Black students and students from low-income families.

Table 5.6 Teen Opinions on Post-Pandemic Schooling (Percentages)

	Completely in person	Completely online	Mix of both online and in person
White	70	9	15
Black	51	15	26
Hispanic	64	6	23
Household income			
Less than $30,000	51	15	23
$30,000–$74,999	60	10	23
$75,000 or more	71	8	15

Source: Data from Pew Research Center survey of U.S. parents conducted April 14–May 4, 2022. https://www.pewresearch.org/internet/2022/06/02/how-teens-navigate-school-during-covid-19/pi_2022-06-02_school-covid19_00-02/

Student and parent satisfaction regarding how their school was handling virtual learning had a mixed response in the survey results, as shown in Table 5.7.

Table 5.7 Teen and Parent Satisfaction Level with How Their School Has Handled Virtual Learning (Percentages)

	Extremely/very satisfied	Somewhat satisfied	A little/not at all satisfied
Teens	28	33	30
Parents	39	33	20

Source: Data from Pew Research Center survey of U.S. parents conducted April 14–May 4, 2022. https://www.pewresearch.org/internet/2022/06/02/how-teens-navigate-school-during-covid-19/pi_2022-06-02_school-covid19_00-03/

The survey results show that parents tended to be more concerned than their teens about falling behind in school as a result of disruptions from the pandemic (Table 5.8). A higher percentage of Hispanic students (28 percent) than Black (19 percent) or white (11 percent) students were extremely or very worried. This was also the case with their parents (Hispanic, 42 percent; Black, 23 percent; white, 25 percent). In families with a household income less than $30,000, teens (27 percent) and parents (44 percent) were more likely to be extremely or very worried than families with an income over $75,000 (teens, 13 percent; parents, 24 percent).

Table 5.8 Worry Level of Teens and Parents That They May Have Fallen Behind in School Due to the Pandemic (Percentages)

	Extremely/very worried	Somewhat worried	A little/not at all worried
Teens	16	22	62
Parents	28	24	48

Source: Data from Pew Research Center survey of U.S. parents conducted April 14–May 4, 2022. https://www.pewresearch.org/internet/2022/06/02/how-teens-navigate-school-during-covid-19/pi_2022-06-02_school-covid19_00-03/

Access to technology, and therefore online learning, was a major issue during the pandemic. The Pew Research Center's survey results showed that 10 percent of teens did not have access to a computer at home, with 20 percent of students from lower-income households (less than $30,000) reporting having no access. In addition to computer access, reliable internet connections were an issue. Teens from lower-income families and children of parents with a high school level education or less were disproportionately affected (Table 5.9).

Table 5.9 Access Issues for Teens, Encountered Often or Sometimes (Percentages)

	Have to do homework on cellphone	Not able to complete homework due to lack of reliable computer or internet access	Have to use public Wi-Fi for homework due to lack of internet connection at home	Encounter at least one of these challenges often or sometimes
All Teens	22	12	6	28
White	20	10	3	24
Black	20	7	7	26
Hispanic	28	16	12	34

Parent's education				
HS or less	27	16	10	34
Some college	20	10	7	25
College+	19	8	3	23
Household income				
Less than $30,000	35	24	17	43
$30,000–$74,999	24	14	7	30
$75,000 or more	19	8	4	23

Source: Data from Pew Research Center survey of U.S. parents conducted April 14–May 4, 2022. https://www.pewresearch.org/internet/2022/06/02/how-teens-navigate-school-during-covid-19/pi_2022-06-02_school-covid19_00-06/

Documents

Press Release from Office of Senator Elizabeth Warren Concerning Letters Sent to CEOs of Online Project Management Companies (2020)

This press release accompanied Senator Warren (MA) and Senator Sherrod Brown (OH)'s sending of letters of inquiry to the CEOs of the five largest Online Program Management (OPM) companies in the country concerning the OPMs' business practices. The senators' concerns revolved around the influence these companies have on higher education, especially given the millions of dollars of federal aid that can be involved.

Senators Warren and Brown Examine Questionable Business Practices of Largest Managers of Online Degree Programs

Aggressive and Deceptive Recruiting Tactics Similar to Those Used by For-Profit Colleges May Undermine Best Interests of Students

Washington, DC—United States Senator Elizabeth Warren (D-Mass.), a member of the US Senate Committee on Health, Education, Labor and Pensions, and Senator Sherrod Brown (D-Ohio) wrote to the five largest Online

Program Management (OPM) companies—2U, Academic Partnerships, Pearson Learning, Wiley, and Bisk—that administer online degree programs for many colleges and universities, raising concerns about their business practices that appear to undermine the best interests of students, and inquiring about their contracts and use of federal student aid dollars.

Colleges and universities often enter into contracts with for-profit OPM companies to administer their online academic programs, but OPM companies can also charge colleges and universities for a variety of non-academic services, like recruitment and admissions services. OPM contracts often stipulate that the college or university must pay most of the tuition revenue from students enrolled in their online programs to the OPM. Because these contracts often delegate recruitment responsibilities to the OPM, this tuition-sharing arrangement may violate federal law, which prohibits colleges and universities from paying commissions for recruiting and enrolling new students.

Available evidence suggests that tuition-sharing arrangements in OPM contracts create perverse incentives that lead to aggressive and deceptive recruiting practices, similar to those that pervade the for-profit college industry. For instance, basic information about the program, including cost, schedule, or admissions policies, may not be available to prospective students until they provide their contact information to the OPM, which the OPM company can then use for aggressive follow-up calls and text messages. An analysis of OPM contract terms found that tuition-sharing contracts often include provisions that prevent colleges and universities from making any changes that would lower revenue, which inflates college costs for students. Because colleges and universities often do not disclose whether an OPM is administering certain programs or advertising and recruiting on their behalf, students often have few ways of knowing whether their online degree program is affected by these troubling practices.

"As the influence of this small handful of companies on the American higher education system has exploded, there is an increasing need for transparency to ensure that students and policy-makers are able to make informed decisions," wrote the senators in their letters. "It is also critical that policy-makers determine if OPM business practices—specifically OPM contracts that require tuition-sharing arrangements—are legal, an appropriate use of federal student aid dollars, and in the best interest of students."

The lawmakers have requested that each OPM respond to questions outlined in their letter no later than February 21, 2020.

Source: Excerpted from "Senators Warren and Brown Examine Questionable Business Practices of Largest Managers of Online Degree Programs." 2020. Elizabeth Warren, January 24, 2020. https://www.warren.senate.gov/oversight/letters/senators-warren-and-brown-examine-questionable-business-practices-of-largest-managers-of-online-degree-programs

Letter Sent by Senators Elizabeth Warren and Sherrod Brown to the CEOs of Five OPMs Concerning Business Practices (2020)

The following excerpt is from the senators' letter to Christopher Paucek of 2U, Inc. The same letter (which was heavily footnoted) was also sent to Randy Best of Academic Partnerships, Mike Bisk of Bisk Education, John Fallon of Pearson Learning, and Ted Zipper of Wiley Educational Services. These are the CEOs of the five largest OPMs in the country. In the letter's final page (not included here), the senators ask the CEOs to produce a series of documents, including contracts, financial arrangements, lists of services provided, same presentation materials, expenditure and revenue figures, and analysis of compliance with the incentive compensation provisions of the Higher Education Act.

Dear Mr. Paucek:

We write to express concern about reports of business practices that Online Program Management (OPM) companies like [insert OPM company name] use, which appear to undermine the best interests of students, and to inquire about your company's use of federal student aid funds in the administration of the OPM services to institutions of higher education that participate in federal student aid programs.

OPM companies like 2U are outside, for-profit companies that run online degree and certificate programs for colleges and universities, including many well-known public and private institutions. OPM companies originated to help brick-and-mortar universities create and administer their online offerings, but they have evolved into businesses that make money by contracting with colleges and universities to provide a variety of services, including recruitment, admissions, and curriculum development services. The OPM industry has experienced striking growth since 2011. More than one-third of colleges with online programs now have contracts with OPMs. Five companies, including 2U, reportedly make up about half the OPM market.

Today, OPM contracts often stipulate that the college or university must share 50% or more of any resulting tuition revenue from students with the OPM. Because these agreements often delegate recruitment responsibilities to the OPM, this tuition-sharing agreement may violate federal law, which prohibits paying commissions for recruiting and enrolling new students. In 2011, the Department of Education (ED) issued guidance allowing for bundled-service contracts between universities and OPMs if enrollment levels were fixed by the institution to prevent illegal financial incentives for recruiting students; however, it is unclear whether colleges, universities, and OPMs are following this guidance. Nor is it clear whether this non-regulatory guidance is consistent with the text of the Higher Education Act.

Available evidence suggests that tuition-sharing arrangements in OPM contracts create perverse incentives that lead to aggressive and deceptive recruiting practices similar to those that pervade the for-profit college industry. If a for-profit, third-party company makes more money when tuition revenue increases, then the obvious incentive is to increase enrollment of students, specifically low-income middle-class students who rely on federal student aid to pay tuition costs by any means necessary.

In some cases, basic information about the program, including cost, schedule, or admissions policies, is not available to prospective students until they provide their contact information to the OPM. The contact information can then be used for aggressive follow-up calls or texts messages. One publicly available OPM contract for an online program at a public institution, for example required the OPM to contact every prospective students at least 13 times per day, for ten days in a row. Once the OPM has prospective students' contact information, it can also target the student for recruitment to programs at other universities that the OPM manages (including those with higher tuition or where the OPM receives a larger share of tuition revenue), or sell the student's information to third parties. A *Forbes* profile of one OPM noted that about half of its employees worked at a call center focused on recruitment and increasingly revenue.

Moreover, an analysis of OPM contract terms found that tuition-sharing contracts often include provisions that prevent colleges and universities from making any changes that would lower revenue for the programs the OPM runs. For example, Purdue University Global, formerly Kaplan University and now a project of Purdue University, is managed by Kaplan Higher Education under a contract that penalizes Purdue if it lowers tuition prices, raises admission standards, or otherwise reduce revenue. These provisions help explain why the promise of online degrees at a lower cost to students have not been realized.

OPM contracts with tuition-sharing arrangements that commit significant portions of students' tuition revenue to the third-party OPM company obviously discourage colleges and universities from offering lower tuitions at online programs, even when they are cheaper to operate. In fact, despite significantly lower overhead costs, online degree programs are actually more expensive on average than brick-and-mortar programs: $277 per online credit, versus $243 per credit earned in person. Many graduate programs at nonprofit universities charge students the same price for the online program as they do for brick-and-mortar programs even though they are cheaper to operate. An analysis of these contractual practices led the Century Foundation to conclude that "by and large, contracted online programs in higher education are wolves in sheep's clothing: predatory for-profit actors masquerading as some of the nation's most trustworthy public universities."

Students and consumers have few ways to know whether their online degree program is affected by those troubling practices. Universities often do not disclose whether an OPM is administering certain programs or advertising and recruiting on their behalf. Although universities are required to provide net price calculators on their websites, these do not typically distinguish between online and in-person programs, masking the irony that online programs can be more expensive for students than their brick-and-mortar equivalents. Furthermore, OPM services often focus on master's degree programs which have fewer disclosure requirements than undergraduate degree programs. Although millions of dollars in federal student aid are directed to online degree programs every year, policymakers and taxpayers have no way to know how many of those dollars are directed to recruiting, advertising, and profit, rather than instruction.

As the influence of this small handful of companies on the American higher education system has exploded, there is an increasing need for transparency to ensure that students and policymakers are able to make informed decisions. It is also critical that policymakers determine if OPM business practices—specifically OPM contracts that require tuition-sharing arrangements—are legal, an appropriate use of federal student aid dollars, and in the best interest of students. To better understand how 2U serves students and manages federal student aid, I ask that you provide the following information no later than February 21, 2020.

Source: Excerpted from letters from Senators Elizabeth Warren and Sherrod Brown to CEOs of OPMs. January 23, 2020. https://www.warren.senate.gov/imo/media/doc/Letters%20to%20multiple%20orgs.%20re%20OPM%20Business%20practices.pdf

National Council on Disability Statement to House Subcommittee Regarding Educational Equity Post-Covid-19 (2021)

In this statement presented to the House Subcommittee on Early Childhood, Elementary, and Secondary Education, Andrés J. Gallegos, Chairman of the National Council on Disability, discusses the particular difficulties faced by students with disabilities during the pandemic as a result of the shift to remote learning. He emphasizes that further research and funding are needed to regain lost ground and prepare for future emergencies, ensuring that students with disabilities are not overlooked.

Lessons Learned: Charting the Path to Educational Equity Post-COVID-19

Chair Member Scott ... On behalf of the National Council on Disability (NCD), we thank the subcommittee for the inclusion of additional funding in the American Rescue Plan of 2021 ... That funding is critically needed to support students with disabilities under the Individuals with Disabilities Education Act (IDEA) for the duration of the Covid-19 public health emergency. As a federal voice for the over 61 million Americans with disabilities, including students with disabilities and their families, NCD, an independent federal agency, provides advice to the President, his Administration, Congress, and federal agencies based on our comprehensive and objective analyses to inform policy development, improvement, and enforcement efforts. We are committed to advancing policy solutions that create a more inclusive society for people with disabilities.

Throughout the Covid-19 pandemic, disability advocates have been outspoken about concerns over the educational needs of students with disabilities during widespread school closures. The full extent of the effects of school closures and remote learning is not fully understood and requires deeper investigation. For this reason, since last year, NCD has been conducting a comprehensive study to examine the effects of the pandemic on people with disabilities across a range of policy topics that will include examination of students' experiences. We will present our findings before this subcommittee at the conclusion of our research in late summer.

The full integration of children with disabilities into society cannot be accomplished without access to a free and appropriate public education. Under ordinary circumstances, students with disabilities—about 14 percent of students from kindergarten to 12th grade, and more than 7 million children—already experienced enormous barriers in their education. Prior to the public health emergency, IDEA funding was sorely inadequate, causing delays and denials of services, and triggering unfair social resentment and discrimination.

While the Covid-19 pandemic caused significant disruptions to the educational experiences of all students, it was especially disruptive for students with disabilities. School districts' sudden reliance on distance learning as the sole option for education exacerbated the exclusion and isolation of students with disabilities. While some students are thriving in a remote classroom, and some have fewer challenging behaviors at home, many more are losing out on educational opportunities during the protracted periods of lockdown and school closures.

The often overlapping problems experienced by students with disabilities include barriers to accessing remote education related to equipment, technology and broadband; the inability of some students with disabilities to focus and learn during remote learning; the failure of schools to accommodate the needs of students with disabilities on remote platforms; the inability to receive services and supports that were provided in person or on school campuses, such as occupational therapy, speech and language therapy, behavioral and mental health supports, small group instruction, and one-on-one aides; among others. Those and other issues will be addressed in NCD's report this summer.

Given the detrimental effects that students with disabilities have experienced as a result of the extended school closures, future federal responses to the Covid-19 pandemic must include additional IDEA funding, as well as provide compensatory education services to allow students with disabilities to regain the skills that were disrupted, delayed or completely lost. In planning for future national emergencies, it is of critical importance that we invest in technology, equipment and connectivity, not only for students with disabilities to have an equal opportunity to engage and succeed in remote learning, if that is the only option, but also to ensure they continue to receive the services and supports that are essential for their academic success.

Most Respectfully,
Andrés J. Gallegos
Chairman

Source: Excerpted from Gallegos, Andrés J. "Statement for the Record to House Subcommittee Regarding Educational Equity Post-COVID-19." 2021. U.S. House of Representatives, Committee on Education & Labor, Subcommittee on Early Childhood, Elementary, and Secondary Education, March 25, 2021. https://www.ncd.gov/letters/2021-03-25-statement-for-the-record-to-house-subcommittee-regarding-educational-equity-post-covid-19/

GAO Report, "Indian Education—Schools Need More Assistance to Provide Distance Learning" (2021)

In a report that includes testimony before the Senate's Committee on Indian Affairs, the Government Accountability Office outlined shortcomings in the Bureau of Indian Affairs' guidance for distance learning efforts during the pandemic in the schools it funds on and near Indian reservations in twenty-three states. The following excerpts from that report summarize the GAO's findings and recommendations.

The Bureau of Indian Education (BIE), within the Department of the Interior (Interior), has not provided BIE-funded schools with comprehensive guidance on distance learning during the Covid-19 pandemic. In March 2020, BIE issued a short memo directing schools to "deliver flexible instruction" and "teach content," but did not offer specific guidance on how to do so. In July 2020, thirteen of the twenty-five schools that responded to GAO's survey said they wanted BIE to provide information on developing and implementing distance learning programs. In addition, twelve schools responded that they wanted information on distance learning methods for areas without broadband internet access. In August 2020, after some schools had already begun the school year, BIE issued a re-opening guide for the 2020–21 school year. BIE's guidance focused primarily on preparations for in-person instruction at schools, although nearly all schools provided distance learning during the fall of 2020. The guidance contained little information on distance learning. Providing schools with comprehensive distance learning guidance will help them better navigate the current pandemic as well as potential future emergencies that lead to school building closures.

BIE helped improve internet access for students at BIE-operated schools during the pandemic, but many students had not received laptops to access online learning by the end of fall 2020. BIE and other Interior offices provided over 7,000 hotspots to students to improve home internet access, but they did not order laptops for most students until September 2020. Interior officials said a nationwide IT supply shortage contributed to the delayed order for about 10,000 laptops. GAO found, however, that delays were also caused in part by BIE not having complete and accurate information on schools' IT needs. Most schools received laptops from late October 2020 to early January 2021, although some laptops still had not been delivered as of late March 2021. Once laptops were delivered, however, schools also faced challenges configuring them, leading to further delays in distributing them to students. BIE officials told GAO that to address schools' challenges with configuring laptops, they are assessing schools' IT workforce needs. Most BIE students did not receive laptops until months after the school year began, according to GAO's analysis of Interior information. Specifically,

- none of the laptops Interior ordered in early September 2020 arrived in time to distribute to students by the start of the school year in mid-September;
- by the end of December 2020, schools had not distributed over 80 percent of the student laptops Interior ordered; and
- as of late March 2021, schools had not distributed about 20 percent of the student laptops Interior ordered.

Without accurate, complete, and up-to-date information on schools' IT needs, BIE was unable to ensure that students received laptops when they needed them. Establishing policies and procedures for assessing schools' IT needs would help guide the agency's IT purchases now and in the future, and position schools to integrate technology into their everyday curricula.
...

GAO is making two recommendations to BIE to (1) provide comprehensive guidance to schools on distance learning; and (2) establish policies and procedures to ensure it has complete, accurate, and up-to-date information on schools' technology needs.

Source: Excerpted from "Indian Education—Schools Need More Assistance to Provide Distance Learning." 2021. United States Government Accountability Office, April 2021. https://www.gao.gov/assets/gao-21-492t.pdf

Press Release from the Office of Senator Edward J. Markey Announcing the Introduction of Legislation Addressing the Online Educational Needs Caused by the Covid Pandemic (2021)

This press release accompanied the introduction by Senator Markey (MA) and Senator Christopher Van Hollen (MD) of legislation addressing the educational needs created by the Covid pandemic. This statement offers one example of the types of proposals that were being offered as Congress sought to address the role of remote learning during the pandemic, as well as the extent of bipartisan, broad-based support for the aid.

Washington (July 22, 2021)—Senator Edward J. Markey (D-Mass.), Senator Chris Van Hollen (D-Md.), and Congresswoman Grace Meng (NY-06), along with 15 additional senators and 25 House members, today introduced the Securing Universal Communications Connectivity to Ensure Students Succeed (SUCCESS) Act to build on the Emergency Connectivity Fund created under the American Rescue Plan and provide schools and libraries with $8 billion a year over five years—for a total of $40 billion—to continue to provide Wi-Fi hotspots, modems, routers, and internet-enabled devices to students, staff, and library patrons following the coronavirus pandemic. The legislation continues the lawmakers' efforts to close the homework gap facing 12 to 17 million students in the United States who do not have internet access at home and support distance learning after the pandemic is over.

Even before the current emergency, students without connectivity were at an educational disadvantage because they could not complete homework assignments that required internet access after class. The coronavirus pandemic only made this situation worse as schools shifted to online learning, leaving students without internet access unable to continue their education. Under the Emergency Educational Connections Act, a part of the American Rescue Plan, Congress provided a one-time, $7.17 billion appropriation to connect students and library patrons struggling to learn at home. The SUCCESS Act will provide crucial additional funding to ensure that the kids who are finally being connected by the Emergency Connectivity Fund are not disconnected once the original funds run dry.

"Even after the coronavirus pandemic finally ends, we cannot ignore a key 21st century educational requirement—internet access. The homework gap is an educational inequity that long predates the current emergency, and we need to put the funding in place to ensure no student is forced to sit in a strip mall parking lot, hoping to connect to a local store's internet in order to finish their homework," said Senator Markey. "This essential funding will build on the newly created Emergency Connectivity Fund and help ensure that the homework gap does not grow into a damaging learning and opportunity gap following the pandemic for our children, particularly those who live in communities of color, low-income households, and rural areas."

"Too many students in Maryland and across our country still lack reliable internet access and face significant barriers in completing their school work. To close this gap, we must get funding straight to where it's needed most. This legislation will build upon the crucial resources we secured within the American Rescue Plan and provide additional support directly to our schools and libraries to get more students online. I will continue working to make sure that every student in every household across our state and nation has access to reliable and affordable internet," said Senator Van Hollen.

"During the Covid-19 crisis, we have seen how crucial internet access has been for learning and completing assignments, and as our nation works to move past the pandemic, we must use this opportunity to help all students get online," said Congresswoman Meng. "Increasing internet access is a vital issue that I have been proud to champion with Senator Markey, and fighting for the $7 billion that was included in the American Rescue Plan was a great victory. But more must be done to build on this critical down payment. As the mother of two young children, I know firsthand how crucial this is. Each and every student must have the tools they need to succeed in school, and the SUCCESS Act is an essential component to permanently closing the homework gap. I urge all of my colleagues in both chambers to help close this digital divide by supporting our effort to secure additional funding for schools and libraries."

[*The bill is also cosponsored by 15 US Senators and 25 Members of the House of Representatives from all part of the United States.*]

[*Numerous supportive statements from a range of educations and community related interest groups were included in support of the proposed legislation. The full list of the organizations expressing their support is below.*]

Endorsers of the SUCCESS Act include AASA, the School Superintendents Association, Advance CTE, Alliance for Excellent Education, American Federation of School Administrators, American Federation of Teachers, American Library Association, American Psychological Association, Association for Career and Technical Education, Association of Educational Service Agencies, Association of Latino Administrators and Superintendents,

Association of School Business Officials International, Children's Health Fund, Common Sense Media, Consortium for School Networking, Council for Exceptional Children, Council of Administrators of Special Education, Council of Chief State School Officers, Education Reform Now, The Education Trust, Family Centered Treatment Foundation, Girls Inc., International Society for Technology in Education, Khan Academy, KIPP, Joint National Committee for Languages, Learning Forward, Magnet Schools of America, MENTOR, National Association of Elementary School Principals, National Association of Federally Impacted Schools, National Association of Independent Schools, National Association of School Psychologists, National Association of Secondary School Principals, National Association of State Directors of Special Education, National Catholic Educational Association, National Center for Families Learning, National Council for Languages and International Studies, National Digital Inclusion Alliance, National Education Association, National Rural Education Advocacy Consortium, National Rural Education Association, National School Boards Association, Parents as Teachers, Project Tomorrow, Public Advocacy for Kids, Schools Health & Libraries Broadband (SHLB) Coalition, State Educational Technology Directors Association, and Teach for America.

Source: Excerpted from "Senators Markey, Van Hollen and Rep. Meng Introduce Bicameral Legislation to Close the Homework Gap, Ensure Students Continue to Receive Needed Internet Access after the Pandemic Ends." 2021. Ed Markey, July 22, 2021. https://www.markey.senate.gov/news/press-releases/senators-markey-van-hollen-and-rep-meng-introduce-bicameral-legislation-to-close-the-homework-gap-ensure-students-continue-to-receive-needed-internet-access-after-the-pandemic-ends

National Science Foundation, "Education Researchers Assess Impacts of Long-term Remote Learning on Students" (2021)

This National Science Foundation article, published in 2021, discusses the organization's efforts to further research into the pandemic effects on education, to assist with online learning efforts during the pandemic, and to support schools with their subsequent return to the classroom. It also looks at the potential long-term impacts of the pandemic on STEM students in particular.

Students and teachers had their routines disrupted when the nation shut down in March 2020 to fight the Covid-19 pandemic. Across the country, educators took their classrooms online to keep students engaged, and as the lockdown continued for many into the following school year, remote learning options became more sophisticated and interactive.

The success of these online learning efforts varied across the country, influenced by an array of factors, leaving many educators and researchers wondering what long-term impact this interrupted year will have on STEM students of all levels and backgrounds.

As the only U.S. federal agency that supports fundamental research across all fields of science and engineering, the U.S. National Science Foundation made more than 1,200 awards totaling over $200 million to study multiple aspects of the pandemic. Among those are projects assessing the impact of lost classroom time, as well as projects helping students and teachers return to face-to-face, group learning settings.

The Pandemic Becomes a Teaching Opportunity

As learning environments shifted from the classroom to the home, teachers and parents looked to take advantage of existing resources, such as NSF-supported STEM activities for students online. There were also multiple NSF awards made to groups developing additional instructional aids for teachers.

Adam Maltese, an associate professor at Indiana University Bloomington, led the launch of a Facebook group—CoBuild19—to deliver STEM activities for kids. Under the NSF grant, the group analyzed how families and children engage with the activities and how STEM content can best be delivered to meet learners' needs and interests. The page now has approximately 5,000 members, including museums, organizations, teachers, librarians and parents.

Researchers from the University of Missouri and the University of North Carolina at Chapel Hill collaborated to develop a curriculum that teaches high school students about viral epidemics as a scientific and social issue. The approach was designed to help students connect their classroom learning experiences with their lives beyond school, a key characteristic of science literacy. A follow-on award will help researchers develop new curriculum for students interested in learning about epidemics to different types of scientific modeling.

Students and professors at University of Houston-Clear Lake expanded the scope of an existing Course-based Undergraduate Research Experience (CURE) award in microbiology to research how the coronavirus might spread among younger adult populations with asymptomatic carriers. This NSF RAPID award enabled students to learn how research is conducted as well as contribute knowledge about how the coronavirus works. Students also developed a virtual reality tool to learn how to sequence DNA fragments, building skills valuable in clinical and research laboratories.

Remote Learning Could Have Long-term Impact on STEM Diversity

Teachers worked harder than ever during the lockdown, but the success of remote learning varied amongst groups and throughout regions. A consistent finding among researchers measuring the impacts was that disparities such as lack of internet access in rural areas, were amplified during the lockdown.

Time away from regular classroom interaction leads to declines in student performance, often referred to as "summer learning loss." The National Opinion Research Center at the University of Chicago is studying the impact on students of the extended loss of classroom time due to the pandemic, or "pandemic learning loss," especially in STEM education. The repercussions are expected to fall disproportionately on poor, minority and underserved students, and initial findings indicate that academic gaps in STEM learning have increased.

A similar study on undergraduate STEM students and the impact of the digital divide found that about 1 in 6 students taking a STEM course often had internet connectivity or other technology problems. This was more prominent among students of color and those from lower-income households. Researchers at Fort Valley State University found that historically Black colleges and universities experienced a range of negative impacts on student retention and learning, due to both a lack of online tools available for students and instructors that had little experience in teaching online courses.

Technology was not the only source of problems for students. Some expressed that they had trouble staying motivated due to the lack of in-person interaction with teachers and classmates as well as concerns about whether remote learning of basic level courses would properly prepare them for higher level classes. Research on the mental health impacts of graduate students conducted by Montana State University found that negative impacts on learning were also created by increasing concerns around food and housing insecurity or more childcare responsibilities. This resulted in an increase in expected delays in completing degree work or a change in career plans.

This long-term impact of pandemic learning could be a further reduction in the quantity and diversity of STEM professionals, with only those students whose families have the resources to easily access e-learning opportunities remaining fully committed to STEM education programs, researchers said.

"The Covid-19 pandemic had a far-reaching impact, affecting students of all ages and educators," said Sylvia Butterfield, acting assistant director for EHR. "Our community rose to the challenges that full-time remote learning created and kept many students engaged throughout a difficult time. But the environment also reminded us of the inequalities faced by our most vulnerable in regard to access to quality educational opportunities, especially in STEM fields."

NSF Funding to Support Return to Classroom and Laboratory

While researchers continue to assess the impact of expanded remote learning, students at all education levels are returning to the classroom. NSF has developed several programs to aid students in these efforts.

As part of the response to Covid-19, the NSF Directorate for Education and Human Resources is funding awards through both regular appropriations and new sources. Existing funding programs will also be used to help students get back on track, such as the EHR Racial Equity in STEM Education program, the Advancing Innovation and Impact in Undergraduate STEM Education at Two-year Institutions of Higher Education, and Supplemental Funding for Postdoctoral Researchers to Mitigate Covid-19 Impacts on Research Career Progression.

Thanks to Congress, funding provided under the American Rescue Plan will be used to support groups most affected—women researchers, underrepresented groups and early-career faculty—as well as individuals at vulnerable career transition points, such as undergraduates preparing to attend graduate school, graduate students nearing the end of their research careers and postdoctoral fellows. In addition, funds will support the nation's science museums and other community-based organizations that provide learning opportunities and have been challenged during the pandemic.

"With students across the US back in the classroom, we must strive to ensure that the tools and proper environments for learning are accessible and equitable for all," Butterfield said. "We can build upon the lessons we learned over the past several months, not just to help students and researchers recover from any setbacks but to create improved opportunities for education that are available to all."

Source: Bates, Jason. 2021. "Education Researchers Assess Impacts of Long-term Remote Learning on Students: NSF Projects Support Return to Classroom." National Science Foundation, September 21, 2021. https://new.nsf.gov/science-matters/education-researchers-assess-impacts-long-term

Excerpt from "Distance Learning in the Pandemic Age: Lessons from a (No Longer) Emergency" (2022)

The following material is excerpted from the discussion and conclusion sections of an article that used the available literature at the time to compare the impacts of distance learning and traditional education resulting from the forced experience of distance learning brought about by the Covid-19 pandemic. The article reviews initial findings from distance learning research during the pandemic age and discusses the potential of well-implemented distance and hybrid efforts for the future of education. The authors' stated goal is to "give the reader a reasonable perspective on how to turn the limitations imposed by the pandemic into new opportunities for the development of teaching/learning processes." The excerpts here summarize the particular care—by teachers, students, and administrators—necessary for the success of distance education efforts and in mitigating the challenges involved with this form of education.

Distance learning can still be a little-known modality for both teachers and students. Preparing students for interactions and emotion management is essential in any teaching mode to maximize the learning and participation of the entire class group. This issue becomes even more critical in distance learning because it lacks those aspects of immediacy and concreteness typical of face-to-face interaction. Students need to understand their responsibility and master their spaces of autonomy, emotions, and feelings to have a successful learning experience. Teaching at a distance is a challenge. The teacher must be creative and imaginative in course design and structure, seeking to place teaching practices and sustainability of educational pathways in a perspective of systemic complexity. A rule of thumb is that learning experiences that work in a traditional classroom may be adaptable to the distance-learning environment but will require more than a few minor changes to slides or handouts. These strategies will likely require more creative and innovative approaches to engage students and keep their attention and motivation high. ... Consequently, teaching at a distance can be an enjoyable experience for everyone involved. Keeping students' interests high and motivating them to stay active can make teaching in distance education a worthwhile and enjoyable learning experience.

Attention to students' needs, including emotional needs, is at the heart of a successful distance learning experience. Quality learning and practical learning experiences depend not only on the efforts and on the expertise of the teacher but are also primarily determined by the efforts and preparation of the students themselves. Teaching and learning are two sides of the same coin, and the learning experiences offered to students should be equivalent but not necessarily equal.

... [T]he shift from the theoretical and practical dominance of traditional approaches to collaborative, creative, and innovative approaches supported by distance learning has created new challenges that have to do with maintaining a clear identity and coherence of purposes and goals of instructional actions.

At the end of the last century, there was an evident shift in thinking from the structural challenges of distance education to considering distance education as a possible method of teaching. The focus shifted from the structural constraints implicit in distance education to an emphasis on the educational experience. Recent developments blending online and face-to-face approaches have further blurred the distinction between the educational experience at a distance and the experience that occurs within school walls, thus contributing to hybrid forms that are difficult to categorize. Attempts to integrate online learning into the traditional paradigm include initiatives such as Massive Open Online Courses (MOOCs), augmented reality learning environments, or educational robotics. However, these initiatives still do not embrace all the possibilities of online collaboration. Traditional teaching is no longer a one-size-fits-all reality or constraint to adhere to but is transformed into the possibility of placing new tools and practices alongside established ones. This appears to be a classic example of a paradigm shift. ... Meeting these challenges will involve a leadership function on the part of school administration through change toward innovation. Progress is only innovation until it becomes the new normal; leadership is needed until the new normal is achieved. This new normal will necessarily involve collaborative partnerships, networked environments, new models of teaching and learning, and ongoing strategic planning. One of the most significant challenges facing institutions is integrating technology into education at every grade level, whether traditional or distance learning is [used]. We have an opportunity to put them at the center of the discussion, not only as an educational method, but as an engine for innovation and change. In this sense, learning communities can play an essential role in this process and can be valuable places of exchange and sharing, benefiting the entire educational community.

...

Currently, it appears that we are transitioning from a pandemic to an endemic phase, when Covid-19 will be one of the most contagious diseases of our time. This suggests that we will need to change our lifestyles to comply with the health safety standards established by the epidemic (for example, the WHO, regardless of infection rates, continues to recommend certain good habits such as social distancing and systematic disinfection of people and workplaces). From the standpoint of distance education, this suggests that we might spend more time in the years to come implementing distance learning technologies as a fundamental and stable component of educational paths in every school, up to and including universities.

Source: Addimando, Loredana. 2022. "Distance Learning in Pandemic Age: Lessons from a (No Longer) Emergency." *International Journal of Environmental Research and Public Health* 19, no. 23 (December): 16302. https://www.ncbi.nlm.nih.gov/pmc/articles/PMC9737831/

Southern New Hampshire University

GIFT OF THE CLASS OF 1993

6

Resources

Resources relating to distance education and remote learning comprise a growth area in the world of publishing and modern media. While books and journals are an important source for some of the historical background and information relating to distance education and remote learning, the speed with which the field has been developing has made the internet and news media an equally important source of information. Indeed, these are the central forums for ongoing debates about the effectiveness of remote learning education efforts as well as broader discussions about the changes, challenges, and advances that sometimes seem to appear at warp speed. Issues at the heart of modern remote learning, including effectiveness, equity, financial factors, and technological advancements, are also forcing discussions about the very nature of modern education. These wide-ranging topics can and should be examined through a variety of lenses.

Also reflective of the constantly evolving nature of the remote and distance education worlds are the multiple editions produced for many of the books on the topic. The following list of books makes clear that, despite the impacts of the pandemic, the idea of online distance education was developing in a very substantive manner early in the twenty-first century, with academics and practitioners seeking to develop appropriate pedagogy and practices that would maximize its educational potential. That process is clearly an ongoing one. Indeed, every time it seemed as though this section of the book was complete, another article of value and relevance appeared. But what follows is at least a substantive start.

Southern New Hampshire University (SNHU) embraced online learning in the mid-1990s, and has since become one of the nation's fastest-growing universities, with 135,000 online students in 2021. (© Rebecca Gragson/Dreamstime.com)

Books and Articles

History, Overviews, and Compilations

Adler, Renata. 1972. "Cookie, Oscar, Grover, Herry, Ernie, and Company: The Invention of Sesame Street." *The New Yorker*, June 3.

An illuminating look at one of the important pre-online "distance education" success stories.

Cotton, Eileen Giuffre. 2000. *The Online Classroom: Teaching with the Internet*. 4th edition. Bloomington, IN: EDINFO Press.

This book helps understand the evolution of teaching and learning to incorporate the internet as it moves toward modern distance education. It offers some insight into some early ideas pertaining to just what the internet could make distance education become.

Darling, Sharon. 1985. "The Electronic University." *Compute*, September. https://www.atarimagazines.com/compute/issue64/electronic_university.php

This article offers an extended look at one of the earliest efforts to create an internet-based distance education institution.

Etherington, Cait. 2018. "What Happened to the Electronic University Network?" elearninginside.com, January 9. https://news.elearninginside.com/what-happened-to-the-electronic-university-network/

A concise but informative look at one of the early efforts to create a distance education-based educational institution.

Euchner, Charlie. 1983. "Business Group Announces Creation of 'Electronic University.'" *Education Week*, September 21. https://www.edweek.org/education/business-group-announces-creation-of-electronic-university/1983/09

An interesting look at one of the early ventures in distance education at the higher education level.

Fusco, Marjorie, and Susan E. Ketcham. 2002. *Distance Learning for Higher Education: An Annotated Bibliography*. Santa Barbara, CA: ABC-CLIO.

This work offers a comprehensive look at the state of distance education as the world headed into the twenty-first century. It offers a great starting point for anyone wanting to see how much and how fast things have changed.

Harasim, Linda M., Starr Roxanne Hiltz, Lucio Teles, and Murray Turoff. 1995. *Learning Networks: A Field Guide to Teaching and Learning Online*. Cambridge, MA: MIT Press.

This book offers an early look at the way early technological developments were beginning to impact the educational world at the primary, secondary, university, and adult education levels. Divided into three sections, the book first surveys the developing field of online learning, then discusses how to best design distance education networks and the role of teacher and learner before considering the potential impact on twenty-first-century education.

Johnson, D. Lamont, Cleborne D. Maddux, and Jacque Ewing-Taylor. 2003. *Distance Education: Issues and Concerns*. Boca Raton, FL: CRC Press.

This collection of essays offers a good overview of the developing world of distance education. Among a range of issues, it looks at the way distance education impacts both student attitudes and behavior as well as the relationship between teacher and student in the virtual learning process.

Kentnor, Hope. 2015. "Distance Education and the Evolution of Online Learning in the United States." *Curriculum and Teaching Dialogue* 17, nos. 1 and 2.

With the arrival of distance education as a bona fide educational option, one that many schools are aggressively developing, it is important to understand its evolution. This work offers a valuable look at that process, tracing its development from early correspondence courses and the use of parcel post, to radio, then to television, and finally to online education in the effort to help better understand where things are headed.

Lesser, Gerald S. 1978. *Children and Television: Lessons from Sesame Street*. New York: McGraw-Hill.

This work by a Harvard professor initially skeptical about the potential of using television as a teaching tool, but who ultimately served as advisory board chairman of the Children's Television Workshop, is a look at the groundbreaking show, *Sesame Street*, and its roots, as well as an early assessment of the show's effectiveness.

Maddux, C. D., and W. D. Milheim, editors. 1992. *Distance Education: A Selected Bibliography*. Englewood Cliffs, NJ: Educational Technology Publications.

This early compilation of work on distance education offers broad general treatments as well as pieces that explore specific areas, including concerns about the approach and research in the field. It is an interesting look at the state of distance education at the time.

Mood, Terry Ann. 1995. *Distance Education: An Annotated Bibliography*. Englewood, CO: Libraries Unlimited, Inc.

This work offers a good compilation of distance education resources from the pre-internet age. It focuses on the pedagogical concerns of distance education with a specific focus on teachers, students, and administrators. Among the subjects included are the history of the approach, its philosophical underpinnings, and its application to non-academic settings.

Moore, Michael Grahame. 2013. *Handbook of Distance Education*. 3rd edition. Abingdon: Routledge.

Moore is one of the recognized leaders in the field of distance education, and this book represents a wide-ranging, research-based compilation of relevant materials. From historical background information to advice for teachers and learners, Moore offers information and guidance for almost anyone with an interest—from whatever perspective—in the area. Whether one is a student or a teacher looking to utilize distance education or someone studying the discipline itself and how it works, including the all-important business aspects, this book has much to offer.

Picciano, Anthony G. 2017. *Online Education Policy and Practice: The Past, Present, and Future of the Digital University*. New York: Routledge.

This book looks at the past, present, and future of networked learning environments and especially the role of faculty within them. With advancing technology making for altered classroom dynamics, this book helps provide an understanding of these changes and how teachers can respond to them. While looking at the history of online education, the book also offers some sense of where distance education in higher education is headed.

Sleator, Roy D. 2010. "The Evolution of eLearning: Background, Blends and Blackboard …" *Science Progress* 93, no. 3: 319–334. https://journals.sagepub.com/doi/pdf/10.3184/003685010X12710124862922

This article offers a look at the historical evolution of distance education before focusing on the modern, more tech-oriented approaches, including discussion of blended learning as potentially the best of both worlds. It closes by reviewing some of the current eLearning platforms.

Ubell, Robert. 2016. *Going Online: Perspectives on Digital Learning.* New York: Routledge.

In this book, respected online learning expert Ubell takes an overarching look at distance education. He goes back to its roots and traces its path into the modern computer age. He discusses what is needed to develop sustainable and successful programs and courses while also addressing the hazards and challenges that teachers and learners must overcome to make the new enterprise an educational success.

Theory, Philosophy, and Developing Practices

Anderson, Terry, editor. 2008. *The Theory and Practice of Online Learning.* 2nd edition. Athabasca, AB: Athabasca University Press.

This collection of essays by practitioners and scholars in the field of distance education offers a full treatment of this longtime but fast evolving area of education. The work provides context and guidance as the rapidly growing field addresses new challenges and embraces new opportunities.

Harry, Keith, Magnus John, and Desmond Keegan, editors. 2014. *Distance Education: New Perspectives.* New York: Routledge.

In bringing together a thoughtful selection of the best and most recent writing on distance education, this book is an important reference for anyone interested in this area. It shines a light on both the introduction of electronic communication technology and its impact on distance education. It also looks at the increasing number of degree programs while generally offering a comprehensive survey of new work in the field.

Holmberg, Borje. 1995. *Theory and Practice of Distance Education.* 2nd edition. New York: Routledge.

This work provides a comparatively early look at the developing world of internet-based distance education. It offers a comprehensive and global survey of distance education, while discussing the different approaches and models that are used. It also puts it in the context of the broader educational landscape.

Keegan, Desmond, editor. 1993. *Theoretical Principles of Distance Education.* New York: Routledge.

This book offers a focused look at the basic principles undergirding the idea of distance education and its attendant abandonment of the educational model centered on interpersonal, face-to-face communication. It explores the problems and opportunities in a more theoretical way, while identifying many of the issues that have subsequently had to be addressed.

Koksal, Ilker. 2020. "The Rise of Online Learning," *Forbes*, May 2. https://www.forbes.com/sites/ilkerkoksal/2020/05/02/the-rise-of-online-learning/?sh=4dd875e272f3

Published at the start of the Covid-19 shutdown, this piece offers a concise but informative take on how online learning is developing and what it has to offer. An advocacy piece to be sure, it also offers good basic information.

Sutton, Brian, and Anthony Basiel. 2014. *Teaching and Learning Online: New Models of Learning for a Connected World*. Volume 2. New York: Routledge.

This work offers practical guidance from a range of figures involved in the multifaceted world of online learning. It avoids technological trends and instead focuses on the development of the teaching and learning theories central to making distance education a distinctive and successful entity in its own right, one aided but not dominated by technology.

Valentine, Doug. 2002. "Distance Learning: Promises, Problems, and Possibilities." *Online Journal of Distance Learning Administration* 5 no. 3. State University of West Georgia, Distance Education Center. http://citeseerx.ist.psu.edu/viewdoc/download?doi=10.1.1.496.2781&rep=rep1&type=pdf#:~:text=Despite%20the%20promises%20and%20obvious,instructors%2C%20students%2C%20and%20administrators

This is a thoughtful look at distance learning, one that addresses just what the title portends: its promises, problems, and possibilities. While changes and developments have come fast and furious since its publication in 2002, the article offers lots of good observations and perspective on the still evolving field.

Teaching Strategies and Tips

Blackburn, Barbara R. 2020. *Rigor in the Remote Learning Classroom: Instructional Tips and Strategies*. New York: Routledge.

This work offers guidance in response to one of the biggest criticisms and fears of the shift from in-person teaching and learning to distance and remote teaching: the maintenance of a rigorous learning experience. The book addresses how to adapt to the new approach while not abandoning the standards that have been central to previous efforts.

Conrad, Dianne. 2018. *Assessment Strategies for Online Learning: Engagement and Authenticity*. Athabasca, AB: Athabasca University Press.

This work argues that the advent of distance education and online learning offers educators the opportunity to develop more authentic and effective assessment techniques and explores how they can do this. It considers how these new methods can recognize more fully the wide range of skills and attributes that each student brings to the learning experience.

Conrad, Rita-Marie, and J. Ana Donaldson. 2011. *Engaging the Online Learner: Activities and Resources for Creative Instruction*. San Francisco, CA: Jossey-Bass.

This book and its follow-up volume (*Continuing to Engage the Online Learner*) offer readers practical advice on how to engage online learners while also sharing numerous activities and ideas that can make the process easier. Building upon their model the Phases of Engagement, the authors look at the differences in a wide range of online and hybrid learning environments, technology tools, and communication styles in an effort to help teachers find the approach that is right for their area of study, school, and capacities. The ultimate aim is to provide teachers with tools appropriate to their needs and resources, while helping them to achieve the most productive online learning experience possible.

Conrad, Rita-Marie, and J. Ana Donaldson. 2012. *Continuing to Engage the Online Learner: More Activities and Resources for Creative Instruction*. San Francisco, CA: Jossey-Bass.

A follow-up to the authors' earlier work (*Engaging the Online Learner*), this book offers more practical ideas to help make the distance education experience all the more effective.

Finkelstein, Jonathan E. 2009. *Learning in Real Time: Synchronous Teaching and Learning Online*. San Francisco, CA: Jossey-Bass.

This book focuses on live online instruction, whether it is a synchronous course or simply a unit. It looks at the tools that can make synchronous instruction most effective while also sharing strategies and ideas that have been used successfully by others. It offers much that can help instructors improve their online offerings.

Fisher, Douglas, Nancy Frey, John T. Almarode, and John Hattie. 2020. *The Distance Learning Playbook for College and University Instruction: Teaching for Engagement and Impact in Any Setting*. Thousand Oaks, CA: Corwin.

This work offers guidance and instruction for university teachers in an effort to help them move beyond the emergency adaptive efforts that typified the early pandemic and instead develop intentional and effective distance education lessons that can be used at any point in an educational landscape.

Fisher, Douglas, Nancy Frey, and John Hattie. 2020. *The Distance Learning Playbook, Grades K-12: Teaching for Engagement and Impact in Any Setting*. Thousand Oaks, CA: Corwin.

This hands-on guide offers a wealth of approaches and ideas that will help teachers develop intentional, impactful, and effective remote learning lessons. It pays special attention to issues of equity as well as the needs of younger children.

Green, Jody Peerless. 2021. *Thriving as an Online K-12 Educator: Essential Practices from the Field*. New York: Routledge.

This concise but comprehensive book offers valuable insights and strategies for those forced to make the transition to remote teaching without the benefits of extended or formal distance education training. It offers much that can help a teacher keep their students engaged and able to learn effectively in the new online world.

Hockenbary, Lindy. 2021. *A Teacher's Guide to Online Learning: Practical Strategies to Improve K-12 Student Engagement in Virtual Learning*. Bozeman, MT: InTECHgrated Professional Development.

This valuable and practical book is aimed at those who have suddenly been forced to teach online. It offers guidance for the K-12 teacher who had to shift on a dime without the benefit of planning and training in the overarching principles of distance education. Including advice on how to address issues ranging from how to engage a class to how to develop personal connection over the internet, it also looks at the challenges of online classroom management, how to develop effective and secure assessments, and so much more.

Kearsley, G. 2000. *Online Education: Learning and Teaching in Cyberspace*. Belmont, CA: Wadsworth.

This book is a comprehensive introduction and overview of teaching and learning in "cyberspace," or online education, a term that the author takes to include any form of learning/teaching via a computer network. It provides its readers with a formal survey of this developing educational paradigm.

Kennepohl, Dietmar, editor. 2016. *Teaching Science Online: Practical Guidance for Effective Instruction and Lab Work*. Sterling, VA: Stylus Publishing.

A look at the specific issues faced by science teachers in the world of distance education, this book covers approaches relevant to each of the core scientific areas—biology, chemistry, and physics. It also considers broader concepts, such as the way online learning impacts labs, collaboration, and instructional activities as well as the potential for greater student access.

Ko, Susan, and Steve Rossen. *Teaching Online*. 4th edition. 2017. New York: Routledge.

This book offers an accessible introduction for anyone looking to teach online. The comprehensive guide centers on the practical aspects of online teaching, offering tools, advice, and examples from experienced practitioners.

Lehman, Rosemary, and Simone C. O. Conceição. 2010. *Creating a Sense of Presence in Online Teaching: How to "Be There" for Distance Learners*. San Francisco, CA: Jossey-Bass.

This book looks at the importance of an online presence in effective distance education, arguing that it contributes much to both student satisfaction and retention. The authors consider both the psychological and social aspects of online presence from the perspective of both teacher and learner. They also offer an instructional framework for developing effective online learning programs.

Lemov, Doug. 2020. *Teaching in the Online Classroom: Surviving and Thriving in the New Normal*. San Francisco, CA: Jossey-Bass.

This book is a response to the pandemic-induced shift to remote learning. It offers educators guidance and strategies that will help them make the transition from in-person teaching to online instruction in an effective manner. The book looks at the challenges central to online teaching and helps teachers and administrators identify and understand best practices both for the short term and in the future, given the reality that distance education is likely to be at least a part of the future educational landscape. This is a practical guide aimed at helping everyday teachers adapt their well-developed teaching skills to the online classroom.

McCabe, Margaret Foley, and Patricia González-Flores. 2017. *Essentials of Online Teaching: A Standards-Based Guide.* New York: Routledge.

This short but informative book offers practical, research-based guidance for teachers in high school, higher education, vocational, and corporate settings who seek to develop and implement standards-based online courses. It offers real-world examples while also addressing central instructional challenges in the modern online education world.

Pedagogy, Curriculum, and Course Design

Burge, Elizabeth J., editor. 2011. *Flexible Pedagogy, Flexible Practice: Notes from the Trenches of Distance Education.* Athabasca, AB: Athabasca University Press.

While remote learning has become an example of educational flexibility, itself a watchword in modern education, making it real is by no means a simple proposition. This book goes beyond assumptions and looks at the reality of the challenge of developing effective pedagogy for remote teaching and learning, paying special attention to the institutional dynamics that are often central to the process.

Cuevas, Rebecca Frost. 2019. *Course Design Formula: How to Teach Anything to Anyone Online.* Learn and Get Smarter, Inc.

This book introduces and explains the Course Design Formula®, a research-based, instructional design process. In integrating best practices from cognitive psychology, information processing theory, instructional design, and more, this process can assist teachers in developing their online courses.

Dalziel, James. 2016. *Learning Design: Conceptualizing a Framework for Teaching and Learning Online.* New York: Routledge.

This book offers a look at the way the field of learning design can be applied to the development of distance learning courses, and especially the way it can be applied to existing pedagogy in productive ways.

Daniela, Linda, editor. 2020. *Pedagogies of Digital Learning in Higher Education.* New York: Routledge.

This work explores numerous educational and pedagogical issues related to the learning process in the modern technological age, including distance learning.

It provides practical offerings that will be useful to those with interests ranging from the collection of research results and digital referencing to the use of online learning tools. Too, it offers ideas aimed at fostering creativity and the use of digital technology in fields ranging from music education to social work education.

Driscoll, Margaret. 1998. *Web-Based Training: Using Technology to Design Adult Learning Experiences.* San Francisco, CA: Jossey-Bass.

This book is aimed at allowing companies to develop their own web-based training and thus serve their own particular professional development needs. An example of much of the early distance education efforts that focused on more professional development and vocational training.

King, Elliot, and Neil Alperstein. 2015. *Best Practices in Online Program Development: Teaching and Learning in Higher Education.* New York: Routledge.

This hands-on guide offers specific strategic guidelines that any academic institution seeking to develop an effective online educational program can use. Beginning with a focus on the importance of the need to integrate distance education with the school's mission, it offers advice in how to make the distance effort an additional asset.

Moore, Michael G., and Greg Kearsley. 2011. *Distance Education: A Systems View.* 3rd edition. Boston: Cengage Learning.

This book focuses on the use of a systems approach to the development of distance education curriculum and its implementation. It shows how distance education is more than simply putting one's classroom lessons in front of a screen.

Palloff, Rena M., and Keith Pratt. 2008. *Assessing the Online Learner: Resources and Strategies for Faculty.* San Francisco: CA: Jossey-Bass.

This work offers guidance for higher education faculty in designing and developing assessments for remote learning classes and includes useful examples and case studies. It also helps instructors develop new ways to assess their new online teaching approaches.

Picciano, Anthony G. 2018. *Online Education: Foundations, Planning, and Pedagogy.* New York: Routledge.

This book offers a comprehensive look at both blended and fully online teaching platforms. It looks at the history, theory, research, planning, and practice of the approach, highlighting the issues of particular importance to the pedagogy and the administration of this developing form of teaching. The book provides historical context for the current efforts while offering some thoughts on what the future holds for the ever-changing educational landscape.

Schreiber, Deborah A., and Zane L. Berge, editors. 1998. *Distance Training: How Innovative Organizations Are Using Technology to Maximize Learning and Meet Business Objectives*. San Francisco, CA: Jossey-Bass Publishers.

Utilizing over a dozen case studies, this book offers readers a look at the way distance education can and has been successfully used by corporations, non-profits, and government agencies to produce effective, efficient, and cost-effective professional development that furthers their corporate and institutional goals.

Schutt, Maria. 2003. "Scaffolding for Online Learning Environments: Instructional Design Strategies that Provide Online Learner Support." *Educational Technology* 43, no. 6 (November–December): 28–35.

This work offers guidance in how to design online courses through a scaffolding approach. Drawing upon research from a variety of areas, it seeks to reach the wide range of interests that are moving towards online and distance instruction.

Vai, Marjorie, and Kristen Sosulski. 2016. *Essentials of Online Course Design: A Standards-Based Guide*. 2nd edition. New York: Routledge.

This book offers a well-designed, step-by-step approach to online course development. Based in standards that reflect best practices in online learning and teaching, it presents pedagogical, organizational, and visual design principles upon which a reader can develop an online course outline.

The Business of Distance Education

Bannon, Lisa, and Andrea Fuller. 2021. "USC Pushed a $115,000 Online Degree. Graduates Got Low Salaries, Huge Debts." *Wall Street Journal*, November 9. https://www.wsj.com/articles/usc-online-social-work-masters-11636435900?mod=djemedu

A look at the business aspect of a university's distance education program and its impact on students.

Bellows, Kate Hidalgo. 2022. "U. of Arizona Is Tightening Its Embrace of Troubled UA Global Campus. Will Reputational Damage Follow?" *Chronicle of Higher Education*, February 2. https://www.chronicle.com/article/u-of-arizona-is-tightening-its-embrace-of-troubled-ua-global-campus-will-reputational-damage-follow

This report highlights some of the potential pitfalls with distance education, even for one of the proven giants of the field. It is a cautionary tale for schools looking to expand their existing but modest programs.

Bramble, William J., and Santosh Panda. 2008. *Economics of Distance and Online Learning: Theory, Practice and Research*. New York: Routledge.

This book offers a comprehensive overview of the world of distance education from an economic perspective. It looks at the benefits enjoyed and costs incurred by the full range of participants who are a part of the ever-growing world of distance education.

Busta, Hallie. 2021. "Southern New Hampshire buys Kenzie Academy to Grow Alternative Credentials." *Higher Ed Dive*, March 9. https://www.highereddive.com/news/southern-new-hampshire-buys-kenzie-academy-to-grow-alternative-credentials/596415/

A news item that highlights the business side of distance education and some of the business reasons for the programmatic decisions.

Finkelstein, Martin J., Carol Frances, Frank I. Jewett, and Bernhard W. Scholz, editors. 2000. *Dollars, Distance, and Online Education: The New Economics of College Teaching and Learning*. Phoenix, AZ: Oryx Press.

This book looks at the way technology and distance learning have changed the very nature of attending college. A series of wide-ranging and authoritative essays analyze the way the college experience has been changed by developing technology, the costs and benefits of these changes, and what they portend for the future, both educationally and economically.

Kim, Paul, editor. 2015. *Massive Open Online Courses: The MOOC Revolution*. New York: Routledge.

A look at the place of MOOCs (Massive Open Online Courses) in the educational landscape with discussions of the many issues they represent as online courses of many types proliferate.

Koenig, Rebecca. 2022. "With Money from Facebook, 10 Colleges Turn Their Campuses into 'Metaversities.'" *EdSurge*, June 1. https://www.edsurge.com/news/2022-06-01-with-money-from-facebook-10-colleges-turn-their-campuses-into-metaversities

A look at the potential future of distance education, one that raises interesting questions about the very nature of the future college experience.

Murphy, John D. 2013. *Mission Forsaken—The University of Phoenix Affair with Wall Street*. Cambridge, MA: Proving Ground Education.

This look back by University of Phoenix co-founder John D. Murphy is an interesting account of the development of the online giant and the many challenges it faced in taking on the brick-and-mortar educational establishment. It offers a thought provoking look at the intersection of business and education in the online world, covering issues that have only become more important with the Covid-19 pandemic fueling more and more distance education initiatives.

Nanfito, Michael. 2013. *MOOCs: Opportunities, Impacts, and Challenges: Massive Open Online Courses in Colleges and Universities*. CreateSpace Independent Publishing Platform.

This good introductory guide offers a look at the MOOC phenomenon, touting what it has to offer and enthusiastically previewing where it may go. While definitely an advocate, the author does not ignore the ongoing challenges and issues that need to be addressed.

Schwartz, Natalie. 2022. "House Committee: End Loophole Allowing Tuition-share Agreements between OPMs and Colleges." *Higher Ed Dive*, June 30. https://www.highereddive.com/news/house-committee-end-loophole-allowing-tuition-share-agreements-between-opm/626433/

This article presents the House of Representatives concerns about the role of Online Program Management (OPM) companies in the delivery of college and university distance education offerings.

Seltzer, Rick. 2021. "Can Colleges Compete with Companies Like Coursera?" *Higher Ed Dive*, September 28. https://www.highereddive.com/news/can-colleges-compete-with-companies-like-coursera/607324/

This article, for the most part a Q&A with noted educator Artur Levine, looks at continuing pressures that colleges are experiencing as they venture deeper into the world of distance education. As higher education is pushed to act like other businesses, this direction has also led educational institutions to rely more and more on outside companies. The piece touches on an intriguing and important set of questions.

Swaak, Taylor. 2022. "A Small, Private College Ups Its Bet on Online Programs. Will It Pay Off?" *The Chronicle of Higher Education*, March 17. https://www.chronicle.com/article/a-small-private-college-ups-its-bet-on-online-programs-will-it-pay-off

This story looks at the way one school has sought to utilize an expanded distance education program to strengthen its financial situation. The final results are not yet in, but the article raises important issues central to such efforts.

Vasquez, Michael. 2021. "A College Found Explosive Growth through Its Online Programs. Now Its Accreditor Has Put It on Probation." *The Chronicle of Higher Education*, November 10. https://www.chronicle.com/article/a-community-college-found-explosive-growth-through-its-online-programs-now-its-accreditor-has-put-it-on-probation

This article offers a cautionary tale about what can happen when the commercial allure of distance education overwhelms a school's core academic mission. The massive expansion of distance education programs resulted in an unprecedented increase in (primarily online) enrollment. Accreditors found that at the same time that Eastern Gateway Community College was enjoying its meteoric rise, its almost unchecked growth was accompanied by a seeming indifference to the quality of the students' academic experience. The result was the school being put on probation.

Vasquez, Michael. 2022. "'They Didn't Care': Inside One University's Sputtering Online Partnership with 2U." *The Chronicle of Higher Education*, June 1. https://www.chronicle.com/article/they-didnt-care-inside-one-universitys-sputtering-online-partnership-with-2u

This article looks at the way business and educational concerns clashed in one university's effort to develop a distance education partnership. It is a case that highlighted the desires as well as the pitfalls that can impact such efforts.

Administering and Developing Distance Education Programs

Catalano, Amy J. 2018. *Measurements in Distance Education: A Compendium of Instruments, Scales, and Measures for Evaluating Online Learning*. New York: Routledge.

As distance education becomes an ever-greater part of the educational landscape, there remains the question of how to assess the rigor and value of such programs. This work tackles that issue head on. In a concise and well-organized manner, it offers a thoughtful review of the numerous instruments, scales, and methods that have been created to assess distance education—the programs, the teachers, and the learners. With more than fifty different surveys, tests, and assorted other metrics, it is a valuable resource for those seeking to understand distance education assessment.

Chute, Alan, Burton Hancock, and Melody Thompson. 1998. *The McGraw-Hill Handbook of Distance Learning: A "How to Get Started Guide" for Trainers and Human Resources Professionals*. New York: McGraw-Hill.

This is a great introduction to distance learning. The guidebook is specifically aimed at helping businesses and other organizations and institutions utilize and adapt distance education to their needs, with an eye to enhancing their efforts in a way that is at once cost-effective and more convenient and effective for employees and customers alike.

Collison, George, Bonnie Elbaum, Sarah Haavind, and Robert Tinker. 2000. *Facilitating Online Learning: Effective Strategies for Moderators*. Madison, WI: Atwood Pub.

A guide to learning the distinctive techniques and skills necessary to effectively facilitate online teaching and learning, this work is aimed at those new to online education and training. It offers both the theoretical framework and practical guidelines that prospective facilitators will need.

Cyrs, Thomas E., editor. 1997. *Teaching and Learning at a Distance: What It Takes to Effectively Design, Deliver, and Evaluate Programs*. San Francisco, CA: Jossey-Bass.

This issue of the quarterly journal *New Directions for Teaching and Learning*, beginning from the premise that distance education is about more than technology, offers thoughtful guidance for the effort to develop skillful instructors and well-designed courses. It draws upon experienced practitioners to address what is needed in the rapidly developing area.

Dillon, Connie L., and Rosa Cintrón, editors. 1997. *Building a Working Policy for Distance Education*. San Francisco: Jossey-Bass.

This special issue of the quarterly journal *New Directions for Community Colleges* offers some early ideas on the ways distance education could impact community colleges.

Fisher, Douglas, Nancy Frey, Dominque B. Smith, and John Hattie. 2020. *The Distance Learning Playbook for School Leaders: Leading for Engagement and Impact in Any Setting*. Thousand Oaks, CA: Corwin.

Believing that distance education is not just about a changing relationship between teachers and students but also about a school culture and approach, this book offers guidance in helping school administrators in the effort to implement distance education where it has not previously been a part of the program. It looks at a wide range of issues including school climate, leader credibility, and caring for self and colleagues as well as instructional leadership teams, while offering administrators research- and evidence-based strategies they can use to ensure that their school offers effective and high-quality online learning programs.

Hillman, Daniel, Robert Schudy, and Anatoly Temkin. 2021. *Best Practices for Administering Online Programs*. New York: Routledge.

This work offers practical guidance for universities looking to develop online programs. It lays out the steps necessary to get a wide range of stakeholders, including program directors, department chairs, teaching faculty, course designers and IT specialists, all focused on and engaged in the effort to develop and offer affordable and accessible online programs.

Means, Barbara, Marianne Bakia, and Robert Murphy. 2014. *Learning Online: What Research Tells Us about Whether, When and How*. New York: Routledge.

This work offers a guide to the types of online learning while looking at the different ways in which it is being utilized from K-12 to higher education. The book draws upon available research to show how different approaches are appropriate for different disciplines and grade levels, highlighting the ongoing importance of the differentiated human dimension of the teaching and learning process, even in distance education.

Porter, Lynette R. 1997. *Creating the Virtual Classroom: Distance Learning with the Internet*. New York: John Wiley & Sons.

This highly informative book goes to the heart of distance education, offering guidance on how to design and manage distance learning programs. Its practical approach covers proposing, planning, and funding a distance learning program for any educational level. It addresses differences in technology and other aspects of distance learning that must be considered when designing a course that is not simply moving an in-person class in front of a screen.

Rice, Kerry. 2020. *Making the Move to K-12 Online Teaching: Research-Based Strategies and Practices*. 2nd edition. Independently published.

This book offers a comprehensive treatment of online education for K-12 teachers. It covers everything pre-collegiate teachers need to make the transition from in-person, in-class teaching to online venues, always with an eye to the many challenges that the shift entails. The book also pays special attention to teaching in a blended classroom.

Rossman, M. H., and M. E. Rossman, editors. 1995. *Facilitating Distance Education*. San Francisco, CA: Jossey-Bass.

This work from the "New Directions for Adult and Continuing Education" series presents a range of perspectives from experienced distance educators concerning the impact of distance education on adult and continuing education. Its goal is to foster in readers a greater understanding and appreciation of how they can facilitate distance education.

Shoemaker, Cynthia C.J. 1998. *Leadership in Continuing and Distance Education in Higher Education*. Boston: Allyn & Bacon.

This work offers extensive and wide-ranging guidance for those seeking to implement and develop a distance education program. While it was published at the end of the twentieth century, the fundamental concerns it addresses remain central to the challenges faced by those working to develop or expand such programs in the aftermath of the Covid-19 pandemic.

Simonson, Michael, Susan M. Zvacek, and Sharon Smaldino. 2019. *Teaching and Learning at a Distance: Foundations of Distance Education*. 7th edition. Charlotte, NC: Information Age Publishing.

The latest edition of an ongoing effort, one that has evolved alongside distance learning itself, this book is intended for those preparing to teach distance education courses. It offers readers the basic information necessary for an individual to be an effective distance educator as well as a leader of an emerging distance education program.

Simpson, Ormond. 2012. *Supporting Students for Success in Online and Distance Education*. 3rd edition. New York: Routledge.

This work seeks to address a major Achilles heel of distance education: dismal completion/graduation rates. Drawing upon substantive research in distance and e-learning, it offers ideas about how retention rates can be improved to the benefit of both students and institutions.

Veletsianos, George. 2010. *Emerging Technologies in Distance Education*. Athabasca, AB: Athabasca University Press.

This book brings together the work of international experts who look at the range of factors—pedagogical, organizational, cultural, social, and economic—that are central to both the adoption and integration of emerging technologies in distance education. It offers important information for educators seeking to launch effective and engaging distance education initiatives, while also addressing the important issues that are central to enhancing the educational practices of distance education.

Verduin, John R., and Thomas A. Clark 1991. *Distance Education: The Foundations of Effective Practice*. San Francisco, CA: Jossey-Bass.

This book offers an early look at the way educators initially began to develop distance education, especially as an option for adult learners. It covers the way the idea has evolved and how it can serve adult learners in particular. It addresses the strengths and limitations already evident in the field's early development, and it explores some of the foundational principles upon which future advancements would rest.

Vivolo, John, editor. 2020. *Managing Online Learning: The Life-Cycle of Successful Programs*. New York: Routledge.

This book offers a comprehensive guide to planning and executing effective online learning programs. Drawing from experienced professionals from both the university and corporate worlds, this work provides educational leaders with the strategies and information they need to address the challenges they face in this changing educational landscape.

Williamson, Ronald, and Barbara R. Blackburn. 2020. *Leadership for Remote Learning: Strategies for Success*. New York: Routledge.

This book offers guidance for school leaders seeking to effectively adapt to remote learning. Among the many issues it addresses are how to maintain a collaborative environment, shaping school culture, and addressing problems of equity in an effort to help teachers and students maximize the teaching and learning experience in the remote environment.

Willis, Barry. 1994. *Distance Education: A Practical Guide*. Englewood Cliffs, NJ: Educational Technology Publications.

This is a "how to" introduction to distance education that can help anyone plan, develop, and implement a distance education program. Offering step-by-step guidance on how to effectively use faculty, materials, media, and teaching strategies to best effect, the book ends by looking at the future of distance education while also highlighting some of the challenges that lie ahead.

Willis, Barry, editor. 1994. *Distance Education: Strategies and Tools*. Englewood Cliffs, NJ: Educational Technology Publications.

This work seeks to address many of the challenges facing distance education. While recognizing how the flexibility of distance education is a plus, the author notes that it can also lead to chaos. He seeks to provide guidance to those educators who will be entrusted with the responsibility of successfully navigating the challenges of this developing educational approach so that they do so in the most productive way possible.

Distance Education versus Remote Learning

Craig, Ryan. 2020. "What Students Are Doing Is Remote Learning, Not Online Learning. There's a Difference." *EdSurge*, April 2. https://www.edsurge.com/news/2020-04-02-what-students-are-doing-is-remote-learning-not-online-learning-there-s-a-difference

This article offers exactly what its title promises, a discussion of the difference between remote learning and online learning. Especially early in the pandemic, these terms were used interchangeably, but the distinction between them is far from minor. Acknowledging the very real differences is especially important as programs are developed and distance education becomes a bigger part of the normal, post-pandemic educational landscape.

Hodges, Charles, Stephanie Moore, Barb Lockee, Torrey Trust, and Aaron Bond. 2020. "The Difference between Emergency Remote Teaching and Online Learning." *EDUCAUSE Review*, March 27. https://er.educause.edu/articles/2020/3/the-difference-between-emergency-remote-teaching-and-online-learning

> Published at the outset of the Covid-19 pandemic, this article offers a comprehensive, thoughtful, and clear discussion of the differences between well-planned online learning experiences that characterize true distance education and the emergency remote teaching and learning experiences to which the nation turned during the pandemic. While recognizing that there were few options in the spring of 2020, the authors seek to make clear what quality distance education can be so that its future usage is appropriate and its impact is maximized to the benefit of countless different constituencies.

Malvik, Callie. 2020. "Online Education vs. Remote Learning: 5 Features of a Quality Distance Learning Program." *CollegisEducation*, May 27. https://collegiseducation.com/news/programs-and-course-content/quality-distance-learning-program/

> This article offers a quick primer on the differences between online education and remote learning. The explanation is concise but clear, and the author explores what needs to be done to turn the temporary remote efforts that saw schools through to the end of the 2019–20 academic year into productive and sustainable distance education programs for students who need or want it and for schools that seek to use it to expand their offerings.

Manfuso, Lauren Glenn. 2020. "From Emergency Remote Teaching to Rigorous Online Learning." *EdTech Magazine*, May 7. https://edtechmagazine.com/higher/article/2020/05/emergency-remote-teaching-rigorous-online-learning-perfcon

> Appearing in the midst of the pandemic-fueled shift to remote learning, this article offers a thoughtful discussion of the difference between remote learning and distance education, a distinction that is critical for all to understand as the nation emerges from the pandemic and the idea of distance education is viewed through a different lens than it had been previously.

Members of the National Council for Online Education, 2022. "Remote Instruction and Online Learning Aren't the Same Thing (Opinion)." *Inside Higher Ed*, February 3. https://www.insidehighered.com/views/2022/02/03/remote-instruction-and-online-learning-arent-same-thing-opinion

This article offers a thoughtful discussion of the difference between the pedagogically and curricularly based field of distance education and the remote teaching and learning that most of the nation experienced during the Covid-19 pandemic shutdown beginning in March 2020. The distinction impacts countless aspects of the educational process at all levels, a fact that was lost during the turmoil of the pandemic.

Stauffer, Bri. 2020. "What's the Difference between Online Learning and Distance Learning?" *Applied Educational Systems (AES)*, April 2. https://www.aeseducation.com/blog/online-learning-vs-distance-learning

This article offers a quick primer on the difference between online learning and distance learning, concisely looking at the pros and cons of both. It can help the reader determine which option is best for them and their learning style.

Voelker, Christine. 2020. "Crossing the Bridge: From Emergency Remote Teaching to Quality Online Learning." *AC&E/Equity & Access*, September–October. https://issuu.com/acecommunications/docs/ace-ed_0920/s/10959636

Coming in the aftermath of the national transition to online teaching that took place in the spring of 2020, this article looks at the way the pandemic-era remote teaching and learning differs from true distance learning while offering insight and suggestions about what must be done to make a successful change to the more thoughtful and polished product that distance education can be.

Pros, Cons, and Assessments

Barnum, Matt, and Claire Bryan. 2020. "America's Great Remote-learning Experiment: What Surveys of Teachers and Parents Tell Us about How It Went." *Chalkbeat*, June 26. https://www.chalkbeat.org/2020/6/26/21304405/surveys-remote-learning-coronavirus-success-failure-teachers-parents

Acknowledging that data related to student learning during the pandemic was non-existent in mid-2020, the surveys discussed in this article offered feedback from students, teachers, and educational administrators on the areas where things had gone well and those where they had not. An interesting look at early opinions about the experience.

Belanger, France, and Dianne Jordan. 1999. *Evaluation and Implementation of Distance Learning: Technologies, Tools and Techniques*. Hershey, PA: Idea Group Publishing.

This is a comprehensive guide to developing and implementing a distance education program. From tips on training teachers, to establishing appropriate learning objectives, to effectively utilizing technology, it addresses the hows and the whys and then offers ways to assess how effective an effort is. It is a very good introductory work.

Berg, Gary. 2002. *Why Distance Learning?: Higher Education Administrative Practices*. Westport, CT: Praeger Publishers.

Utilizing both a national survey of higher education institutions and interviews with administrators, this book looks at key issues of distance learning, including why higher education institutions are pursuing such ventures and how administration and management practices are affected by these motivations. It also investigates the pedagogical impacts and the impact on school culture of such efforts. It is a thoughtful look at some of the issues central to any decision to adopt or develop a distance education program.

Fisher, Douglas, Nancy Frey, Vince Bustamante, and John Hattie. 2020. *The Assessment Playbook for Distance and Blended Learning: Measuring Student Learning in Any Setting*. Thousand Oaks, CA: Corwin.

Recognizing that assessments that are effective in face-to-face learning may not be appropriate to distance learning, this work offers guidance, as well as an array of examples and strategies, for how to develop and implement assessments that will work in remote and blended classroom settings.

Herman, Peter C. 2020. "Online Learning Is Not the Future." *Inside Higher Ed*, June 10. https://www.insidehighered.com/digital-learning/views/2020/06/10/online-learning-not-future-higher-education-opinion

This is an early entry in the developing debate over the effectiveness of remote learning efforts during the pandemic and what they portended for the future. It highlights the divide between educators and public policy people, many of whom are on a constant search for the educational silver bullet. It is an interesting contribution to the debate.

Kilburn, Don. 2022. "President Speaks: Stop Asking Whether Online Learning Is 'Worth It.' Start Focusing on How It Helps Working Adults." *Higher Ed Dive*, February 7, 2022. https://www.highereddive.com/news/president-speaks-stop-asking-whether-online-learning-is-worth-it-start/617705/

An impassioned plea from the president of UMass Online to have educators and policymakers move beyond the wide-ranging quality of online learning programs that was revealed by the pandemic—a range that, as he notes, is no less apparent in in-person instruction—and instead to recognize the value of distance education, focusing on and drawing from the quality programs that do exist so their methods can be applied more broadly and more effectively for today's students, especially adult learners already in the working world.

Lederman, Doug. 2020. "What Do We Know about This Spring's Remote Learning?" *Inside Higher Ed*, June 10. https://www.insidehighered.com/digital-learning/article/2020/06/10/what-do-we-know-and-what-should-we-try-learn-about-springs

An early work on the debate over the effectiveness of the remote learning efforts to which the nation turned after the onset of the Covid-19 pandemic in the spring of 2020. In raising important questions, the article helps develop the agenda for discussions that follow.

Moore, M. G., and M. M. Thompson. 1990. *The Effects of Distance Learning: A Summary of Literature*. University Park, PA: American Center for the Study of Distance Education.

After briefly reviewing the characteristics of distance education, this work looks at the research of the 1980s on issues like teaching, learning, and educational planning as they relate to the role of communications technology in modern distance education. The main focus is on audio, video, and computer teleconferencing. Issues addressed relate not to the effectiveness of the communications media per se, but rather to their impact on certain educational variables, especially both learners' and teachers' achievements and attitudes, as well as course design and curriculum issues, among others.

Schnieders, Joyce, and Raeal Moore. 2021. *First-Year College Students' Online Learning Experiences during the Pandemic*, ACT, June. https://www.act.org/content/dam/act/unsecured/documents/pdfs/First-Year-College-Students-Online-Learning-Experiences-During-Pandemic.pdf

One of the major standardized test providers looks at the experience of first year college students during the pandemic's first full academic year. This work raises many issues of importance for all involved in the teaching and learning process at a time when the educational world moves ever more deeply into distance learning.

"7 True Stories from Virtual School." 2021. *The New York Times Magazine*, September 9. https://www.nytimes.com/2021/09/09/magazine/stories-virtual-school.html

This set of personal perspectives reflects on what virtual school was like during the first stages of the pandemic-fueled shutdown. It offers a poignant insight into the human toll of the experience on a range of people.

Turner, John G. 2021. *The Pros and Cons of Online Learning in Higher Education*. Independently published.

This book introduces readers to the basic benefits of an online educational experience while comparing it to the in-class experience. It looks at the impact of the online experience for students before and after the pandemic. In weighing the pros and cons, it seeks to help students make more informed choices about their future education.

Higher Education and Distance Education

Bannon, Lisa, and Rebecca Smith. 2022. "That Fancy University Course? It Might Actually Come from an Education Company." *The Wall Street Journal*, July 6. https://www.wsj.com/articles/that-fancy-university-course-it-might-actually-come-from-an-education-company-11657126489?mod=hp_featst_pos4

This article looks at the often complicated relationship between higher education and the corporate interests that are now central to supplying, or at least delivering, their content. The article explores the business side of distance education.

Hannah, Donald E., Chris Dede, Donald Olcott, Jr., Janet Poley, Kathy Schmidt, and John Tallman. 2000. *Higher Education in an Era of Digital Competition: Choices and Challenges*. Madison, WI: Atwood Pub.

Published, as the authors note, "at the dawn of a new millennium," this book looks at the critical knowledge and perspectives that will help shape higher education in the future. The book offers a framework in which new technologies can serve as a positive change agent, a powerful tool for enhanced teaching and learning in the new age.

Lederman, Doug. 2022. "What Have We Learned about Online Learning?" *Inside Higher Ed*, July 6. https://www.insidehighered.com/news/2022/07/06/what-have-we-learned-about-online-learning

A look at what the pandemic years have taught the higher education community about online and distance learning. Among the important takeaways is the critical importance of training in the effort to make online teaching and learning a positive force for educational equity.

Nichols, Mark. 2020. *Transforming Universities with Digital Distance Education: The Future of Formal Learning.* New York: Routledge.

This book looks at the way higher education can utilize and maximize the benefits of online learning. Addressing system-wide issues that go beyond instructors and academic programs, the book seeks to help managers and decision makers avoid the problems that can lead to dysfunction and undermine best efforts.

Ubell, Robert. 2021. *Staying Online: How to Navigate Digital Higher Education.* New York: Routledge.

This work offers important insights into how we can reimagine digital higher education. As the pandemic has hastened a developing movement towards greater online programming, higher education leaders must address how to create and develop effective programs. Ubell looks at the dynamics of current online learning practices and offers forward thinking suggestions that will help educational leaders in ways that maximize technological capabilities while preserving core values of the educational process.

Hybrid and Blended Learning

Horn, Michael B., and Heather Staker. 2014. *Blended: Using Disruptive Innovation to Improve Schools.* San Francisco: Jossey-Bass.

This book offers practical advice for implementing blended learning techniques in K-12 classrooms. A hands-on guide, it provides practical guidance for those seeking to incorporate online learning into their traditional classroom time.

Schwartz, Natalie. 2022. "Chief Online Officers Predict Shift to Hybrid Education by 2025, Survey Finds." *Higher Ed Dive*, August 9. https://www.highereddive.com/news/chief-online-officers-predict-shift-to-hybrid-education-by-2025-survey-fin/629136/

As another school year begins, education technology leaders offer an assessment of where higher education is going in terms of online education.

Issues and Impacts

Belsha, Kalyn, and Matt Barnum. 2022. "Sticking Around: Most Big Districts Will Offer Virtual Learning This Fall, a Sign of Pandemic's Effect." *Chalkbeat*, June 6. https://www.chalkbeat.org/2022/6/6/23153483/big-school-districts-virtual-learning-fall-2022

An article that highlights both the way online teaching has become an acceptable option while at the same time noting the continuing problems with remote teaching and learning. As a fallback and a short-term panacea, the approach is not doing what distance education at its best can do. The divide between remote learning and distance education remains a source of contention.

Campbell, Patricia B., and Jennifer Storo. 1996. "Reducing the Distance: Equity Issues in Distance Learning in Public Education." *Journal of Science Education and Technology* 5, no. 4 (December): 285–95. https://www.jstor.org/stable/40188564?seq=1

This work looks at the way that, while distance learning and educational equity have been founded on the principles of access, changing and expanded definitions of equity and new developments in distance education have made the issue of equity an even greater source of concern in the field. Although the authors agree that distance education has been a tool for increasing access to education, they also warn that efforts to advance equity must continue along with efforts to improve educational quality.

"Education in a Pandemic: The Disparate Impacts of Covid-19 on America's Students." 2021. Office for Civil Rights, U.S. Department of Education, June 9. https://www2.ed.gov/about/offices/list/ocr/docs/20210608-impacts-of-covid19.pdf

This report offers some important early data related to the effectiveness of the remote teaching and learning that took place with the onset of the Covid-19 pandemic. While reflecting only the early stages of the efforts, the report raises numerous and important questions about both access and equity in the online educational experience of students at all levels during that period and offers much for policymakers to consider as remote and distance education play more prominent roles in future educational endeavors.

Gallagher, Sean, and Jason Palmer. 2020. "The Pandemic Pushed Universities Online. The Change Was Long Overdue." *Harvard Business Review*, September 29. https://hbr.org/2020/09/the-pandemic-pushed-universities-online-the-change-was-long-overdue

This article looks at the impact of the pandemic on colleges' approach to online learning. Noting that many colleges and universities were already moving in that direction, the authors argue that the pandemic sped up that transition and discuss the reasons why, especially from a business perspective, the change is a good thing, as well as what it portends for the future.

Gusman, Michaela, Kevin J. Grimm, Adam B. Cohen, and Leah D. Doane. 2021. "Stress and Sleep across the Onset of the Covid-19 Pandemic: Impact of Distance Learning on U.S. College Students' Health Trajectories." *Sleep Research Society*, July. https://www.researchgate.net/publication/353608691_Stress_and_Sleep_Across_the_Onset_of_the_COVID-19_Pandemic_Impact_of_Distance_Learning_on_US_College_Students'_Health_Trajectories

This article looks at one aspect of the health concerns brought on by the pandemic-fueled remote learning shift of the spring of 2020 and raises some interesting points about the impact of remote and distance education beyond the teaching and learning elements.

Mauriello, Tracie. 2022. "Michigan Students Forced Online by Covid Learned Less Than Those in Schools." *Chalkbeat Detroit*, January 10. https://detroit.chalkbeat.org/2022/1/10/22875336/epic-remote-learning-loss-michigan-test-scores-achieveme

This report on the challenges and the limited effectiveness of remote learning in at least part of Michigan during the pandemic highlights the way the process impacted some groups more than others.

Merod, Anna. 2022. "District Outreach Critical as 10M Households Benefit from Affordable Connectivity Program." *K-12 Dive*, February 16. https://www.k12dive.com/news/district-outreach-critical-as-10m-households-benefit-from-affordable-connec/618954/

A look at the importance of government programs in creating greater equity and access to online learning.

Merod, Anna. 2022. "White House Eyes Digital Divide with Discount for Low-income Families." *Higher Ed Dive*, May 11. https://www.highereddive.com/news/white-house-eyes-digital-divide-with-discount-for-low-income-families/623506/

A news report of early government efforts to address the economic-based inequities impacting the potential effectiveness of distance education.

North, Anna. 2020. "The Shift to Online Learning Could Worsen Educational Inequality." *Vox*, April 9. https://www.vox.com/2020/4/9/21200159/coronavirus-school-digital-low-income-students-covid-new-york

An early look at the ways in which equity and inequity are issues that dog the remote learning experience, concerns that distance education must address in the future.

"Pandemic Gave Teachers New Insight into Ed Tech. Now, It May Be the Next Big Thing in 2022—and Beyond," 2022. *The 74*, January 4. https://www.the74million.org/article/pandemic-gave-teachers-new-insight-into-ed-tech-now-it-may-be-the-next-big-thing-in-2022-and-beyond/

This article looks at the way the pandemic increased educators' awareness of the way technology, both in the classroom and through distance learning, can impact the educational process while opening new possibilities for the future.

Schwartz, Natalie. 2021. "Pandemic Fueled Huge Online-only Enrollment Growth, Report Finds." *Higher Ed Dive*, October 20. https://www.highereddive.com/news/pandemic-fueled-huge-online-only-enrollment-growth-report-finds/608522/

This article offers an early look at the impact on enrollment of the pandemic-fueled shift to remote learning. Now that students have been introduced to the process, they are more open to it. The piece raises many questions that will be part of the debate going forward.

Smalley, Suzanne. 2021. "Philanthropies Help HBCUs Take Their Education Online." *Inside Higher Ed*, October 26. https://www.insidehighered.com/news/2021/10/26/philanthropies-help-hbcus-take-their-education-online#:~:text=United%20Negro%20College%20Fund%20and,their%20unique%20educational%20offerings%20digitally

A look at how the recent upsurge in philanthropic gifts to HBCUs has helped one sector in the effort to address concerns about equity in remote teaching and learning and distance education.

Smith, Carl. 2022. "How Can States Plan for the Long Game of Digital Equity?" *Governing*, June 15. https://www.governing.com/next/how-can-states-plan-for-the-long-game-of-digital-equity

This article looks at early, but future-oriented, efforts of states in the aftermath of the pandemic to ensure digital equity at a time when digital-based education is becoming an ever-greater part of the educational landscape.

Smith, Carl, and Dustin Haisler. 2020. "What States Can Do to Improve Broadband Access." *Governing*, March 4. https://www.governing.com/next/what-states-can-do-to-improve-broadband-access.html

This assessment was published just before the Covid-19 pandemic shutdown. It lays out the existing digital divide, the ramifications of which were exacerbated with the pandemic-induced move to online remote learning. Equity issues are made clear, as is the need for governmental action to address the issue.

Sublett, Cameron. 2020. *Distant Equity: Promises and Pitfalls of Online Learning for Students of Color in Higher Education*. American Council on Education (ACE).

This work provides a look at the range of issues surrounding distance education, particularly questions of equity. It looks at the promise the approach holds for narrowing the equity gap in higher education as well as what has been done so far. Although distance learning has the ability to close both opportunity and achievement gaps, the author notes that thus far, it has fallen short.

Swaak, Taylor. 2022. "Will Virtual-Reality 'Metaversities' Risk Students' Data Privacy? We Asked for Contracts to Find Out." *The Chronicle of Higher Education*, June 17. https://www.chronicle.com/article/will-virtual-reality-metaversities-risk-students-data-privacy-we-asked-for-contracts-to-find-out

As a group of schools pioneer the idea of "Metaversities," questions arise about what it entails for the students involved.

Toppo, Greg. 2021. "Hybrid Learning Sparks New Worries about Cheating. Can Assessment Evolve?" *Higher Ed Dive*, December 22. https://www.highereddive.com/news/hybrid-learning-sparks-new-worries-about-cheating-can-assessment-evolve/616476/

This article looks at concerns related to the integrity of assessments that have arisen with the growth of distance education and remote learning and whether there is an opportunity to reevaluate the very nature of assessment in modern education.

Opportunities for the Online Learner

Atieh, Sam. 1998. *How to Get a College Degree Via the Internet: The Complete Guide to Getting Your Undergraduate or Graduate Degree from the Comfort of Your Home*. Shreveport, LA: Prima Publishing.

This is an early work touting the benefits of distance education and laying out options for those wanting to pursue a degree in that way.

Bear, Mariah, and Thomas Nixon. 2006. *Bear's Guide to Earning Degrees by Distance Learning*. Berkeley, CA: Ten Speed Press.

This book is a comprehensive guide to earning degrees of all kinds through distance education. Offered by a longtime leader in helping navigate the challenges of nontraditional education, this book helps readers understand what is available in a field that is seeing a massive increase in the number of schools developing and offering accredited online degree programs.

Burgess, William E. 2000. *The Oryx Guide to Distance Learning: A Comprehensive Listing of Electronic and Other Media-Assisted Courses*. Phoenix, AZ: Oryx Press.

This early guide to available media-assisted course credits is a starting point and allows readers to see how far things have progressed in the last two decades. The book includes thousands of distance learning courses from hundreds of post-secondary institutions and makes clear that the idea of distance education was developing well before the Covid-19 pandemic shifted it into overdrive.

Dixon, P. 1996. *Virtual College: A Quick Guide to How You Can Get the Degree You Want with Computer, TV, Video, Audio, and Other Distance-Learning Tools*. Denver, CO: Petersons Guides.

An early guide that offers readers a sense of the different early efforts to provide alternative, technology-based types of education, with each being a forerunner of the modern types of distance education.

"U.S. News Unveils 2022 Best Online Programs Rankings." 2022. *U.S. News & World Report*, January 25. https://www.usnews.com/info/blogs/press-room/articles/2022-01-25/u-s-news-unveils-2022-best-online-programs-rankings

Reflective of the growth of distance education, *U.S. News* has added the ranking of distance programs to its offerings. High rankings are trumpeted by schools that do well.

Websites

American Center for the Study of Distance Education (AC4SDE) https://sites.psu.edu/acde/

Founded in 1988, AC4SDE is an inter-institutional, multidisciplinary center that seeks to facilitate collaboration among institutions and individuals in the United States and overseas for the purpose of promoting distance education research, study, scholarship, and teaching, while also serving as a clearinghouse for the dissemination of knowledge about distance education.

The Association for Distance Education and Independent Learning (ADEIL) https://adeil.org/

An organization serving professionals working in distance education, ADEIL's mission is to provide distance educators with opportunities for collaboration with other members as well as professional development.

Competency-Based Education Network (C-BEN) https://www.cbenetwork.org/

A national consortium that designs, develops, and scales new models for student learning, C-BEN consists of a diverse membership that is dedicated to working together to foster greater use of competency-based learning—an approach that has been a hallmark of many of the developing distance education programs—through research, experience sharing, and conferencing.

Distance Education Accrediting Commission (DEAC) https://www.deac.org/Resources/Associations.aspx

DEAC is a private, nonprofit organization that serves as an accreditor of institutions that primarily offer distance education. It offers accreditation for educational entities from primary school through graduate and professional degree granting institutions. Founded in 1926, the DEAC is recognized by both the U.S. Department of Education and the Council for Higher Education Accreditation.

Educause https://www.educause.edu/

Educause is a nonprofit association whose mission is to advance higher education through the use of information technology. Its work is central to the tech basis of modern distance education.

Federal Government Distance Learning Association (FGDLA) https://www.fgdla.us/

The FGDLA is a nonprofit, professional association that promotes the development and application of distance learning in the federal government. It actively promotes collaboration and understanding among those involved, furthering the education and training needs of the federal government and supporting federal agencies involved in distance learning.

Florida Distance Learning Association (FDLA) www.fdla.com

A nonprofit association formed to promote the development and application of distance learning in the public and private sectors and all levels of education: K-12, area education agencies, higher education, continuing education, information sciences, corporate training and education, and the military.

Garden State Distance Learning Consortium (GSDLC) https://sites.google.com/a/stockton.edu/gsdlc/home

The GSDLC is a nonprofit, educator-founded organization that promotes the development of distance learning in New Jersey, as well as the application of video conferencing within a classroom setting for education and training.

Instructional Technology Council (ITC) https://www.itcnetwork.org/

Affiliated with the American Association of Community Colleges, ITC seeks to advance distance education by providing the leadership and resources necessary to expand and enhance distance learning through the effective use of technology.

Maryland Distance Learning Association (MDLA) http://www.marylanddla.org/

The MDLA is an association of learning professionals who advocate and promote the coordination and use of distance education in Maryland

and throughout the region. Its members represent over two dozen organizations, and the group's focus is to provide professional development, networking, and collaborative opportunities for educators at all levels.

Missouri Distance Learning Association (MoDLA) https://www.modla.org/

The Missouri Distance Learning Association is the state chapter of the United States Distance Learning Association. It serves as the voice for distance education in the state while promoting the effective application of distance learning strategies to maximize access, equity, and quality of educational resources for all.

National Council for Online Education (NCOE) https://www.nationalcouncil.online/

NCOE is a partnership between the Online Learning Consortium (OLC), Quality Matters (QM), University Professional and Continuing Education Association (UPCEA), and WICHE Cooperative for Educational Technologies (WCET).

Through their joint effort, NCOE has become a formidable voice for online and digital education within higher education policy and thought leadership. It brings diverse perspectives on the process of online learning, diversity that helps address the rapid changes that are a part of the modern distance education and higher education landscapes.

New York State Distance Learning Consortium (NYSDLC) https://www.nysdlc.org/

The NYSDLC provides opportunities, services, and professional development related to distance learning and e-learning. Utilizing twenty-first-century learning technologies, it seeks to enrich the teaching and learning process by expanding the role and reach of education through virtual environments.

Northeast Digital Learning Association (NEDLA) https://nedla.org/

The regional chapter (serving Northeastern and Mid-Atlantic states from Maine to Virginia) of the USDLA, NEDLA is committed to the development and application as well as the free exchange of ideas related to digital educational technology so as to enable effective learning experiences in areas ranging from K-12 to corporate, government, and higher education settings.

Ohio Distance Learning Association (OhioDLA) https://www.ohiodla.org/

The OhioDLA seeks to promote and foster the formation of partnerships among schools and affiliates in order to further the effective use of distance learning.

Online Learning Consortium (OLC) https://onlinelearningconsortium.org/

Starting in 1999 as Sloan Consortium, OLC is a leading professional online learning society committed to advancing quality e-Education in mainstream education. The nonprofit was rebranded in 2014 as the Online Learning Consortium (OLC) to better align with its mission: creating community and knowledge around quality online, blended, and digital learning while driving innovation.

Quality Matters (QM) https://www.qualitymatters.org/

QM is a nonprofit self-described quality assurance organization that seeks to help institutions develop well-conceived, designed, and presented distance courses and programs. It also engages in ongoing reviews and appropriate improvements while offering a certification of its quality.

Texas Distance Learning Association (TDLA) https://www.txdla.org/

A nonprofit association whose membership is open to all individuals, TDLA promotes the development and sensible application of digital and distance learning to maximize opportunities and the quality of educational resources for teachers and learners at all levels.

United States Distance Learning Association (USDLA) https://usdla.org/

A nonprofit organization, USDLA is committed to creating quality online and distance education with a focus on both research and training of educators.

UPCEA https://upcea.edu/

UPCEA is the leading association for professional, continuing, and online education. Founded in 1915, it offers conferences and seminars, as well as research, information, networking opportunities, and publications relevant to its field. It serves hundreds of institutions.

coursera

381

Chronology

While the internet has revolutionized the concepts and practices central to remote learning and distance education, they are concepts that can trace their roots back centuries. As depicted in this chronology, the evolution of distance learning, like that of formal education itself, has been the result of changing technologies combined with an entrepreneurial bent that has long had an eye on and sensitivity to the changing audiences it aimed to serve. At the same time, the field's development was also a product of an increasingly broad definition and democratic concept of education. Remote learning and distance education, both through their differences and in the ways they overlap, have been a force helping to drive change—while also responding to changes in the local and global communities in which they operate.

1728 — In a bid to start the first correspondence course, Caleb Phillips runs an advertisement in the *Boston Gazette* offering to teach shorthand to students in a process that would involve the exchange of letters. There is no available evidence as to whether Phillips' undertaking was successful.

1833 — Swedish newspapers across the nation carry advertisements for correspondence composition courses, a practice which soon spreads across Europe.

1840s — Sir Isaac Pitman offers correspondence courses that teach his "Pitman shorthand" style, one still widely used today.

Silicon Valley headquarters of Coursera, a massive open online course (MOOC) provider founded in 2012 that partners with higher education institutions and other organizations to provide courses, certifications, and degrees. (© Andreistanescu/Dreamstime.com)

1856	Instructors Charles Toussaint and Gustav Langenscheidt begin to offer language classes from Germany via the mail.
1858	Queen Victoria of Great Britain signs a charter that allows the University of London to provide distance-learning degrees to people no matter where in the world they study. The university establishes the External Programme through which it becomes the first university to offer a degree via distance learning.
1873	The first correspondence course in the United States, an enterprise headed by Ana Eliot Ticknor and named The Society to Encourage Studies at Home, is founded.
1892	In a pamphlet produced by the University of Wisconsin-Madison, the term "distance learning" is first used.
1892	The University of Chicago begins offering correspondence courses, becoming the first traditional, brick-and-mortar, residential college to do so.
1900	Cornell University teacher and suffragette Martha Van Rensselaer organizes a remote education program that reaches out to women in the rural areas of New York state. In just five years the program enrolls over 20,000 women.
1906	The Calvert School in Baltimore becomes one of the first primary schools to offer correspondence courses.
1906	The University of Wisconsin begins recording lectures that are then sent to students in the form of phonograph records.
1911	The University of Queensland in Australia founds a Department of Correspondence Studies with materials being exchanged through the country's postal system.
1920s	With initial licenses issued to the University of Salt Lake City, the University of Wisconsin, and the

University of Minnesota, colleges become active users of radio as a vehicle to conduct remote teaching and learning. Ultimately, over 175 radio stations are constructed at some of the nation's educational institutions to facilitate this process. The radio broadcasts are most often used as a complement to correspondence courses, with the students actually being able to hear the teacher.

1922 Pennsylvania State University begins broadcasting some courses over radio.

1923 Almost 10 percent of all broadcast radio systems are owned by educational institutions.

1927 Congress passes the Radio Act of 1927 in an effort to regulate the broadcasting industry, including educational use.

1928 The Ohio Department of Education develops the Ohio School of the Air program, which offers daily programming in literature, history, science, and music.

1928 The National Broadcasting Company (NBC) starts the Radio Corporation of America (RCA) Educational Hour, an effort to use commercial radio for educational purposes.

1930 The Columbia Broadcasting System (CBS) starts the American School of the Air, its first venture into educational programming.

1930 The Rockefeller Foundation and the Carnegie Foundation organize and fund the National Advisory Council for Radio in Education (NACRE).

1930 The Institute for Education by Radio (IER), an organization which focuses on techniques used in educational broadcasting, is founded in Columbus, Ohio.

1930	The National Committee on Education by Radio (NCER) is founded by a group of educators fighting for the preservation of nonprofit educational radio stations at a time when commercial radio programming is experiencing a meteoric increase.
1934	The University of Iowa begins broadcasting courses, launching an effort that will open the door to future learning via public broadcast channels whose costs are underwritten in the 1960s by the FCC's Instructional Fixed Service.
1943	The United States Armed Forces Institute uses correspondence courses to train individual servicemen.
1946	The University of South Africa begins offering Correspondence Education courses.
1953	The University of Houston begins offering the first televised college classes utilizing KUHT, the first public television station in the United States. The station runs 13.5 hours of educational material a week, representing just under 40 percent of the station's weekly broadcasting content.
1958	Renowned newscaster Edward R. Murrow gives his television as "wires and lights in a box" speech, challenging the industry to use television in ways that allow it to be the productive educational tool of which it is capable.
1960	PLATO (Programmed Logic for Automatic Teaching Operations) a computer-based education system is created by Donald L. Bitzer at the University of Illinois at Urbana-Champaign (UIUC). PLATO serves as a successful teaching tool in various iterations for four decades, but the cost and its cumbersome hardware prevents it from ever becoming a large-scale success. However, in its spawning of the

Chronology

	first successful online communities, it foreshadows the ultimate development of the internet.
1965	The University of Wisconsin launches a telephone-based distance learning program for doctors.
1967	Congress passes the Public Broadcasting Act of 1967, which establishes the Corporation for Public Broadcasting (CPB). The announced mission of CPB is "to encourage the growth of public radio and television broadcasting including the use of media for instructional, educational, and cultural purposes."
1968	The University of Nebraska-Lincoln begins offering an accredited high school diploma through distance education.
1968	The Children's Television Workshop is founded under the leadership of Joan Ganz Cooney. Its hit show *Sesame Street* premiers in November 1969 on public television stations across the country.
1971	The United Kingdom's Open University, the first distance learning only university, admits more than 24,000 students in its first year.
1972	By this time, 233 educational television stations are in existence.
1972	WGBH-TV in Boston launches *Zoom*, a *Sesame Street*-inspired children's show notable for its mostly unscripted, audience initiated and inspired plays, poems, and other creative undertakings.
1976	Coastline Community College, based in southern California, becomes the first "virtual" college. It has no campus and broadcasts all its courses.
1982	The United Kingdom's Open University begins offering distance learning courses overseas.

1982	Western Behavioral Sciences Institute's School of Management and Strategic Studies provides a distance education program for business executives.
1983	Former Atari president Ron Gordon launches the Electronic University Network, which makes online courses available to people who have access to personal computers.
1984	National Technological University (NTU) based in Fort Collins, Colorado, is founded as a nonprofit organization offering graduate courses via satellite TV. This method allows for the delivery of a combination of live and recorded course material, while also making it possible for students to call their instructors by telephone and get their questions answered on the air in real time.
1985	Nova Southeastern University in Fort Lauderdale, Florida, offers the first electronic classroom through an accredited online graduate program.
1986	The National Science Foundation Network (NSFNET) launches the first open computer network, a precursor to the internet, which enables institutions to create and distribute electronic information.
1987	The United States Distance Learning Association (USDLA), the first nonprofit distance learning organization in the United States, is founded. Its creation is a development that recognizes both the potential of distance education as a force for change in the world of the education as well as the movement's growing presence and influence in the educational world.
1987	Entrepreneur Glen Jones launches the cable television network Mind Extension University (ME/U, later Knowledge TV), a venture which enables 30,000 students to take courses from more than thirty colleges and universities via television.

1989	The University of Phoenix becomes the first fully online institution of higher education, offering courses leading to both a bachelor's and master's degrees.
1993	Glen Jones and Bernard Luskin launch Jones International University, the first accredited and fully web-based university.
1992	Michigan State University introduces the Computer Assisted Personalized Approach (CAPA). This system creates individual assignments for each student while also allowing them to get individual personalized feedback.
1994	The Open University in the United Kingdom becomes the first accredited school to offer a course over the internet when it offers an experimental Virtual Summer School (VSS) to some of its Cognitive Psychology students.
1994	CALCampus launches the first online-only curriculum featuring synchronous learning—real-time instruction and student participation.
1995	A bipartisan group of nineteen US governors come together to create Western Governors University, a private nonprofit, all online institution, in an effort to maximize educational resources through distance learning.
1997	The Interactive Learning Network (ILN) is created and released to numerous schools as the first eLearning platform. Early users include Yale, Cornell, and the University of Pittsburgh.
1997	Blackboard Inc., is founded. The content management system developed a standardized platform for course management and delivery, a model that made it possible for many additional schools to come online. It is still used at many universities to manage their online courses.

1998	California Virtual University opens its doors, launching a website that promises access to online and distance education with approximately 700 online classes from the state's accredited colleges and universities.
1998	New York University (NYU) creates NYU Online, an online, for-profit subsidiary of its existent continuing education program. It ends operations in 2001.
2002	Massachusetts Institute of Technology (MIT) announces its OpenCourseWare Project, which offers free MIT courses to people across the globe.
2005	YouTube is launched. By 2009, YouTubeEDU is offering thousands of free lectures online.
2006	Apple introduces iTunes U which offers lectures on a wide range of subjects to anyone willing to purchase them.
2008	Khan Academy, which offers basic classes in math, science, and other areas, is founded. Initially begun as a tutorial type of resource, it subsequently expands so that, by 2020, it offers a comprehensive collection of school classes from kindergarten through high school and also becomes an active partner with the College Board, offering review classes and review materials as well as test prep materials for the SAT, MCAT, and LSAT.
2012	Udacity and EdX begin to offer hundreds of university level MOOCs (Massive Open Online Courses), an initiative that allows learners to take classes asynchronously at their own pace.
2012	The University of Wisconsin's Flexible Option begins offering competency-based bachelor's degrees.
2014	UF (University of Florida) Online, the first online-only public university in the United States, is launched. The

	school's mission is to offer "high quality, fully online baccalaureate degree programs at an affordable cost" to either first-time or transfer students.
2017	Purdue University acquires the online for-profit institution, Kaplan University.
2019	California launches Calbright College, an online-only institution that awards certificates, not degrees. It is intended to be a public option for adult and low-income workers seeking to improve their skills with the aim of getting better paying jobs. Previous options have too often been limited to expensive, for-profit institutions.
March 2020	The Covid-19 pandemic leads the overwhelming majority of American colleges and universities, as well as most elementary and secondary schools, to move their instructional programs online. Much of this would continue through the 2020–21 academic year as well.
Fall 2021	2U acquires edX as it seeks to gain a greater presence in the established educational world.
2021	Major OPMs Coursera and Udemy go public.
November–December 2021	A nationwide surge of Covid-19 Omicron variant infections sends hundreds of schools and colleges across the United States rushing back to online and virtual learning, but not without resistance in many quarters.
2021–22	With many schools returning to in-person learning in 2021, the percentage of students enrolled in distance learning courses dropped to about 59 percent—still much higher than in pre-pandemic years. Online learning rates again fell in 2022 but remained over half.

January 2022	Arizona State University announces the launch of a new initiative that promises to reach 100 million learners worldwide by the year 2030.
October 2022	Numerous reports reveal major drops in state-wide academic achievement test scores nationwide during the academic years impacted by the pandemic.
2023	Idaho State Board of Education approves plan to have University of Idaho buy University of Phoenix. As of the spring of 2024, the sale was not yet finalized as issues were still being addressed by the Idaho Legislature.
2023	University of Arizona completes deal to acquire former for-profit Ashford University, which enrolls 35,000 students, becoming the new, online nonprofit University of Arizona Global Campus.
June 2023	The math and reading performance of American thirteen-year-olds in the United States hits the lowest level in decades, according to the National Assessment of Educational Progress (Nation's Report Card). Math scores are the lowest since 1990, and reading scores are the lowest since 2004.
April 2024	Amidst increased talk about the financial status of OPMs, the U.S. Department of Education issues a statement saying it was "concerned" about the impact that a potential financial failure of 2U and other OPMs would have on students.

Glossary

Asynchronous learning: Learning experience in which the instruction is presented in a way that does not require all students to be present at the same time. Students may complete their work at their own pace, and communication and interaction is accomplished through online discussion boards, emails, or telephone communication.

Blended/hybrid learning: Educational offering in which a student's learning experience consists of a mix of standard teacher-supervised, in-person instruction in a formal school building away from home, as well as a remote component. In the remote segment, lessons are shared through an online delivery system and students generally have some control over the timing, pace, and place where the learning takes place, although some remote learning may be as synchronous as it would be in person.

CD-ROM courses: Classes in which instruction comes from students interacting with already created content shared with them via disks loaded onto a computer.

Competency-based learning: Educational approach in which progress towards a degree is measured by acquired skills and learning in contrast to the traditional approach based on time completed. Rather than being tied to a definitive academic calendar with the completion of a term or semester being the benchmark of progress, competency-based learning students can progress through a course as soon as they are able to demonstrate their mastery of the material. Mastery is demonstrated through a range of assessment types, from written exercises and papers to tests and projects, as appropriate for the curriculum being studied and the degree program in which the student is enrolled.

Correspondence courses: The oldest form of remote learning, this form of teaching and learning involves the exchange of learning materials through the mail from teacher to student and back again. The student receives and studies the lessons and uses return mail to ask questions and seek clarification as well as to submit completed assessments to the instructor.

Course management system (CMS): A collection of software tools that provide an online environment for course interactions. These tools typically include areas for faculty to post class materials such as a course syllabus and handouts, areas for students to post papers and other assignments, a gradebook where teachers can record grades for students to see, a means for communication between teachers and students and within smaller groups within the course, and a chat tool that allows for synchronous communication among class participants. A thread board allowing for communication among asynchronous students is also often part of the package.

Educational television: Television programming developed and offered with a clear educational purpose in mind. While virtually any form of documentary has an educational component, such efforts usually come under the umbrella of news. In contrast, the most common examples of modern educational television are programs offered by public broadcasting stations aimed at young children as either substitutes for formal preschools or as a complement to them.

Learning management system (LMS): A technology platform through which students access online courses or digital instructional materials in a traditional educational setting.

MOOCs (massive open online courses): Distance learning classes characterized both by their unlimited number of participants and a format that enables student to learn asynchronously at their own pace.

Online boot camps: Intensive, accelerated programs in which students are able to learn the in-demand technical skills required in an ever-changing workplace.

Online learning: An overarching term for all courses delivered via the internet. These courses can be offered synchronously and/or asynchronously. The teaching and learning processes are conducted 100 percent virtually as a distinctive curricular component.

Online Program Management (OPM) companies: External providers that colleges and universities contract with to take their academic programs online. The contractual arrangement can be based on a "tuition revenue share" or a fee for service model. Often, OPMs are used to jumpstart an online program for those schools that do not have the necessary in-house capacity.

Radio: A form of broadcasting that transmits audio sounds to receivers owned by individuals, a public audience. Initially achieving widespread public acceptance in the 1920s, radio is most commonly used to broadcast various types of entertainment as well as public addresses and educational programs.

Remote learning: A broad term for any type of teaching and learning activity in which the participants—teachers and students—are located some distance from each other, occupying separate spaces. The term can apply to any learning situation, regardless of whether or not the teacher and students are separated in time.

SMOCs (synchronous massive online courses): Distance learning classes characterized both by their unlimited number of participants and a format that calls on students to participate synchronously, in real time.

SPOCs (small private online courses): Distance learning in which the number of students per class is limited and the learning takes place in an asynchronous manner.

SSOCs (synchronous small online courses): Distance learning in which the number of students per class is limited and the participating students are required to follow along with the lessons in real time.

Synchronous learning: Learning experience in real time, like a traditional, in-person class, but one that is presented through an online platform. All students are in attendance at the same time, and the teacher–student and student-to-student interactions occur in real time.

Telecourses: Courses where the educational content is delivered from instructor to student(s) via either a radio or television broadcast.

Television: Form of broadcasting that transmits visual images and audio sounds to receivers owned by individuals, a public audience. First achieved widespread public acceptance in the aftermath of the Second World War, and by the mid-1950s a television set was a staple of the average American home.

Webinar: A web-based, online educational offering distinctive for its interactive nature, with viewers able to ask questions and offer comments in real time.

Index

Academic integrity 71–4
Academic Partnerships 19–20
Access and Equity
    access for students with learning
        disabilities/differences 55
    cities with inadequate internet access
        availability 56
    college students' access to adequate
        internet 56
    concerns about Indian education
        164–5
    early concerns 24
    government efforts to expand
        broadband access 52–4
    legal challenges to inadequate access
        57–8
    legislative efforts 166–8
    plans to improve equity post-pandemic
        162–4
    post-pandemic broadband deficiencies
        58
    racial and socio-economic disparities
        54–6
Arizona State University 30, 36–7
    ASU Online 125–6
Attitudes towards online and distance
    education 25, 38–9, 63, 85–6

Bisk Education 19–20
Bitzer, Donald L. 11
Blackboard Inc. 16
Brown, Governor Jerry 18–19
Brown, Senator Sherrod 19, 151, 159
Business aspects of distance education
    78–80

CalBright College 18–19
California Virtual University 16
Calvert School 6
Chautauqua Movement 5
Children's Television Workshop (CTW)
    10, 113–15

Coastal Community College 12
College Board 17, 70, 130
Competency-based learning 134, 142
Cooney, Joan Ganz 10, 113–15
Corporation for Public Broadcasting
    (CPB) 9
Correspondence courses 1, 4–6
Course Management System (CMS) 79–80
Coursera 34, 36, 38, 126–8

Daniels, Mitch 18
Distance education
    access and equity, 52–8
    concerns about academic integrity
        71–5
    costs 75–6
    definition 2–3
    flexibility 51–2
    heightened profile 23
    impact on teaching and learning
        65–71
    necessary distinctive teacher training
        62, 68
    rankings 36–7
    term first used 5

Eastern Gateway Community College 28
edX 17, 36, 126, 127, 138–9
Edison, Thomas 8
Educational television 9–11
Electric Company, 10–11, 114–15
External Programme 4

Federal Communications Commission
    (FCC) 8
Financial costs 75–6
Future of Distance education and remote
    learning 67–71, 85–6

Gordon, Ron and Electronic University
    Network 12, 135–7
Grand Canyon Education, Inc. 20

Index

Harper, William Rainey 5
Health concerns 76–8
Hybrid classes 65–6

Impact of distance education on teaching and learning 64–5
Impact of pandemic-induced virtual learning 83–5, 153–7, 169–74
Impact on schools of Omicron strain of Covid 31–4
Improvement of post-pandemic equity 162–8
Improving access for Indian Schools 164–5
In-person *vs.* remote learning 51
Interactive Learning Network 15–16
International Correspondence Schools (ICS) 1, 5

Jones, Glen and the Mind Extension University 14
Jones International University 15

Kaplan University 17–18, 20, 30
Kendall, Janet Ross 118–21
Khan, Sal 17, 51, 70, 128–30
Khan Academy 17, 51, 70, 128–30

Massachusetts Institute of Technology (MIT) OpenCourseWare Project 17
Massive Open Online Courses (MOOCs) 17, 31, 36, 126
Moore, Michael Grahame 115–17
Murrow, Edward R. 9, 11

NYU distance efforts 13, 16
National Assessment of Educational Progress (Nation's Report Card) 39–40
National Science Foundation 218
National Technological University 13
Nova Southeastern University 13

Oaks, Muriel 118–21
Online Learning Consortium (OLC) 130–2
Online enrollment changes 21–3, 39–40, 151–3

Online Program Management (OPM)
   companies 19–20, 79–80
   controversy 81
   governmental concerns about role and influence 79, 82, 157–61
   impact of the pandemic on their operations 34
   increased corporatization 36, 38–9
   increased use 81–2
   profitability 128
   role/function 27–8, 82
Online teaching and learning
   approaches: asynchronous *vs.* synchronous 25–6
   concerns about experience 35
   definition 2
   early challenges 20–5
   effectiveness of pandemic based experience 60
   impact on student health 76–8
   personal teacher and student experiences 95–111

Pandemic-driven teaching and learning experience 60
Pandemic learning loss 39–40, 166–8, 168–72, 172–4
Pearson Learning 19–20
Pennsylvania Colliery School of Mines 5
Pennsylvania State University 6, 117
Phillips, Caleb 4
Pitman, Sir Isaac 4, 121–2
PLATO Program 11–12
Purdue University 17–18, 30

Quality of distance education 38, 59–64
Queen Victoria 4

Radio and education 6–8
Remote learning definition 1–2
Remote learning experience 95–111

Security and distance education 54–5
Sesame Street 10–11, 113–15
Sloan Consortium 131
Southern New Hampshire University (SNHU) 27, 30, 79, 132–5, 177
Swedish newspapers 4

2U, Inc. 19–20, 137–9
Telelearning Systems and the Electronic University Network 135–7
Television as educational tool 8–11
Ticknor, Ana Eliot 5

Udacity 17
Udemy 27, 36
United Kingdom Open University 15, 217, 219
University of Arizona 39, 222
University of California 5, 31
University of Chicago 5
University of Florida 17
University of Houston 9
University of Illinois Urbana-Champaign 11
University of Iowa 216
University of London 4
University of Maryland 16
University of Nebraska-Lincoln 12
University of North Carolina Project Kitty Hawk 28–30
University of Phoenix 14, 16, 27, 35, 139–41
University of Queensland Department of Correspondence Studies 6
University of South Africa 216
University of Southern California 137–8
University of Wisconsin Madison 5, 6, 8, 69, 116–17, 122–4

Van Rensselaer, Martha 6

Warren, Senator Elizabeth 19, 151, 159
Washington State University 118–21
Wedemeyer, Charles A. 8, 122–5
Western Governors University 15, 18, 27, 30, 141–3
WGBH, Boston 11
Wiley Education Services 19–20

Zoom 10–11
Zovio 20, 39

About the Author

William H. Pruden III is the Director of Civic Engagement, a college counselor, and an instructor in history and social studies at Ravenscroft School in Raleigh, North Carolina. He earned an AB in History from Princeton University, a JD from Case Western Reserve University, and master's degrees from Wesleyan University and Indiana University. In an educational career that spans four decades, he has taught students from fifth grade through college, although the overwhelming majority of his work has been at the high school level. In addition to his many years in the classroom, he has served in a number of administrative positions, ranging from high school principal to athletic director. He has also complemented his years of teaching history and government with active involvement in the political system. He twice ran for local office and he also did stints as a legislative assistant to both a state senator and a member of the US House of Representatives, as well as serving on the staff of a US Senator. Pruden has written widely on US history, politics, and education. The author of a biography on feminist activist Gloria Steinem, Pruden has contributed chapters to a number of books while also writing numerous op-eds. In addition, he has written hundreds of articles for historical encyclopedias and reference works. He has also made presentations and given lectures on historical and education-related subjects at numerous conferences and professional gatherings.